Concepts of Fit

Concepts of Fit

An Individualized Approach to Pattern Design

Bonnita M. Farmer
Department of Foods and Nutrition/ Home Economics
California State Polytechnic University, Pomona

Lois M. Gotwals
Department of Consumer Science and Retailing
Purdue University

Macmillan Publishing Co., Inc.
New York

Collier Macmillan Publishers
London

Copyright © 1982, Macmillan Publishing Co., Inc.

Printed in the United States of America

All rights reserved. No part of this book may be reproduced or transmitted in any form or by any means, electronic or mechanical, including photocopying, recording, or any information storage and retrieval system, without permission in writing from the Publisher.

Macmillan Publishing Co., Inc.
866 Third Avenue, New York, New York 10022

Collier Macmillan Canada, Inc.

Library of Congress Cataloging in Publication Data

Farmer, Bonnita M.
   Concepts of fit.

   Includes bibliographical references and index.
   1. Dressmaking—Pattern design. 2. Tailoring—Pattern design. I. Gotwals, Lois M. II. Title.
TT520.F28   646.4'072   81-8275
ISBN 0-02-336260-X   AACR2

Printing: 1 2 3 4 5 6 7 8   Year: 2 3 4 5 6 7 8 9

Preface

Theories are unifying statements within disciplines that not only order the existing knowledge but stimulate inquiry into the unanswered. As a specialized area of study within home economics, clothing construction has accumulated a vast amount of knowledge in construction methods. Books, extension publications and private newsletters that offer a variety of construction methods are numerous. However, fewer texts discuss pattern drafting or altering. At this stage, progress can be achieved by theory development and by comparative analysis of the methods used to achieve fit in garments. Our purpose in writing this text has been to systematize this knowledge and offer a theory about *why people sew*.

We theorize that people choose to sew to achieve individualized fit in their clothing and that fit is a primary factor in clothing satisfaction. The standardization techniques required for effective mass production cannot accommodate the individual differences and needs in fit. Garments must be made to statistical models, not real people. Therefore persons acquire the skills needed to construct garments hoping to achieve fit. They must then opt to alter a commercial pattern or create their own pattern to reach their ultimate goal. A comprehensive text book that compares alteration methods and presents pattern-drafting procedures is needed by the student who has acquired sewing skills and is ready to advance to individualized fit and design.

We believe this book will meet the needs of many audiences. It has been organized for classroom instruction at the university, junior college, technical vocational, and adult education levels. We hope clothing-construction teachers and extension home economists will use the book as a text and reference for advanced clothing-construction classes and for pattern-drafting and clothing-design courses. However, an individual who has had sewing experiences can use the book for self-instruction in altering and drafting. Professional tailors, dressmakers, and pattern makers will find the information helpful in their work. Because the chapters address specific sections of the garments independently the book may be successfully used as a reference.

Growing concern about the needs of handicapped persons has prompted us to incorporate specialized information related to fit. Teachers of the handicapped may use this text to help handicapped persons design or alter patterns to suit their particular needs. Properly fitted clothing should help these persons gain greater independence and self-confidence and thereby increase both their opportunity for employment and their earning capacity.

The book is divided into three major sections: the conceptual framework—what fit is and how it varies, a comparative analysis of pattern alteration techniques, and drafting procedures for basic patterns. By developing an appreciation for good fit, the student will be motivated to study the various methods for achieving fit. An informed choice can then be made between altering a commercial pattern to fit and drafting a pattern from personal measurements.

Material in the book has been drawn from the latest information in the field and from the author's experiences. All the pattern-drafting and altering procedures have been tested by the authors in classroom situations. For their time, interest, and concern about the quality of this book we are indebted to Indiana Cooperative Extension Home Economists who specialize in clothing, adults in Indiana Extension classes, students at Riverside City College, Riverside, CA, and California State Polytechnic University, Pomona, CA. They clarified our confusion, caught our mistakes, and convinced us that this was a worthwhile endeavor. We wish to acknowledge Sandra Adams, Rhoda Holleman, and Charlie Hand for their help in preparing both the illustrations and the manuscript. We appreciate their commitment to seeing this project through to completion.

Textbooks don't just happen; they evolve over time as a result of working in a subject-matter area. Working together as extension specialists at Purdue University, we were challenged by Dr. Eva Goble, State Extension Leader and later Dean of Home Economics, whose philosophy was that programs grow and prosper only insofar as they meet the needs of people. With this perspective, we concur and although our careers are now separated by many miles, our direction remains the same. We wish also to recognize the contribution of Miss Leah Weidman, Professor Emeritus, Indiana University, Bloomington, Indiana, for her instruction in pattern drafting. Her attention to detail, precision in procedure, and interest in students made pattern drafting an exciting skill to master.

We cannot close without a special thank you to our families. Our husbands, Dr. Walter Farmer and Dr. John Gotwals, were a constant source of encouragement and strength. Margaret and Melissa Farmer helped in many ways as we wrote—mainly by being very special daughters. And, thank you to our parents who taught us to be sensitive to the needs of others and to value the individual differences of people.

B. M. F.
L. M. G.

Contents

Part One
Introduction to Fit in Clothing

1. **The Importance of Good Fit** 3

    Good Fit – Why? 3
    Good Fit for the Family 3
    Good Fit – How It Is Achieved 4
    Good Fit – Recognizing the Characteristics 4
    Good Fit Through Fabrics 4
    Fit – A Process or a Product? 5

2. **Fit and Social Variables** 6

    Socioeconomic Status 6
    Age 7
    Sex Roles 7
    Religion 7
    Race and Ethnicity 8
    Fashion Change 8

3. **Body Changes During One's Lifetime** 9

    The Early Years 9
    The Middle Years 10
    The Later Years 11
    Obesity 11
    Disabilities 12

4. **Structural Features That Contribute To Fit** 17

    Garment Features 17
    Fabric Features 18
    Guides to Good Fit 20

5. **Measurements, Proportions, and Body Curves** 23

    How to Measure 23
    Body Proportions and Curves 25

Part Two
Comparative Analysis of Pattern Alteration Techniques

6. **Pattern Alterations: General Techniques** 31

    Size and Ease 32
    Pattern Preparation and Measurements 33
    Alteration Methods 33
    General Principles 34
    Ready, Set, Alter 34

7. **Altering Bodices** 36

    Length Changes 36
    Lengthening Only at Center Back or Front 39
    Changing Bustline Darts 41
    Raising or Lowering Darts 41
    Bustline Width Changes 42

Eliminate Armhold Pouch 48
Round Shoulders 49
Very Erect Back 50
Broad Back 51
Narrow Back 53
Hollow Chest 54
Pigeon Chest 55
Narrow Shoulders 55
Broad Shoulders 57
Square Shoulders 58
Sloping Shoulders 58
Large or Small Neckline 59
Neckline Too Low 60
Waistline Changes 61
Test the Fit 62

8. **Altering Shirts** 63
Length Changes 63
Chest Width Changes 63
Round Shoulders or Very Erect Back 65
Narrow or Broad Shoulders 66
Square or Sloping Shoulders 67
Collar Too Tight or Loose 68
Waistline Changes 69
Test the Fit 69

9. **Altering Sleeves** 70
Length Changes 70
Increase Sleeve Width 72
Decrease Sleeve Width 75
Sleeve Cap Alterations 77
Large or Tight Armscyes 79
Test in Fabric 80

10. **Altering Basic Skirts** 81
Length Changes 81
Hip and Thigh Width Alterations 83
High Hip Bones 86
Prominent or Flat Seat 88

Swayback 92
Prominent Stomach 93
Waistline Alterations 96
Skirts with Yokes 98
Flared and Bias Skirts: Width Alterations 99
Flared and Bias Skirts: Seat and Stomach Alterations 100
A Fitting Shell 101

11. **Altering the All-in-One Dresses** 103
Length Changes 103
Raising or Lowering the Bustline 103
Bustline Width Changes 104
Hollow or Pigeon Chest 107
Round Shoulders 108
Very Erect Back 108
Broad or Narrow Back 109
Narrow and Broad Shoulders 110
Square and Sloping Shoulders 111
Waistline Changes 112
Hipline Changes 113
Prominent or Flat Stomach 114
Prominent or Flat Seat 115
Swayback 116
Test Your Skill 116

12. **Altering Pants** 117
Crotch Depth Alterations 117
Leg Length Alterations 120
Hip and Thigh Width Alterations 122
Stomach or Seat Alterations 124
Swayback 127
Dropped Seat 128
Hollow Pubic Area 128
Waistline Alterations 128
Culottes and Hostess Pants 128
Jumpsuits 129
A Master Pattern 129

Part Three
Drafting Your Own Basic Pattern

13. **General Drafting Techniques** 133
Supplies and Equipment 133
Terms and Procedures 137
Procedures for Establishing Lengths and Widths 139

14. **Drafting Bodices** 141
Procedure for Drafting Bodice Back 141
Procedure for Drafting Bodice Front 145
Designing Bodices 147

15. **Drafting Sleeves** 158
Procedure for Drafting Sleeves 159
Designing Sleeves 162

16. **Drafting Shirts** 173
Procedure for Drafting Shirt Back 173
Procedure for Drafting Shirt Front 176
Designing Shirts 178
Adapting the Shirt Drafts for Children 181

17. **Drafting Skirts** 182
Procedure for Drafting the Skirt Front 182
Procedure for Drafting the Skirt Back 185
Designing Skirts 186

18. **Combining the Basic Drafts for the All-in-One Dresses** 195
    Procedures for the All-in-One Dresses 195
    Designing All-in-One Dresses 198

19. **Drafting the Basic Pants** 201
    Procedure for Drafting Pants 201
    Designing Pants 205

Part Four
Designing Skills in Use

20. **Adapting Clothing Designs for the Handicapped** 212
    Assessing the Needs of the Individual 212
    Design Adaptations 213

21. **Fit of the Future** 217
    Lifestyle Changes 217
    Special Needs 219

Technological Advances 219
Career Options 220

Appendix 222

Bibliography 227

Part One
Introduction to Fit in Clothing

1
The Importance of Good Fit

GOOD FIT: WHY?

Recall a memorable moment in your life. Now see if you can remember the most embarrassing event in your life? These are typical questions posed to students as they begin their study of clothing and textiles. Interestingly, the responses have a consensus often unexpected by the teacher. The description of these events frequently mentions clothing—what was worn at the particular time and place. It is striking how persons can remember what they wore at the important happenings of their lives. Clothing is an extension of the self—helping us define who we are, what we like, and how we feel about ourselves. Because it plays such a key role in our lives, it is not surprising that we associate both the happy and the unhappy times with what we wore on those occasions.

What qualities of clothing do we associate with positive feelings? Qualities often listed by students include attractive appearance, comfort, freedom of movement, and fashion. We recognize one basic quality underlying all of these attributes: *fit*. How well or how poorly a garment fits appears to be the variable on which all other qualities depend. The concept of fit varies with individuals, but everyone has an opinion about what feels good, looks good, and is right for her or him. We have all experienced the dissatisfaction of wearing a mass-produced garment in the "right" size for us that actually did not fit at all. We think how nice it must have been in the days when clothing was made by private seamstresses and tailors—custom-made clothing, the answer to our fitting problems. Or we speculate about the future and predict that machines will be able to produce garments to an individual's measurements. Alvin Toffler, in *The Third Wave* (1980), stimulates our imagination by suggesting that "It may be possible to read one's measurements into a telephone, or point a video camera at oneself, thus feeding data directly into a computer, which in turn will instruct the machine to produce a single garment, cut exactly to one's personal, individualized dimensions!" (p. 200). Thus experts agree as to the goal—clothing that fits the individual—but it is the means for achieving this goal that remains obscure.

How can today's consumer resolve this dilemma? We suggest that one option open to those persons with basic clothing-construction skills is to make their own clothing. Technology has given us beautiful fabrics and sophisticated sewing machines; technology has not yet been able to give us clothing customized to the individual at an affordable price. Therefore consumers can maximize their resources by converting time and energy to skill in making clothes that fit. This is the rationale for the text that follows. Consumers need, want, and enjoy clothes that fit. Essential to this goal is information about how good fit is achieved.

GOOD FIT FOR THE FAMILY

All family members, of whatever age or sex, require good fit in clothing. Men and women, boys and girls require clothing that allows them to function in their roles. Roles involving extensive physical activity require fit for comfort and ease of movement. Professional roles often suggest more conservative fit in clothing. In the theater, costume designers use fit as a means of projecting character images. The "poverty" look is associated with oversized, baggy clothes. The "sexy" look is portrayed by tight, body-accentuating clothing. Fit in clothing is so ingrained in our thinking that we tend to impart personality traits to individuals based on the way their clothes fit, although this relationship may not actually exist. Social scientists have not been able to demonstrate a correlation between actual behavior and such attributions, but they have documented the associations that people believe exist.

Clothing can become a factor in role performance and in determining life chances.

GOOD FIT: HOW IT IS ACHIEVED

Judging the fit of a garment requires that you recognize certain qualities in it when it is worn. The garment should hang freely and easily as you move. Adequate ease should be provided for comfort, but wrinkles, folds, and bulges of fabric are unacceptable. The amount of ease desired will vary with your size, your age, and the style of the garment. Current fashion also influences our perception of what is a desirable amount of ease in a garment. One season's fashionable garments may fit tightly and closely to the body whereas loose, easy fit will be chic the next season. Development of your own personal guidelines for fit is therefore extremely important. The fit of a garment should flatter you by skillfully accentuating positive features and making problems less noticeable. Seam placements, dart positions, and hemlines are key points to check in judging a garment's fit.

GOOD FIT: RECOGNIZING THE CHARACTERISTICS

Our experiences in teaching clothing construction have convinced us that you can achieve good fit by understanding the basic principles of pattern making. This understanding makes it possible to alter commercial patterns for individual fit or to draft patterns from personal measurements. Each of these methods has advantages, and by understanding the basic principles, you can select the method that suits the particular situation. Often it is desirable to combine the two methods to achieve good fit and to improve the design quality. We should therefore, not want to present one method without the other. Being able to use both techniques makes it possible to achieve individualized fit in garments with ease and confidence. Further, this information will help you recognize an ill-fitting garment and to correct the fitting problems. Thus you will have improved your consumer skills as well as your construction skills through the learning process. Using these techniques provides a creative experience that is both satisfying and rewarding. You may not become a professional designer by mastering these techniques, but you will gain a feeling for line, design, fabric, and fashion. Then again, these may be the very technical skills you need to activate a latent gift or talent for clothing design.

GOOD FIT THROUGH FABRICS

Woven fabrics have lengthwise and crosswise grainlines created by the yarns' interlacing at right angles to each other. Experts check the positioning of grainlines when judging the fit of a garment. Lengthwise grainlines must hang perpendicular to the floor and crosswise grainlines parallel to the floor. Special attention must be given to preventing distortion of these grainlines. Irregularities in body proportions or posture may lead to fitting difficulties resulting from shifting grainlines. Techniques for resolving these problems are discussed in the chapters that follow. The proportions of the left and right sides of the body may differ, causing grain distortions. Fitting should be done with the garment right side out and for each side independently. Fitting one side and then transferring the markings to the other side cannot yield custom fit.

Although knitted fabrics shape to the body more easily than woven fabrics, fit is still an important consideration. The elastic quality of these fabrics may lead to instability and ever-changing fit. These fabrics are also subject to distortion in manufacturing process. Particular attention should be given to the lengthwise and crosswise lines created by the loops in the fabric, which are known as the *wales* and *courses* of the fabric, rather than as *grainlines*. The placement of these lines in the garment is critical to fit. In purchasing knitted fabrics, be alert to distortion, as you cannot correct it when constructing the garment. Heat setting in the final stages of fabric production locks in the shape of fabrics that are made of synthetic fibers or treated with chemical finishes.

A motto displayed in a music store says, "The bitterness of poor quality remains long after the sweetness of low price is forgotten." This wisdom is applicable to fabrics. Your investment of time, energy, and money in constructing garments makes the selection of quality fabrics essential. The fabrics you purchase will influence the ultimate pleasure you experience from the clothing you make. Select fabrics on the basis of fiber content, yarn structure, construction, finishes, colorfastness, and the care required. Fiber content and care information are provided to consumers in compliance with labeling laws. Recognizing other quality features requires training and experience in evaluating fabrics. Time invested in the study of textiles will contribute to your overall expertise in clothing construction.

FIT: A PROCESS OR A PRODUCT?

Definitions of good fit change, but people consistently desire and demand comfort, attractive appearance, freedom of movement, and fashion in their clothing. Think of good fit as being a process rather than a product. Although it has been achieved in one garment, the emphasis may be slightly different in the next. Or a cherished garment may be altered several times during its life span. Good fit is a process—a process that meets the clothing needs of people.

2
Fit and Social Variables

Scholars from many disciplines have been intrigued by clothing behavior. Historians trace the progress of dress over the centuries hoping to find clues to what prompted clothing choices in a particular era. Anthropologists see clothing as one of the important cultural indicators. Sociologists study clothing as an integral part of group behavior. Psychologists are concerned about clothing's impact on the individual. Yet, so general has been the interest of these disciplines that specific facets of clothing that distinguish similar garments have been overlooked. Such is the case with "fit." Although clothing construction teachers dwell on the importance of fit and emphasize techniques for achieving fit, little empirical work has been done to link standards of fit to social variables. We suggest that this is a fertile area for inquiry and offer some theories for testing. These associations have been observed in various settings but lack empirical documentation. Exploring the relationships between "fit" and the following social variables is an exciting challenge.

SOCIOECONOMIC STATUS

Proper fit in clothing has long been associated with high social status. *Proper* does not imply close fit; rather it means the fit that is judged fashionable at a given time. Persons of wealth, power, and prestige have the resources to acquire proper fit. Not only can they pay the price, but they have the time to shop, are able to travel to find the appropriate choice, or have access to a private designer, dressmaker, or tailor who can create or alter garments to suit them. The expressions "fits to a T," and "fits like a glove" emphasize the value placed on this facet of clothing in our culture.

We are all familiar with the stigma associated with hand-me-down clothing in large families. The objection to these clothes among siblings is often not that the clothing is worn or unattractive but that it does not fit the different children. Poor fit announces to the world that you are poor or deprived. Therefore only clothing items that are properly altered for the individual receive acceptance.

The designer-label appeal used in merchandising also promotes the status-symbol aspect of fit. Designer jeans, hosiery, and sweaters claim superiority because of better—or at least, more fashionable—fit.

In analyzing the content of historic fashions, we note that the elite displayed the fitted clothing. The peasantry were not allowed this symbol of rank.

Governmental agencies and educational groups have sought to standardize sizes of clothing in an effort to provide fit for more persons. Underlying the objectives of these programs has been the assumption that fit or the availability of good fit is one of the existing inequalities in our society. It is further assumed that by eliminating this means of discriminating against persons in different socioeconomic positions, one can reduce prejudice and move toward greater equality. Unfortunately standardization of sizes has not been entirely successful in accomplishing these lofty objectives. In many cases, the reverse outcome has occurred, and consumer choice has actually been reduced because of standardization.

AGE

Different age groups accept different standards of fit. We are familiar with the preoccupation of many teenagers with appearance and social acceptance. Body changes are so rapid at these ages that fit is a constant problem. Pants and sleeves are too short; garments become constricting and tight. The peer group closely monitors the appearance of all members and feeds back acceptance or rejection. Group standards of fit and those of parents may often be in conflict at this age level. We are all aware of or have experienced the typical generation-gap conflict over fit in clothing. The teenager constantly searches for the true mirror image. Do my clothes really fit, and by what standards should I judge or will I be judged?

Fit poses a different problem for the mature adult. Priorities may be comfort and freedom of movement, and as a result fashion may be compromised. Persons suffering from obesity or a disability may forgo the pleasure of properly fitted clothing altogether. Age may be seen as a limiting factor, for example, "A person my age can't wear a short skirt." However, age distinctions in clothing have blurred as the elderly have become more socially involved. Personal appearance, including good fit in clothing has become a priority.

Whatever the standards of fit accepted by different age groups, recognition of the role of good fit in personal satisfaction with clothing cannot be denied.

SEX ROLES

Social scientists have shown that sex-role definitions begin early in life and are widely accepted in societies (Oakley, 1972; Walum, 1977). Clothing, particularly the fit of clothing, has been a part of sex-role distinctions, and as sex roles change, parallel changes occur in concepts of fit. Women viewed as sexual objects have been associated with clothing fitted tightly to accentuate the body. Women viewed as men's possessions were dressed to display the man's economic and social success. Veblen (1899) wrote of women's clothes being restrictive to the degree that they could not work. Confining, impractical clothing said to the world that this person did not have to work and was dependent. Views of women's roles and clothing choices have changed, and women are now experiencing greater independence, freedom, and mobility. They are gainfully employed and seeking professional advancement and satisfaction. What changes have occurred in the fit women seek in their clothing?

One assumption is that success in the professional world and proper fit in clothing are related. This association is described by Korda (1977), as he warns men to pay particular attention to fit in the business suit. "When you have found it, be ruthless about alterations. It is not all that important how much the suit costs, *but it must fit.* Nothing makes a man look more like a failure than a poorly fitted suit (p. 156-7). This statement attaches great significance to fit as a vehicle for personal achievement. As women redefine their roles to include achievement, we might predict greater concern about fit in their clothing. Prescriptions for "appropriate" dress for the working woman abound in popular literature. They require fit as one of the subtleties not to be overlooked—a crucial factor in upward mobility.

RELIGION

Because organized religion stresses values and attitudes in living, the stance of various groups on the issue of fit in clothing is of interest. Overall we note that garments worn by the clergy in most religious ceremonies are void of fit. The robes are straight-cut, long, and flowing. In certain religious sects, not only the leaders but also the followers forgo fitted garments and don the religious vesture. One can theorize that fit is associated with worldliness and pleasure-seeking or has a sexual connotation in many religions. Religions often specify what is acceptable and unacceptable, for example, sleeve, jacket, and skirt lengths and types of necklines. One's religious background greatly influences one's concept of fit. Religious norms established early in life often persist in adulthood.

RACE AND ETHNICITY

The effect of race and ethnicity on concepts of fit are less easily identified. If we look at costumes represented as "national" costumes, certain characteristics are observed, for example, tight-fitting waistlines, or wrapping as opposed to stitching to achieve fit. Viewing international beauty contests would lead one to believe that fit has become universal in definition. However, these contests have cultural assimilation as their goal, and contestants tend to cater to the judges' Western taste. One may hypothesize that the more closely an individual identifies with his or her race or ethnic group, the more readily he or she adopts the group's standards of fit. These standards may be subtle nuances identifiable only by group members.

FASHION CHANGE

Studying fashion over time gives insight into its changes. Fashions originate, are promoted by change agents, and become highly visible in the media. Some gain mass acceptance: they are worn by all ages, are produced at different price levels, and are judged acceptable for many occasions. This wide acceptance leads to fatigue or boredom, and the fashion is displaced by another on the rise. Concepts of fit change as fashions change. Skirt lengths dramatically support this theory, as do waistlines, which come and go or move above and below the body's natural waist. The fashion question is not simply, "Are skirts in fashion?" but "What type of skirt is in fashion and how is fit achieved in the design?"

We propose that fit is related to several social variables that help explain differences among individuals, groups, and cultures. We find these relationships intriguing and believe there is much to be gained from an examination of these variables.

3
Body Changes During One's Lifetime

As you progress through life, your body will change—sometimes suddenly, as the result of an accident; sometimes rapidly, as during a growth spurt; and sometimes very slowly, as with aging. These changes may affect only the size, shape, and proportion of your body, or they may bring limited ability and a need to readjust basic living skills. Thus, as the body changes, clothing must be adapted to fit as well as to meet one's need for independence, convenience, safety, comfort, and looking like one's peers. Most of us take some of these needs for granted, but when we are unable to dress ourselves or to take care of our toileting and personal hygiene, clothing that gives independence becomes a high priority.

This chapter discusses the physical changes that occur throughout life, and we have grouped them into five subgroups: the early years, the middle years, the later years, obesity, and disabilities. Each subgroup is discussed briefly so that you can begin to observe the changes as they occur in yourself and others. Space does not permit us, nor is it the purpose of this book, to delve deeply into the topic; however, we would encourage you to read further and to study human physiology and clothing for special needs. Only as you study and observe how the body develops and changes, as well as how some conditions limit it, will you be able to draft or adapt patterns that fulfill particular personal and physical needs.

THE EARLY YEARS

Bodies are constantly changing. Newborn babies have large heads in proportion to their bodies and very short arms and legs. Growth is very rapid and a baby usually triples its birth weight and doubles its height by the end of the first year. During the first year, the baby's head continues to grow and develop, so that it is apt to be larger in circumference than the chest by the end of the year. Besides rapid growth, the baby is learning to sit up, crawl, feed itself, and walk. Thus clothing needs to provide plenty of space for movement, as well as easy access for diapering. Fabrics must be absorbent, warm, lightweight, washable, and nonallergenic.

Toddlers (eighteen months to two-and-a-half years) grow by spurts. After growing very rapidly for the first year or so, the child slows down during the next few years. As the child grows out of babyhood, noticeable changes take place in its body proportions. The child gradually loses its baby chubbiness and grows lengthwise. As it begins to be very active, its weight is made up of more muscle than fat. The child's abdomen is prominent, the chest is round, and the neck is short. Clothing should be large enough to accommodate this rapid growth but not so large as to be troublesome. As coordination develops, the child begins to dress herself or himself. The toddler has little patience with clothes, so clothing should be easy to put on and take off; it should also be washable.

The preschoolers (two to five years) are "doers." They can run, jump, and climb; they are never still a minute. They gain consistently in height and weight, and the arms and legs continue to grow more rapidly than the torso. The amount of growth increase depends on body build and heredity, but overall the child increases in height more rapidly than in width and circumference. Boys and girls have much the same body proportions during this period. The abdomen decreases in size and the shoulders begin to broaden. The child's ability to coordinate eye-and-hand movements continues to improve until the child can dress and undress herself or himself if the clothes are easy enough to manipulate. Preschoolers can button buttons that are a half inch (13 mm) or more in diameter and that are easy to reach. By the end of the preschool period, children may be able to tie bows that they can see.

By the time the child begins elementary school, body proportion is much like that of an adult. During the elementary school years, growth decelerates, but the child's legs and arms continue to lengthen. Each child will grow at his or her own pace during this period, producing variations in general body types: tall and slender, stocky, short and thin. At about the midpoint of this period, weight and height may increase very slowly, sometimes allowing clothing to be worn for two to three years.

Just before puberty, growth accelerates. Weight may increase, and legs, arms, and feet grow very rapidly. Girls usually mature before boys. In girls this maturation is noticeable as the hips broaden, the waistline becomes smaller, the shoulders widen, and the nipples and later the breasts develop. When sexual maturity is achieved, girls may almost cease to grow.

Puberty for boys is not as physically noticeable; however, the voice deepens, the shoulders broaden, and hair appears on the face. Growth does not stop with sexual maturity for boys; they continue to grow in height, weight, and strength until their early twenties.

Periods of rapid growth bring clothing problems for preadolescents and adolescents. Garments are quickly outgrown, sleeves become too short or too tight, pants are soon above the ankles, and skirts are quickly too short. For girls, waistlines and crotch length become too short, and close-fitting dresses become too tight between the armscyes. Drafting or adapting patterns for the rapidly growing child and adolescent is a constant challenge.

THE MIDDLE YEARS

Growth in height ceases in adolescence or in the early middle years, but the body may continue to change in size and proportion as it matures and during pregnancy.

Pregnancy

During the first three months of pregnancy, the body proportions remain almost normal even though breasts may begin to increase slightly as early as one and one half months after conception. The waistline begins to increase and rise after the fourth month, and it continues to rise until about two weeks before the baby is born (Tate and Glisson, 1961). At this time, the baby drops lower in the abdomen and the waistline lowers. As the abdomen expands, the curvature of the lower spine increases to help maintain body balance, and the hips and upper thighs increase in size. This posture change lengthens the front of the figure. Thus jackets, dresses, and tops should be wider through the waistline and abdomen and longer in front to keep the hemline even. Skirts, pants, and shorts need to be fuller through the hip and thigh areas and longer in front unless they are designed with front stretch panels. Maternity outerwear will probably not be needed until about the fourth month; however, this need will depend on the snugness of the existing wardrobe and the weight gain and proportion of the pregnant woman.

General Changes

Weight gain is often associated with the middle years, when both men and women tend to enlarge at the waistline. Body fat migrates downward even in the face, and the contour becomes more angular. Wrinkles also begin to appear and then enlarge and deepen after the midpoint of life. During the middle years, both men's and women's hair begins to gray, and many men begin to notice bald spots. Women generally increase in bust, hip, and thigh measurements, and the bustline lowers as the breasts begin to sag. Often the shoulders begin to round and a slight swayback may develop. Garments need more fullness through the back armscye as well as more length in the back bodice. The buttocks also flatten, especially in women, requiring pants to be shaped differently if they are to fit correctly. Men, even those with a slender build, find fat deposits around the abdomen and the hips, making pants tight through the thighs and across the stomach. Coats, too, may need adjustment through the waist and hipline. These changes are all affected by heredity and may be delayed by good nutrition, attitude, and exercise.

THE LATER YEARS

The later years cover a phase of life lasting twenty years or more, and there is a great variation—physically, socially, and psychologically—among people in this age group. Again, how rapidly the body seems to age depends on heredity, nutrition, attitude, and excercise.

During the early part of the later years, the abdomen, hips, and thighs become heavier and more prominent. Later the body may become thin, and as muscle tone decreases, the legs and arms become less shapely. The slouching posture that began in the middle years may become more slouched, developing into a dowager's hump. This stance thrusts the head forward, increases the neck circumference, and hollows the chest. Both men and women may need clothing that is longer and wider in the upper back area and shorter in the front waist length. Women's breasts continue to sag, and clothing styles that do not emphasize the bustline are becoming. There is a reduction in total height (as much as five inches), partly from a slouching of the posture and partly from a reduction of cartilage in the spinal column (Goodrick and Meadors, 1977).

The contours of the face change, and facial features become more pronounced as hollows are created at the temples and alongside the cheeks. More wrinkles appear on the face and neck as the skin becomes dry, thin, and inelastic. Existing wrinkles continue to enlarge and deepen, giving the face distinctiveness and character. The skin tends to become more yellow in tone, and blood vessels dilate and become more visible through the thinning skin. These changes, along with graying hair, call for clothing designs that give softness to the face and a new selection of becoming colors.

As one ages, he or she becomes more susceptible to extreme heat and cold because of changing body conditions and the older person's tendency to move or exercise less. Thus garments with long sleeves, jackets, and sweaters are comfortable. Joints begin to stiffen as the person ages, and the resulting decreased mobility in the arms and fingers requires garments that are easy to manipulate and that have front closures.

Despite many health problems that develop with increasing age, most older individuals do not consider themselves seriously handicapped. When they are asked to compare their health with others in their age group, the majority rate their health as "good" or "excellent" (Harris, 1978). However, almost half of the people over sixty-five years old suffer some limitations of activity due to a chronic condition, and almost 40 percent are limited in carrying out major activities (Harris, 1978).

Many older people continue to care about their appearance, and they want clothing that accents their good features and gives a psychological lift. Gilbert (1952) considers general appearance the first thing to remember when working with older people. She believes that when one looks good, it is difficult not to feel well. Thus the more older people see an alert and fresh image in the mirror, the more inclined they are to feel good about themselves. Appearance has a great deal to do with mental attitude, keeping socially active, seeking new experiences, and being a useful member of society, regardless of age.

OBESITY

Obesity has become a problem in every age group. People are considered obese if they are 20 percent overweight for their height and age. Some overweight people are large all over and are well proportioned. Others are full only through the hips and thighs and have a relatively trim chest or bustline. Others are topheavy: large through the chest and shoulders, but trim through the waist and hips. Still others, especially women, have an hourglass figure: heavy through the bust and hips with a small waistline. Obese men are often largest through the abdomen. Some people are large-boned and muscular and have firm flesh, whereas others have very mobile flesh that shifts and bulges over any snug-fitting garment, such as a bra or a bathing suit.

Designs that do not make obese people appear larger and that give the illusion of a better-proportioned figure are good choices. For example, obese women with heavy hips and thighs should keep the center of interest close to the face with an attractive neckline. Men with large stomachs should avoid decorative belt buckles, which draw the eye to the overweight area. Grooming is especially important for all obese persons if they are to overcome the stereotype that they are sloppy in all aspects of their lives. Proper fit is important for both men and women, as girth is emphasized by clothing that fits too tightly and gaps between buttons.

Women may find raglan and cut-on sleeves and dresses without waistline seams easier to fit, as their body-contour lines, especially at the shoulders and the waistline, become indistinct. Armscye seams are especially difficult to locate if the shoulders are sloping. When using or drafting patterns with set-in sleeves for obese women with narrow shoulders, locate the armscye seam slightly further out on the shoulder to help balance the hipline. Many obese women have protruding stomachs, and a dress with little or no waistline shaping is more slenderizing than a dress with a waistline seam or a bodice and skirt of different colors.

Generally an overweight woman's bustline is lower, but it could be higher than normal. Any deviation calls for a pattern alteration and for styles with bustline fullness, which are more flattering than those that follow the contour of the bustline. Because overweight people may have short, full necks, V necklines, shirts with open collars, and flat collars are more pleasing and comfortable than high necklines or mandarin collars.

Overweight women who have difficulty bending will find dresses that go over the head easier to manipulate than those that have full-length front openings. However, front openings of full or three-quarter length are better for women who cannot raise their arms above the head. Obese people should dress as attractively as possible and wear colors that give them a psychological lift.

DISABILITIES

Independence in dressing and caring for their own needs are probably the most important clothing priorities of people who are disabled. Of course, wearing garments similar to those of their peers is important, too, as long as these garments provide independence, safety, and comfort. Approval gives everyone, including the handicapped, self-confidence and a feeling of well-being, so wearing attractive clothing can lift the spirits and lessen feelings of tension, anger, hostility, and depression. Clothing becomes very important to people with physical handicaps because they want observers to see an attractive person with a handicap rather than just a handicapped person (Hoffman, 1979).

A disability is defined as a physical impairment that may result in a handicap, whereas a handicap is the inability to function normally without help. Thus a disabling condition is not always a handicap; it depends on one's perception of the disability. Some conditions that bring about the need for special clothing are

- disabilities that result in limited motion.
- disabilities that result in the inability to stand, walk, or balance.
- figure irregularities.
- mastectomies.
- incontinence.

Limited Motion

Limited motion can result from rheumatoid arthritis, osteoarthritis, a stroke, or a disabling disease. Whether one can function independently depends on the type and severity of the condition.

Mobility can be inhibited by swelling, stiffness, tenderness of the joints, inability to move the fingers or to grasp anything with them, inability to rotate the shoulders or the hips, and intense pain when moving the joints.

Clothing that is designed for easy dressing, undressing, and toileting is necessary. Thus garment openings may need to be longer or larger and conveniently located. Openings should be closed with medium to large buttons, zippers with large pulls (Figure 3.1), large skirt or fur hooks (Figure 3.2), and Velcro (Figure 3.3). Patterns may need to be designed with extra-large armscyes or raglan sleeves and wrap around features.

Safety is also of prime importance to those with limited motion. Safety related to clothing means garments that will not catch on objects, that will not catch fire or burn readily, and that will not catch in wheelchairs or crutches. Flame-resistant fabrics should be used for garments worn by people who smoke or who heat their homes with wood stoves or space heaters. Garments with short sleeves or long, close-fitting sleeves are less apt to catch on objects or to flame if brushed across a burner on the range. Properly placed, flat pockets, the absence of drawstrings and ties, and moderately full skirts and pants, all contribute to clothing designed for safety.

Inability to Stand, Walk, or Balance

This condition may be the result of a stroke, paralysis, cerebral palsy, poliomyelitis, multiple sclerosis, birth defects, or an accident. All of these diseases and conditions can result in the use of adaptive equipment such as braces, crutches, a wheelchair, or casts. Clothing may need to be adapted for limited motion as well as to accommodate the equipment.

Braces are bulky and awkward, and they cause friction and wear on clothing. Any fabric chosen for wearing over a brace must be durable and abrasion-resistant. Clothing worn over the brace should be simply designed; it should have a loose fit and be free of bows or other trim that might catch or cause an accident. Long zippers may need to be inserted in the seams of pants legs and of sleeves so that dressing is easier. To reduce friction and wear, fusible patches can be used on the wrong side of the fabric, or a protective cover can be worn over the brace. Garment seams and hems should be double-stitched and finished to eliminate loose threads. Flat-felled seams are a good choice.

Crutches create a lot of wear and abrasion in the underarm area of garments. Extra width is needed between the back armscyes and may be needed around the upper sleeve because the arms and shoulders are used extensively. The use of crutches also causes garments to pull up, making it difficult to keep shirts and blouses tucked into waistbands. Garments need to be designed with high-cut armscyes or gussets, and sleeveless garments should be cut high under the arm to prevent skin abrasion. Underarm areas should be lined or reinforced with double-stitching of twill tape in the seams. Action pleats or designs with back fullness increase the roominess needed between the armscyes. Shirts and blouses may stay in place better if designed to be worn over the waistband or attached to another garment, creating bodysuits or jumpsuits. Two piece dresses and dresses with elastic at the waistline give women more freedom of

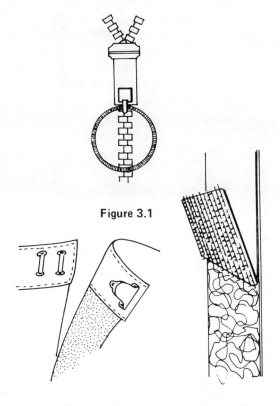

Figure 3.1

Figure 3.2   Figure 3.3

movement. Coat sleeves must also be cut high under the arm and without much bulk for crutch users. Skirt patterns may need to be altered because continued use of crutches may change the posture and cause hemlines to curve upward in back.

Wheelchair users have difficulty dressing, so clothing needs to be designed with convenient closures, and some outerwear, such as coats and robes, can be designed without a back seat area (Figure 3.4) Continual sitting enlarges the waist and the hipline, lengthens the back, and shortens the front torso. Also, the shoulders may become broader from operating the wheelchair. Thus most patterns need to be drafted or altered to fit correctly. In addition, wheelchair users may desire garments that conceal leg deformities and are designed for easy access to urinary devices such as catheters. Sleeves and skirts should not be too long nor so wide that they catch in the chair or become soiled from the wheels. Raglan sleeves, back-action pleats, and back gathers below a shoulder yoke are shirt and blouse designs that can be easily adapted for wheelchair users. Jackets and coats that are shaped at the hemline—longer in back to reach the chair seat and short enough in front just to brush the top of the thigh when seated (Figure 3.5)—or that have side slits are most comfortable (Figure 3.6). Pants and skirts need to be shortened in the front crotch length and lengthened in back to accommodate the figure (Figures 3.7 and 3.8). Fabrics need to be slick enough for easier turning in bed and for sliding in and out of the wheelchair, but not so slick that the person slides when seated.

Arm and leg casts call for clothing that is adapted to fit over the cast. Stretchy knit T-

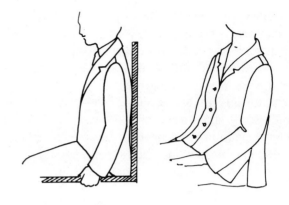

Figure 3.5   **Figure 3.6**

Figure 3.7 Before alteration

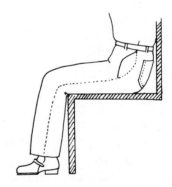

Figure 3.8 After alteration

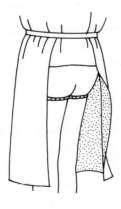

Figure 3.4

shirts and blouses may fit over arm casts if the sleeve is opened or made larger to accommodate the cast. If the arm cast is temporary, the sleeve seam may just be ripped and an extra piece of fabric inserted to make the sleeve wider. However, for more permanent use, the sleeve pattern can be drafted or altered to fit over the cast, and a zipper can be inserted in the underarm seam to make dressing easier.

Leg casts call for pants with full-cut legs, such as warm-ups, and zippers or Velcro inserted in the leg seams. A tape loop may need to be stitched inside the waistband so that a hook can be used to pull up the pants if the person cannot bend over. Skirts for women must be designed with a moderate amount of fullness so that they fit over the cast but do not hinder the use of crutches or a walker. If crutches are used, clothing must also be designed for wear and abrasion in the underarm area.

Figure Irregularities

These problems are the result of abnormal curving of the spine—lordosis, kyphosis, and scoliosis—birth defects, and other physical deformities. Lordosis is the inward curvature of the spine at the lower back; a mild condition is called *swayback*. More extreme conditions result in a raising of the buttocks and a rounding of the upper back. Thus garments wrinkle across the back below the waistband and are too tight across the buttocks. Skirts curve upward at the center back hemline and the side seams swing toward the back. Kyphosis is the outward curving of the spine, generally in the upper back area, which results in the "caving-in" of the chest. Thus shirts, blouses, and bodices need to be made wider and longer in back and shorter in front. Skirts and pants also need to be shortened below the front waistline. Some fullness designed into the front chest area helps to balance the figure and creates a more pleasing look (Mead, 1980).

Scoliosis is a lateral curving of the spine, which causes one side of the back and one hip to be more prominent. The prominent hip and one shoulder may also be higher than the other. Garments with back fullness and straight-cut jackets and overblouses help to conceal the curves. Patterns usually need to be drafted or altered differently for each side of the figure. If a brace is worn for scoliosis, garments will need to be sized larger to fit over the brace, and necklines will need to be larger, or styled with convertible collars that stand away from the neck. Separates and dresses with waistline seams are easier to adapt than one-piece jumpsuits and A-line dresses for anyone with an abnormal curvature of the spine.

Midgets are rarely over 3 feet 4 inches tall, but they are well proportioned, and females are generally small-breasted (Hoffman, 1979). Thus drafts and patterns sized for children can be adapted providing the style is appropriate for an adult. Some children's patterns need to be increased in the front bustline for small, but developed breasts.

Dwarfs have nearly normal torsos with short arms and legs, making them less than 4 feet, 8 inches in height (Hoffman, 1979). It is generally easier to draft than to alter patterns for the dwarf figure; however, a basic pattern may be altered and used to create various styles. Generally dwarfs look better in simple styles without high necklines and with moderately full skirts, shorter jackets, tapered sleeves, and slightly tapered pant legs. An illusion of increased height is achieved with one-color outfits and smooth fabrics with little design.

Mastectomies

Regardless of the type of mastectomy, associated problems may include tenderness of the scarred tissue; swelling of the arm, which may be permanent or may vary from day to day; difficulty in raising the arm; and a sunken area. Before clothing can be adapted, one should be fitted with the correct prosthesis and a bra that is designed with bra bands that do not rub across sensitive areas. Most women find that they can wear many garments from their existing wardrobe providing that the sleeves are large enough and that the garment is easy to put on. If the swelling persists, garments designed with raglan or cut-on sleeves will accommodate the larger arm. Select lingerie, evening wear, and swimsuits with wide shoulder straps, less revealing necklines, and sleeveless armholes that fit close around the arm. Slightly gapping necklines may sometimes be made to fit if several rows of elastic thread are sewn inside the neckline. Sleeveless garments may have a piece of fusible interfacing fused to the garment under the armhole to bridge the hollow area. Otherwise a padded armhole shield that fills the hollow may be made and attached to the bra. As long as dressing is a problem, select styles and patterns with front openings and large armscyes.

Incontinence

Incontinence includes the total or partial loss of bowel or bladder control, and the person may

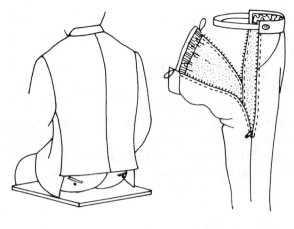

Figure 3.9   Figure 3.10

feel embarrassment and shame. Clothing needs to provide access to collection devices, absorbent pads, and waterproof pants. Loose-fitting garments conceal the device or padding. Pants with wide legs and inseam zippers permit easy cleaning of the urine bag. Gored skirts give women the needed concealment, and those that wrap in back can be pulled aside for easier changing. Cutouts or short back panels in coats, robes, dresses, and skirts are helpful for both men and women who are wheelchair-bound (Figure 3.9). Pants for both men and women may need zippers from the waistline to the hip and down both side seams, as well as an inside waistband (Figure 3.10), for access to the stoma (artificial opening created through the abdominal wall for removing the contents of the bowel).

Today, people with disabilities, as well as the elderly, are more able to work at meaningful jobs and to become active in community life. Thus clothing gains importance as people want to be recognized for their contributions instead of being viewed with pity and curiosity. We urge students to learn as much as possible so that they can draft and alter clothing to meet the special needs of individuals and to help contribute to the self-worth of others.

4
Structural Features That Contribute to Fit

GARMENT FEATURES

As you look at an attractive garment design, it is essential that you recognize which details of that design contribute to the fit of the garment and which details are purely decorative. The shape (often called the *silhouette*) and the style of the garment are created through seams. To interpret a silhouette in a pattern, seams and darts are placed within the contour in harmonious space relationships to the lines of the silhouette. Structural seams and darts thus create the distinctive outline of the garment, at the same time determining fit. Deciding which seams are structural and which seams are decorative is your first step in pattern design. Major vertical structural seams are usually placed at the center front, the center back, and the sides. The basic pattern used for fitting relies on these seams. Major horizontal seams are usually placed at the shoulder, at the waist, and occasionally at the hip. Special attention must be given to fit in these areas also. Purely decorative seams are often included in a garment to create unusual design lines—the matching of plaids and stripes, the introduction of two or more colors of fabric, or the inclusion of trim. Often seams serve both structural and decorative purposes, for example, princess seams, skirt gores, and yokes.

Seams are not the only structural details for achieving good fit. Darts or dart equivalents are also used for shaping fabric over body curves. The purpose of darts is to release fullness over body curves while controlling the fullness at the seams so that adjoining pieces match. Darts begin at a seamline and are directed toward the fullest part of the body curve. The stitching line at the front of the dart stops before reaching the fullest part of the curve. Typical dart locations are the shoulder, bust, waist, hip, and elbow. Basic patterns rely on these structural darts for fit. Once fit is established via darts, interesting designs may be achieved by substituting dart equivalents, for example, gathers, tucks, or pleats. Dart equivalents are softer and less form-fitting in appearance. Care must be taken to retain the fit previously established with structural darts.

Garment openings are usually placed within major structural seams. Zippers placed within major seams (e.g., center front, center back, or side seams) do not change the fit of the garment if properly installed. Disregarding seam allowance widths when installing zippers is a common error that does change the garment's fit. Zipper installation techniques that begin with the seam basted closed at the seamline help eliminate this difficulty. The decision about where the zipper is to be placed should be based on the ease of getting into and out of the garment as well as on the total design effect. In constructing women's garments, it is often easier to insert the zipper at the center back because the seam is less apt to pucker or ripple, and fitting can be accomplished at the side seams. This position is less acceptable if arm movement is limited. Often, selecting a zipper of maximum length aids the wearer. For example, the choice of a 9- or 11-inch (23- or

28 cm) zipper for a skirt side seam may be preferable to the traditional 7-inch (18-cm) skirt zipper.

When buttons and buttonholes are used as garment closures, the seamline becomes the position where the button should rest when the garment is buttoned. Therefore, it is necessary to design an extension beyond the seamline to accommodate the width of the button. Failure to add or maintain this extension alters the fit of the garment as there will be no overlap at the opening. Recommendations for the width of the extension vary from 3/4 to 1 1/2 inches (2 to 3.8 cm) for dresses but must always allow for the width of the button. It should be possible to place the button between the seamline and the garment's edge except when very large buttons have been selected for design effects. The width of the extensions on coats or jackets varies from 1 1/2 to 3 inches (3.8 to 7.5 cm) or up to 8 inches (20.5 cm) for double-breasted garments. The facing pattern to be used at the opening must also include this extension. Particular attention must be paid to building in an adequate extension when designing a bodice with a cut-on facing. The extension width is double because the facing folds back on the garment. When altering a commercial pattern, it is also necessary to redesign the facing patterns to include all alterations.

Other possibilities for garment closures include the use of hooks, Velcro, or snap tape within the seam. As long as seam-allowance widths are observed, these closures should not alter the fit of the garment and may contribute greatly to the ease of getting into and out of the garment.

Openings may be merely slashes with or without ties or opened seams. Because these edges butt together rather than overlap, they seldom pose a fitting problem. However, if the garment has been fitted too closely in other areas or not designed or altered to accommodate figure characteristics and problems, these openings tend to gap and not lie flat. Carefully constructed facings on slashed openings contribute to good fit.

Occasionally it may be necessary to enlarge a garment opening (e.g., a neckline) to allow it to slip easily on and off the body. This is accomplished by slashing the pattern to open it the desired amount. Enlarging techniques will be discussed later. Elastic, drawstrings, and belts may be used to regain the fit once the garment is on the body.

FABRIC FEATURES

Fabrics vary greatly in stretchability versus stability. Generally, knitted fabrics have more "give" than do fabrics that are woven. Knitted fabrics are constructed from one set of yarns that form an interlocking loop structure. Woven fabrics are constructed from two sets of yarns interlacing at right angles to each other. The loop structure of the knit permits greater stretchability than is found in woven fabrics because the give in the woven fabric is limited to the intersections of the lengthwise and crosswise yarns, referred to as the *bias* of the fabric. The pattern envelopes of commercial patterns distinguished between designs appropriate for knits and those appropriate for woven fabrics because of the differences in fit between woven and knit fabrics. The pattern designer must be able to recognize the differences between these fabric structures. It is usually recommended that the basic fitting pattern be tested by sewing it in a closely woven fabric.

Within the categories of woven and knitted fabrics, great variation in the amount of stretchability is found. Generally, the more closely woven a fabric, the lower the stretchability. Fabrics of low thread count tend to have more give. Created with stretch yarns used in one or both directions of the fabric, woven stretch fabrics offer the stretchability and comfort of many knits. Using these fabrics requires consideration of both the direction of the stretch and the amount of the stretch. This information is seldom provided at the point of sale, and therefore the amount of stretch is difficult to evaluate.

Knitted fabrics offer varying amounts of stretch depending on their compactness and type of structure. Those used in apparel are mainly double knits, single knits, and warp knits. The double knit pictured in Figure 4.1a is a firm knitted structure, whereas the single knit in Figure 4.1b has much give. Double and single knits have stretch in both horizontal and vertical

Figure 4.1a

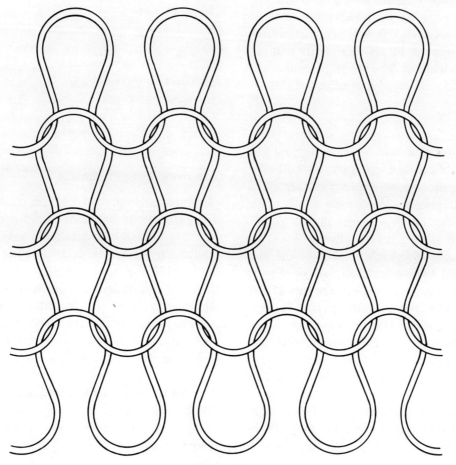

Figure 4.1b

directions. Warp knits (e.g., tricot) are constructed on machines that knit vertically and therefore offer stretch properties predominantly in the horizontal direction. When stretched horizontally, the warp knit rolls toward the right side of the fabric. Within each type of knit are fabrics engineered with varying amounts of stretch. Careful analysis of the stretch characteristics in each fabric is essential to achieving fit in a design.

Fit is dependent on several structural features of the garment, including seams, darts, dart equivalents, fabric, and openings. All must serve the dual purpose of contributing to the total design and shaping the fabric to the figure. Thus the fit of the garment becomes aesthetically pleasing and comfortable.

GUIDES TO GOOD FIT

Developing an awareness of those features that contribute to good fit is the first step in drafting or altering patterns. As your awareness of these features increases and your skill in adjusting fine details grows, the fit of your garments will improve. Special features you must recognize are described in the following sections.

Grainlines

The center front and back grainlines should be vertical to the floor and centered on the body, dividing the body in half. Bias-cut garments and some design details are exceptions to this rule because the grainline lays diagonally across the body. On the sleeve, the lengthwise grainline should be straight down the center of the arm from the top of the sleeve to the elbow (Figure 4.2). In pants, the front leg creases should follow the grainline, and the creases should hang straight (Figure 4.3). The crosswise grainlines should be parallel to the floor around the bust or chest, hip, and upper arm. Any deviations in the vertical or horizontal grainlines indicate that the body characteristics have not been accommodated and the pattern must be changed or that the pattern was not laid correctly on the fabric before cutting.

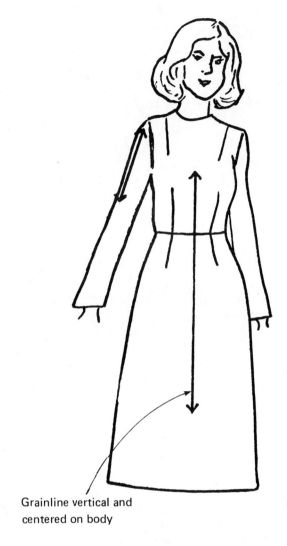

Grainline vertical and centered on body

Figure 4.2

Seam and Edge Placement

Side seams begin at the center of the armpit and hang straight to the floor, curving toward neither the front nor the back (Figure 4.4). Center front and back seams are perpendicular to the floor and divide the body in half. Vertical seams (e.g., princess line seams) should hang straight to the floor with an even amount of flare. The armscye seam should lie across the end of the shoulder bone (where the arm joins the body) and continue downward with a smooth curve to the underarm. The shoulder seam lies in a straight line on the top of the shoulder, slanting toward neither the front nor the back. If the pattern contains a shoulder yoke, the shoulder area should still be positioned as indicated. The neck-

STRUCTURAL FEATURES THAT CONTRIBUTE TO FIT • 21

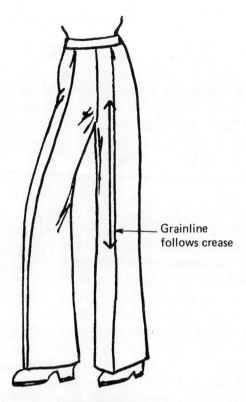

Figure 4.3
Grainline follows crease

Seam-vertical from armpit to hem

Figure 4.4

line seam should fit close to the base of the neck without feeling too tight. Be sure the seam allowance is clipped before fitting so that the neckline lies flat. If you are unaccustomed to a close-fitting neckline, the basic fitting garment will feel tight and uncomfortable even though it fits properly. The waistline seam should follow the natural waistline and fit close to the body. Check this by tying a string or a 1/4-inch (6-mm) elastic around the waist and wiggle so that the string or elastic slips to the natural waistline. The waistline seam should lie under the string or elastic.

Empire waistlines should lie directly under the breast and should be fitted close to the body. A dropped waistline seam should hang parallel to the floor and fit close to the body without wrinkling. The waistline on women's pants should reach the natural waistline unless the pants are designed to be worn below the waist. Because men's waistlines are not sharply defined, pants fit above, below, or at the natural waistline, whatever is comfortable and right for the style. A full-length sleeve hem or cuff should cover the wristbone when the arm is slightly bent. Short sleeve lengths and other variations should be flattering to the figure. Shirts and blouses should be long enough to remain tucked in after the wearer bends over. Casual shirts designed to be worn over waistbands are usually hemmed at the hipline. The length of skirts and pants depends on the style and the current fashion trends. For women this length sometimes varies yearly. Men's pants usually touch the shoe in front without breaking and reach the top of the shoe heel in back.

Ease and Fullness

The bodice front and back should be smooth and without wrinkles in the shoulder area or around the chest. The body of the shirt or blouse should have adequate ease around the chest and waist so that it does not bag, pull across the back, or gape open in front. There should be enough ease across the back shoulders and in the sleeves to provide adequate movement. On basic fitting garments, there should be enough ease across the back for you to comb your hair, but not enough for you to extend both arms fully. Work and sports garments should be fitted with more ease than formal wear unless stretch fabric is used. All sleeves should hang smooth and free of wrinkles; however, puffed and gathered sleeves should contain enough fullness for the design to be recognized. Cuffs should be tight enough to maintain the drape of the sleeve, yet loose enough to allow the arm to extend. The fitted waistline should fit close to the body but allow breathing room. The skirt should have enough ease so that it is free of wrinkles and does not cup under the seat nor wrinkle above the hipline. Pleats should hang vertically to the floor and not swing open nor to one side. In pants, the crotch length should be comfortable, neither too short nor too long. Any wrinkles in the crotch area are an indication of improper fit. The seat should not bag or pull, and it should be comfortable when the wearer is sitting, bending, or standing. The pant legs should hang freely on the body without binding, regardless of the width or the style.

Darts and Their Placement

Shoulder, underarm, and waistline darts should be directed toward the fullest part of the bust and end 1/2 to 1 1/2 inches (1.3 to 3.8 cm) short of the fullest part of the bust.

Any gathers or tucks used as either dart equivalents or design features should hang evenly and provide adequate ease. Elbow darts should be directed toward the center of the elbow. Darts and dart equivalents in skirts and pants should be directed toward body curves and end before reaching the fullest part of the curve. They should adequately control fullness at the waistline.

The golden rule of fitting (actually, a law of physics) states that for every *action,* there is a *reaction.* Thus, for every change, another part or parts of the garment will be affected. For example, if you increase bustline width to accommodate full breasts, the dart depth will need to be increased. Adjustments made in skirts to accommodate large hips or abdomen may change the position of the side seams. Or, lengthening a flared skirt will increase the hem's circumference. As you work with these fitting guides—grainlines, seams and edges, ease and fullness, darts and dart equivalents—you will see their interrelationships. Accuracy in fitting depends on your ability to perceive this chain reaction.

5
Measurements, Proportions, and Body Curves

Knowing the precise size and shape of your body is probably one of the most difficult factors in achieving good fit. It may be difficult to be objective about your body size and shape without being overly critical of each curve, but very few bodies are perfect. Most of us wish we had "a little more here and a little less there." However, well-fitted clothing in becoming styles hides a multitude of figure problems. Accept the "shape you are in" and make the best of it!

Before you take your measurements, put on the undergarments suited to the outfit. This is especially important for women because a different style of bra or control-top panty hose may shift the curve of the breast or the seat enough to change the body measurements. Wear shoes that have appropriate sole thickness and heel height for the outfit.

Women should have their measurements taken over a slip and/or the undergarments they plan to wear with the outfit. Men should be measured while wearing undergarments and a thin shirt, with two exceptions. The inseam and side-seam measurement for pants should be taken over similarly styled pants without a belt. Measurements are inaccurate when taken over bulky clothing.

While being measured, stand comfortably with your weight equally balanced on both feet. Assume a natural stance, with your legs positioned as you normally stand. Let a friend do the measuring and the moving while you stand still.

HOW TO MEASURE

Before measuring mark the following places on your body:

1. Tie a string or piece of 1/4-inch (6-mm) elastic around your waist and wiggle so that the cord or elastic slips to your normal waistline.
2. Locate the base of your neck with a choker-length chain, or knot a longer one so that it outlines the bottom of your neck.
3. Mark a dot at the first neck bone (back vertebra). If you bend your head forward, you can feel this top vertebra. Also mark the neck-shoulder point. If you shrug your shoulders, a hollow will form at the side of the neck where this point is located.
4. Mark the end of the shoulder bone. If you have trouble locating this point, raise your arm to shoulder level; a dimple will form at this location.
5. Place rubber bands around each arm so that they lie on top of the end of the shoulder bones and form straight lines down to the armpits.

Have a friend help you measure all of the points designated. Have your friend hold the tape measure flat against your body and take snug, but not tight, measurements. He or she should work at eye level to make sure that the tape measure is parallel to the floor. Record your measurements and the date the measurements are taken. Use the measurement worksheets in the Appendix. Do not cheat on body measurements, and do not record a measurement of 1 to 2 inches (2.5 to 5 cm) smaller than your actual measurement, thinking that you will lose a few pounds before the garment is sewn. Take the following measurements.

These are general measurements for men, women, and children, regardless of the garment:

1. Height: stand against the wall without shoes. Place a flat object (a ruler) on top of the head, parallel to the floor. Measure the wall from below this object to the floor.
2. Waistline: measure around the natural waistline, over the string or elastic.

Measurements for Bodices and Shirts

3. Bust or chest: measure around the fullest part of the breast or chest, keeping the tape parallel to the floor.
4. High bust (women only): measure under the arms and straight across the back, bringing the tape to the front and above the breast (Figure 5.1)
5. Neck (men and boys only): measure around the neck at the Adam's apple to determine the neckband size (Figure 5.2).
6. Back waist length: measure down the center of the back from the first neck bone to the waistline (Figure 5.3).
7. Front waist length: measure from the shoulder at the side of the neck to the waistline.
8. Shoulder to bust (women only): measure from the shoulder at the side of the neck to a line even with the bust point (fullest part of breast).
9. Shoulder length: measure from the side of the neck to the end of the shoulder bone.
10. Back width: measure across the shoulder blades between the armscye locations. Men should measure 6 inches (15 cm) below the

Figure 5.1   Figure 5.2   Figure 5.3

neck base; women, 5 inches (12.5 cm) below the neck; teenagers, 4 1/2 inches (11.5 cm) below; younger girls and boys, 4 inches (10 cm) below; children, 3 inches (7.5 cm) below; and toddlers, 2 3/4 inches (6.4 cm) below (DuBane, 1978).

11. Arm length: measure from the end of the shoulder bone to the wristbone over the bent elbow.
12. Shoulder to elbow (women, girls, and children only): measure from the end of the shoulder bone to the middle of the bent elbow.
13. Shirt-sleeve size (men and boys only): measure from the first neck bone along the shoulder and down the arm, over the bent elbow, to the wristbone.
14. Upper arm: measure around the fullest part of the upper arm.

Measurements for Pants and Skirts

15. Hips: measure around the fullest part of the hipline, keeping the tape parallel to the floor. Women should also measure 9 inches (23 cm) below the waistline for misses', women's, and junior patterns and 7 inches (18 cm) below for half-size and petite patterns.
16. Thigh (for pants): measure around the fullest part of the upper leg. Also measure and record the distance along the side of the body from the waistline to the thigh measurement.
17. Thigh (for skirts): measure around the fullest part of the thigh area (include both legs). Also measure and record the distance along the side of the body from the waistline to the thigh measurement.
18. Crotch depth: sit on a flat chair or table and measure down the side of the body from the waistline to the table or chair (Figure 5.4). Be sure to use a tape measure and follow the body curves.
19. Crotch length (women and girls only): measure from the center back waistline between the legs and up to the center front waistline (Figure 5.5).
20. Pants side length: measure from the waistline along the side of the body to the desired length. Men should measure over a pair of similarly styled pants from the waistband seam to the desired hem.
21. Inseam length (men only): measure the inseam of a pair of similarly styled pants from the crotch to the desired hem.
22. Back skirt length (women and girls only): measure from the center back waistline to the desired length.

Check your body measurements periodically; not only does your weight change, but your body proportions may shift. We suggest that adults be measured two to three times a year, and more often if they have been ill or are changing weight. Children during the growth years may need to be remeasured for every garment that is sewn.

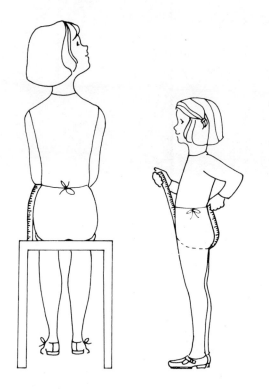

Figure 5.4   Figure 5.5

BODY PROPORTIONS AND CURVES

Even though your body measurements may be standard or nearly so, you may find figure variations in the proportion of one part of your body as compared with another part. For example, three men may be the same height, but one may have a back waist length of 19 inches (48.5 cm) and a pants side-seam measurement of 38 inches (96.5 cm); another may have a back waist length of 18 inches (46 cm) and a pants measurement of 39 inches (99 cm); and the third may measure 17 and 40 inches (43 and 102 cm). Thus the first man is long-waisted, the third man is short-waisted, and the second man has standard proportions.

Stand before a full-length mirror and analyze your posture and figure characteristics. Wear your normal undergarments or leotards and turn sideways as well as facing front to check your silhouette. Check the back view, using a full-length, three-way mirror, if available. As you check your body, be honest with yourself and remember that all people think they have figure problems!

First, check your posture, as the standard figure has good posture that is comfortable and healthful. If your posture is overly erect, the distance from the base of the neck to the fullest part of the breast or chest is lengthened, thereby causing fitting problems. If the posture is slumped, the chest drops and round shoulders result. Also a protruding stomach and swayback may occur (Figure 5.6).

Test your posture by standing with your back against the wall and your weight evenly distributed on both feet. If your posture is good, neither overly erect nor slumped, your shoulders, shoulder blades, and seat (buttocks) should touch the wall. You should barely be able to insert your hand between the wall and the small of your back. Always work at maintaining good posture, as your posture can change over a period of time, for either the better or the worse.

As you continue to analyze your figure, decide whether you are well proportioned, tall or

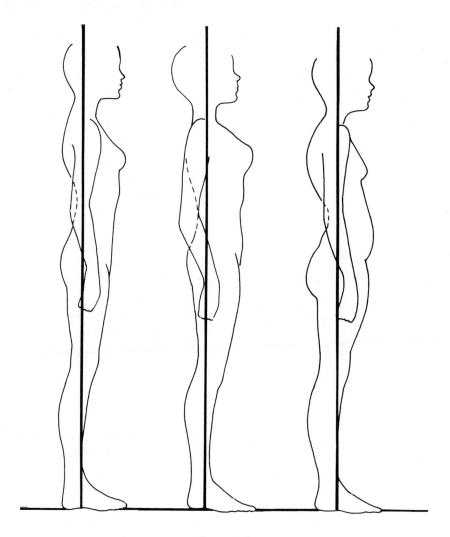

Figure 5.6

short, long- or short-waisted, full through the waist, the hipline, and so on. Continue before the mirror and check your body curves for shape, size, and placement. For example, do your thighs bulge more at the sides or in the front? Is your seat curve high and full or low? Is your stomach flat or round? Are your breasts high, low, or widely spaced, and is your chest above the breast full or hollow and sloping? All of these characteristics differ for each person, and all of them affect the way your clothes fit. When you draft a pattern, you will design it for your special body measurements and characteristics. If you are using a commercial pattern, purchase the one that corresponds most closely to your measurements and figure type. Then alter it to fit.

Ready-to-wear or unaltered garments sewn from patterns will also help indicate your body characteristics. For example, if a dress is too short-waisted, the waistline will lie above your natural waistline and may be too tight around your rib cage. If the crotch depth of pants is proportioned differently than your figure, the waistband of the pants may not come high enough for your waistline, or the crotch may hang several inches below your body.

Be precise and accurate when measuring and analyzing your body. Errors and oversights now will create problems later. The more clothing you fit and sew for yourself, the more aware you will become of your body size and shape.

Part Two

Comparative Analysis of Pattern Alteration Techniques

6
Pattern Alterations: General Techniques

As you perfect your sewing skills now and over the next several years, you will work with many patterns. Being able to alter these patterns for your current and future body characteristics is a skill that will enhance your appearance and your feelings about yourself. Clothing that fits detracts attention from undesirable body characteristics, especially if it is designed to emphasize good or desirable body characteristics. Clothing that fits poorly, especially in the area of an undesirable body characteristic, draws attention to the figure problem.

This section is written to help two types of readers: those who desire to personalize the fit of a basic pattern so that they can create various designs; and those who wish to alter fashionable commercial patterns to fit their figure characteristics. Whatever your goal in reading this section, you will learn more if you alter a basic pattern. Because basic patterns fit closer to the body, figure characteristics are more easily seen and the pattern can be readily adjusted. Thus, as a student, you are more apt to learn the principles of pattern alteration that can be adapted to other patterns and to other people.

Only two pattern companies offer basic dress patterns. If you desire to alter a basic pattern, you may need to choose a fashion pattern in your favorite brand and/or figure type with the following characteristics. Choose a pattern that fits close to the body and has structural seams and darts that follow the natural lines of the figure. Patterns for women should be designed with armscye and waistline seams and should have a minimum of design features, such as pockets, collars, and yokes. When learning to alter, avoid patterns with unusual seam placement, curved and bias seams, and a lot of flare and fullness. Men will need to purchase a shirt pattern with traditional styling: a collar, separate neckband, long sleeves, and cuffs. Both men and women should purchase pants patterns that use only structural seams (no yokes), a fitted waistband, and a minimum of pockets.

Women's patterns are available in various figure types: women's, misses', half-size, miss petite, junior, junior petite, and young junior/teen. A figure type is a general body shape based on body proportions, not age. Use your body measurements, especially height and back bodice length, to determine your figure type. Compare the figure-type diagrams and the measurement charts in any commercial pattern book with your body measurements and shape. Some companies also offer proportioned and easy-to-adjust patterns. If these patterns are basic in design and fit close to the body, they will indicate needed pattern adjustments. However, if you plan to apply the alteration techniques to other commercial patterns, it is better to choose a more common figure type because several styles are available.

Choose the pattern that most nearly corresponds to your body measurements as well as your figure type. For a dress, blouse, coat, jacket, or multiple-garment pattern, choose your size by the bust measurement. However, if your bust measurement is 2 inches (5 cm) or more larger than your high-bust measurement, use the high-bust measurement for selecting the pattern. This means you have a small frame in proportion to your bust, and you need to purchase a pattern that fits your body through the shoulders and neck area. Of course, you will need to alter the pattern for your bust measurement. For skirts, pants, shorts, and culottes, choose the pattern by your hip measurement, as this is the most difficult area to fit.

Men's patterns are available in only two body types: men's and teen boys'. Each type specifies body build, not age. Take accurate body measurements as instructed in Chapter 5, "Measurements, Proportions, and Body Curves," and study the body-type diagrams and measurements in any commercial pattern book. If your measurements are between two pattern sizes, choose the smaller size for easier pattern adjustments. Choose shirt patterns by your neckband size, as the sleeve length and other alterations are easier to make. Use your chest measurement to determine the size for jackets and vests, and your hip measurement for pants patterns.

Children's patterns are available in toddlers', children's, girls', chubbies', and boys' figure types. Toddlers' and children's patterns are available for both girls and boys, whereas chubbies' patterns are designed only for girls. Children are difficult to measure because they are apt to wiggle, but they must be measured accurately. Take children's measurements as directed on the Measurement Worksheet (see the Appendix), but disregard the figures listed in the "Ease Needed" column. Remeasure children for every garment sewn, especially if they are growing rapidly. Select patterns that are closest to their chest and back waist-length measurements. Because children have fewer curves than adults, pattern alterations mainly involve length changes. The instructions for pattern alterations given in Chapters 6 to 12 are for children as well as adults.

SIZE AND EASE

The Measurement Committee of the Pattern Fashion Industry established current standard body measurements that have been adopted by most pattern companies. The companies that have adopted these measurements use them for their patterns—every design and type of clothing—unless otherwise stated in the pattern catalog. Thus you will select the same size of pattern, regardless of brand name, providing that all of the pattern companies within your selection have adopted the standard body measurements. Because a few companies do not use standard body measurements, it is wise to check the measurement charts of any unfamiliar company.

Body size is consistent among most pattern companies, but this is the only factor that is controlled. Ease, which is the extra length and width provided in a pattern for movement and style, is not standardized. Every garment has two types of ease, known as *wearing* and *design ease*. Without both types of ease, garments would pull, and you would not be able to sit down comfortably, breathe, nor move your arms. Design ease is fullness added beyond that needed for comfortable wear, and it is an integral part of the garment's style or design. The amount of design ease needed in any pattern is not standardized and is left to the discretion of the pattern designer. Thus patterns of different brands, but in similar styles, may fit very differently. Design ease is also dependent on the style of the garment. For example, a blouse that gathers from a yoke will be wider across the bust than a fitted style. A dirndl skirt will have more design ease at the hip than an A-line or straight skirt. A blouson top will be fuller above the waistline than a fitted one, and trouser-style pants have more ease in the hip area than jeans.

Wearing ease is a bit more universal, as it is only the fullness needed to permit comfortable movement. Just about all commercial patterns contain both wearing and design ease, with the exception of those for swimwear and some evening wear. Bodices and skirts designed for fitting and alteration classes contain a minimal amount of ease and thus fit closer to the body than most street wear. Minimal amounts of ease for patterns are stated on the worksheet for commercial patterns (see the Appendix). Use the worksheet for recording your body measurements now as well as the pattern measurements later. Then refer to the worksheet for needed pattern alterations.

PATTERN PREPARATION AND MEASUREMENTS

After you have selected the pattern, sort the pieces and return to the envelope those pieces you will not be using. Press the pieces to be used with a warm, dry iron so that they lie flat.

Measure the pattern by one of these methods. Either pin together darts and pleats and measure over them, or measure the pattern deleting the darts and pleats. Gathers need to be folded into small pleats, reducing the area so that it matches the corresponding pattern piece. With either method measure between seam lines. Take pattern measurements that correspond with those taken on the body. Remember that on most pattern pieces, you are measuring only half of the finished garment; thus these measurements must be multiplied by two.

Record the pattern measurements alongside the body measurements using the measurement worksheet (Appendix). Do not forget to allow for ease, so that your garment will be comfortable. If the total of body measurement plus ease differs only slightly from the pattern measurement, the needed adjustments can probably be made after the garment is basted togther. If there is considerable difference in the measurements, the pattern should be altered. Complete the worksheet, marking a "+" in front of the alteration needed if it is an increase and a "−" for decreases.

ALTERATION METHODS

There are several methods for altering garments, but we have selected three for this book. None of these methods are ideal for every alteration problem. Sometimes two methods give identical results and do not vary appreciably in the time and effort spent in the alteration process. In these situations, we prefer to let you, the reader, choose the method to use. At other times, when one method works for a specific figure characteristic or for a certain amount of change, we will discuss this in the comparison-of-methods section. We would suggest that you study all techniques for a specific alteration and read the comparison-of-methods section before you decide which method best suits your needs.

Internal Method

The internal method is often used by educators because it involves making the alteration within the pattern at the source of the problem, not at the side seam. For example, if the bust needs enlarging, the pattern is cut apart in the bust area and spread the needed amount. Thus the paper pattern is increased or decreased across the body curve or hollow, whichever is causing the problem. The drawback in this method is that a lot of time and effort are involved for minor alterations, and many students hesitate to cut or, as they say, "destroy" the pattern. There is less acceptance of this method outside the classroom and among adult groups. This method is still the best of the three methods for major and/or difficult alterations because greater changes can be made and darts are altered appreciably to accommodate prominent curves.

Slide Method

The slide method involves marking the original corners or edges of the pattern on tissue paper as well as marking the needed alterations. The pattern is then slid to the alteration marks, and the new cutting edge is drawn or cut from the tissue. The pattern is then returned to the original position and taped in place.

The slide method is quick and easy to learn, and the pattern remains in one piece. Experienced students will discover that many alterations can be made while they are cutting the fabric, so that they can dispense with the tissue paper. However, cutting directly on the fabric is not recommended for beginning students who are learning the method. The method does not alter dart depth as much as the internal method; therefore major alterations will not accommodate prominent curves.

Seamline Method

The seamline method is workable for small adjustments that change each pattern piece one inch or less. Techniques for this method involve drawing new cutting lines along the edges of the pattern with straight and curved rulers. Although the method is very quick and easy, it does not change dart depth and therefore is not workable for major alterations. Also the method is seldom accurate when one is making large adjustments.

GENERAL PRINCIPLES

Before altering, know the specific alteration and the amount of change needed. *Do not guess* any more than necessary, and make complete notes as you proceed. Not only may you need to explain the process to your professor or to another student, but your notes should enable you to make the identical alteration on a similiar pattern later.

Accuracy and thinking of the complete pattern save time. Be sure to alter each pattern piece affected by the figure characteristic. For example, most shoulder alterations must be made on both the back and the front pattern pieces. Also alter any adjoining pattern piece, such as a facing.

If they are confusing, trim the margins from the pattern. Margins are helpful when the seamline method is used, but some students find them more confusing than helpful while learning.

Make alterations so that the pattern lies flat. Remember that the pattern will be laid on flat fabric; so keep it flat for greater accuracy. However, small pleats created in the seam allowance are permissible when you are using the internal method but always keep the body of the pattern flat.

Keep "straight-of-grain" marks straight. These arrows are placed in the most critical area of the pattern. Thus the garment will hang better if that area is cut straight with the lengthwise threads of the fabric. If altering a pattern section changes one end of the arrow, ignore the direction of the short cut-off point, and extend the main part of the arrow. When using the slide method, always return the pattern to the original position. This automatically keeps the grainline arrow straight.

Do not alter the shape of the shoulders, armscyes, or neckline any more than necessary. These areas are difficult to reshape and alter. It is usually best to purchase a pattern that fits these areas and then to alter the bust, waist, and hips.

It is less confusing to make one alteration at a time, especially if you are a novice. When making difficult alterations or several alterations using the internal method, cut the pattern out of tissue paper, then alter the tissue and compare it with the original pattern. When using the slide method, draw the changes needed rather than cutting the tissue. This way you can make several difficult alterations, one at a time, on the same tissue.

After completing all alterations, double-check to see that the altered seamlines match the corresponding pieces. Also check to see that the dart stitching lines and extensions have been redrawn and that the symbols and notches have been transferred to the altered pattern.

Test the altered pattern by pinning it together at the shoulder and side seams (except for 3 inches [7.5 cm] directly under the arms) and fitting it on the figure. After the paper pattern is on the figure, pin the remaining side seams together and pin the center front and back to the wearer's undergarments. If the pattern is a bit too small around, remember that paper does not stretch as fabric does; the garment will probably fit. If the pattern fails to reach by 3/4 inch (2 cm) or more, recheck the pattern size and remeasure.

Check the length of the garment while the paper pattern is on the figure. Also check the location of the darts, tucks, design lines, and pockets. Check the sleeve by pinning the underarm seam together. Then slide the arm into the sleeve and pin it to the shoulder seam. Check both the length and the width of the sleeve.

Test the altered pattern in fabric. If you are using a new brand of pattern or if many alterations are needed, it is wise to sew the garment or muslin to check the fit. Sew or machine-baste the major seams and then fit the garment on the figure.

READY, SET, ALTER

Now that you have a little information on each method and you know the alterations needed, you are ready to begin. Work on a sizeable table and have an adequate supply of tissue paper. Other needed supplies are straight and curved rulers, scissors, a seam guide, straight pins, a tape measure, transparent tape (the kind you can write on), soft-leaded pencils, and notepaper.

The following chapters will give you detailed information on each method and a comparison of the methods. Read all of the information on each alteration before you decide which method to use. Then gather your courage and begin.

7
Altering Bodices

Each person has his or her own height, weight, and set of body curves. Thus patterns must be adjusted to fit each individual so that the garments made from them will be both aesthetically pleasing and comfortable. Several kinds of adjustments for fit can be made on basic bodices.

This chapter explains various figure characteristics, outlines two or more ways of altering the pattern to fit each characteristic, and compares these alterations. It gives you, the reader, a chance to learn each method and how it differs from other methods. You can then determine the best alteration method to use for your figure.

Before attempting to use any method, be sure to read Chapters 5 and 6, which explain how to take pattern and body measurements, how to recognize figure characteristics and how to select a pattern. Make alterations only where changes are needed, remembering that when the body curves vary from those on the pattern, changes may be needed in both the length and the width of the pattern.

LENGTH CHANGES

Adjusting the length of the bodice is easy, and it should be the first adjustment made. Even though your total height may be the same as the height indicated by the pattern for your figure type and size, your bodice length may be shorter or longer than that in the pattern.

Internal Method

Most patterns have a printed line or guide on the lower portion of the bodice front and back pieces that indicates where length adjustments should be made. If not, draw a length-adjustment line across the front and back pieces just above the waistline at right angles to the grainline arrows (Figure 7.1).

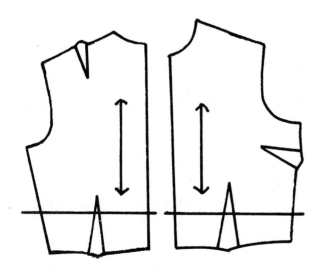

Figure 7.1

ALTERING BODICES • 37

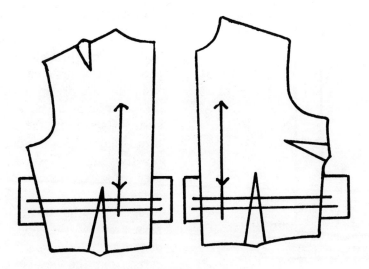

Figure 7.2

To *lengthen* the bodice, cut the pattern apart on the length-adjustment line. On tissue paper, draw two parallel lines, making the distance between the lines equal to the amount you want the pattern lengthened. Tape the upper part of the pattern to one of these lines. With a ruler, extend the grainline arrow and the center front or back line onto the tissue paper. Tape the lower part of the pattern to the second line, matching the grainline arrow and the center front or back line (Figure 7.2). Redraw the dart stitching lines and the cutting line at the side seam. Be sure to make identical changes on the front, the back, and the corresponding facing patterns.

To *shorten* the bodice, draw a second line across the pattern, parallel to the first line, making the distance between the lines equal to the amount you want to shorten the pattern (Figure 7.3). Fold along one line and bring the fold to the second line, creating a tuck. Tape the tuck in place and correct the dart stitching lines and the cutting line at the side seam (Figure 7.4). Be sure to make identical changes on the front, the back, and the corresponding facing patterns.

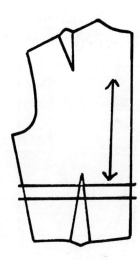

Figure 7.3

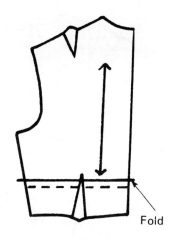

Figure 7.4

Slide Method

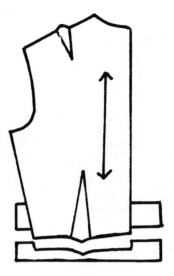

Figure 7.5

Pin tissue paper under the lower portion of the pattern. Cut through the tissue paper along the pattern's waistline cutting edge and for about 1/4 inch (6 mm) up both sides. Transfer all pattern markings—darts, tucks, and so on—to the tissue paper along the waistline. Unpin the pattern (Figure 7.5). To *lengthen,* slide the pattern up the amount of additional length needed, measuring several places along the waistline cutting line to ensure that the added amount is even. Tape the tissue to the pattern. With a ruler, redraw the side cutting lines from the underarm to the waistline edge. Redraw any darts from the points to the marks along the lengthened waistline (Figure 7.6).

To *shorten* the bodice, pin tissue under the pattern and cut along the waistline edge as instructed for lengthening (Figure 7.5). Transfer the markings to the tissue paper. Unpin the pattern and slide it down the amount needed (Figure 7.7). Pin the pattern to the tissue paper and check the bodice length. If it is correct, fold up the lower portion of the bodice pattern and tape it to the tissue paper (Figure 7.8). With a ruler redraw any dart stitching lines and the side cutting line from the underarm to the waistline edge.

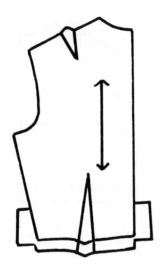

Figure 7.6

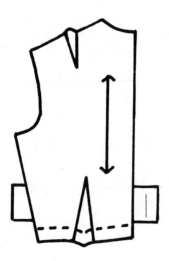

Figure 7.7

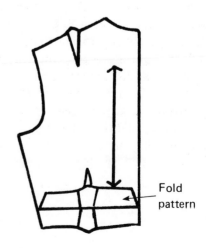

Figure 7.8

Seamline Method

Pin tissue paper under the lower portion of the pattern if the margin is not sufficient. Extend the grainline arrow to the bottom of the tissue paper. Measure down or up the amount needed to lengthen or shorten the pattern (Figure 7.9). Be sure that the measurement at each side of the pattern is the same distance from the grainline arrow as the original marking so that the waistline width is not changed. With a ruler, redraw the waistline cutting line, the side cutting lines, and the dart stitching lines. Recheck the pattern width by remeasuring the new and the original patterns along the waistline seam. If these widths are not equal, correct the measurements between the grainline arrow and side cutting lines.

Comparison of Methods

Patterns altered correctly with any of these three methods should be identical; however, if the length change is greater than 1 inch (2.5 cm), it may be difficult to maintain the waistline shape when using the seamline method. You may prefer one method over the other because you personally find it more efficient and/or more accurate.

LENGTHENING ONLY AT CENTER BACK OR FRONT

Some patterns need to be altered in length only at the center front or back because of a prominent stomach or a curved back. If you have rounded shoulders, you may need to add length to the center back and to shorten the center front. However, the alteration for people with round shoulders (see the section on "Round Shoulders") should be made before the following alteration is used to lengthen the lower back.

Internal Method

To *lengthen,* cut the pattern from the center back or front just to the side seam on the length-adjustment line. Place tissue paper under the pattern and tape the upper portion in place. Spread the cut at the center front or back the needed amount and tape the bottom portion to

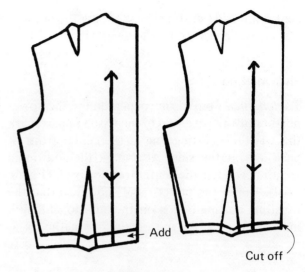

Figure 7.9

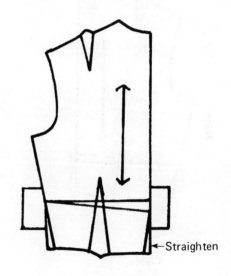

Figure 7.10

the tissue paper (Figure 7.10). Use a ruler to redraw the center and side seams and to straighten the dart stitching lines. This alteration makes the waistline larger. If the addition is not needed at the waistline, remove the increased amount at the side seam.

To *shorten,* cut the pattern as directed for lengthening, but lap the amount needed at the center front or back. Use a ruler to straighten the center and side cutting lines, adding the amount lost at the center to the side seam (Figure 7.11).

Slide Method

To *lengthen,* pin tissue paper under the lower portion of the pattern. On the tissue paper, mark the waistline cutting line at the center front or back and at the side. Also mark the additional length needed at the center front or back (Figure 7.12). Unpin the pattern and slide it so that the waistline cutting line is on the additional length mark at the center and on the original mark at the side seam (Figure 7.13). Pin in place and cut the tissue paper along the waistline cutting line and for about 1/4 inch (6 mm) up both sides of the pattern. Transfer all pattern markings—darts, tucks, and so on—to the tissue paper along the waistline. Unpin the pattern and return it to the original position. Tape the tissue to the pattern. With a ruler, draw the side cutting lines from the underarm to the waistline and any darts from the point to the marks at the waistline (Figure 7.14).

To *shorten,* pin tissue paper under the lower portion of the pattern. On the tissue paper, mark the waistline cutting line at the center front or back and at the side. Unpin the pattern and mark the amount of length to be removed (alteration mark) at the center front or back (Figure 7.15). Lay the pattern on the tissue paper so that the waistline cutting line is on the alteration mark at the center and on the original mark at the side. Pin in place and cut the tissue paper along the waistline cutting line and for about 1/4 inch (6 mm) up both sides of the pattern. Transfer all pattern markings—darts, tucks, and so on—to the tissue paper along the waistline. Unpin the pattern and return it to the original position, folding up the center portion so that the waistline cutting line of the tissue can be seen. Tape the tissue to the pattern. With a ruler, draw the side cutting lines from the underarm to the waistline, and the darts from the original point to the waistline marks.

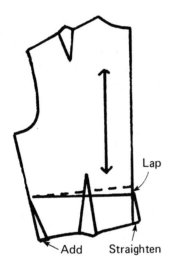

Figure 7.11

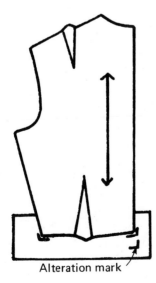
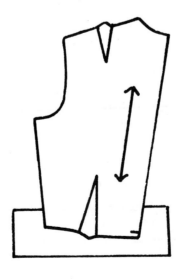
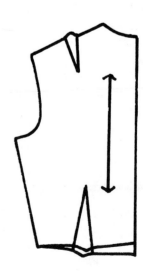

Figure 7.12   **Figure 7.13**   **Figure 7.14**

Seamline Method

Pin tissue paper under the lower portion of the pattern if the margin is not sufficient. Measure up or down the amount of length adjustment needed at the center front or back, keeping the center back or front line straight. With a ruler, draw the waistline cutting line, the side cutting line, and the dart stitching lines. Check to make sure that you maintained the original waistline width (Figure 7.16).

Comparison of Methods

Patterns altered correctly with any of these three methods should be identical; however, you may find it difficult to maintain the shape and width of a curved waistline edge when using the seamline method. Also you may have a personal preference for choosing one method over the other.

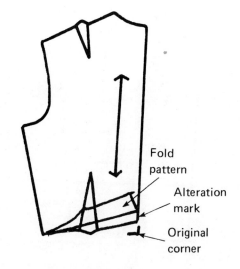

Figure 7.15

CHANGING BUSTLINE DARTS

The bustline area of the bodice should fit smoothly and comfortably across the breast without pulling. If it does not, first check the location of all bustline darts, as they are easy to alter and often cause a bodice to fit incorrectly.

Bustline darts should point toward the fullest part of the breast, never above nor below. The dart point should come to within 3/4 (2 cm) to 1 1/2 inches (3.8 cm) of the fullest point of the breast and should never extend beyond this point. The base of the dart can be located at any point on the side seam from approximately 1 inch (2.5 cm) below the armscye to the waistline seam. If the dart is too deep, the fabric will appear puffy and too full over the breast. If the dart is too shallow, the fabric will pull over the breast and dartlike folds may automatically form under the arm. Darts will also appear puckered at the point if they are incorrectly pressed or are stitched with a blunt instead of a tapered point.

To determine the proper dart location, pin the back and front pattern pieces together at the side and shoulder seams and try on the pattern. Be sure to align the pattern with your figure at the shoulder and the center front. Mark the

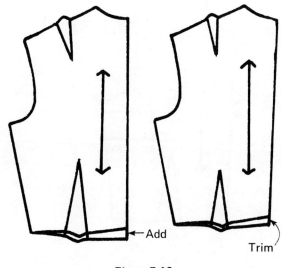

Figure 7.16

fullest point of the breast on the pattern with a pin or a fine-point, felt-tip pen.

RAISING OR LOWERING DARTS

Internal Method

Draw a box around the dart by drawing a horizontal line 1/2 inch (13 mm) above the dart and a second horizontal line 1/2 inch (13 mm) below. Connect the two lines with a vertical line at the point of the dart (Figure 7.17). To *raise* the dart,

42 • COMPARATIVE ANALYSIS OF PATTERN TECHNIQUES

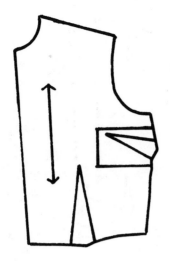

Figure 7.17

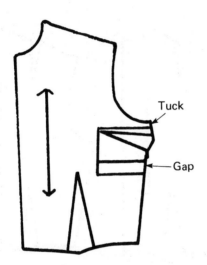

Figure 7.18

cut along the lower horizontal line and the vertical line. Fold a tuck along the horizontal line above the dart, creating a gap below the dart that equals the amount the dart should be raised (Figure 7.18). Redraw the side seam. To *lower* the dart, cut along the upper horizontal line and the vertical line. Fold the tuck below the dart, creating a gap that equals the amount needed (Figure 7.19).

Slide Method

On the pattern at the dart point, measure up or down the amount the dart is to be moved. Redraw the center and stitching lines of the dart from this point to the original dart lines at the seam. If this procedure causes the dart to slope downward or to slant abruptly upward, measure up or down a like amount along the side seam at both dart stitching lines. Connect all three marks, lowering or raising the whole dart (Figure 7.20). To reestablish the dart extension at the side seam, tape extra tissue paper underneath the pattern if the margin is not sufficient. Pin the new dart together as it will be stitched and hand press the dart tuck toward the waistline seam. Draw a straight line from the armscye to the waistline and cut along it (Figure 7.21). Remove the pins and unfold the dart.

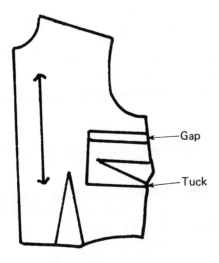

Figure 7.19

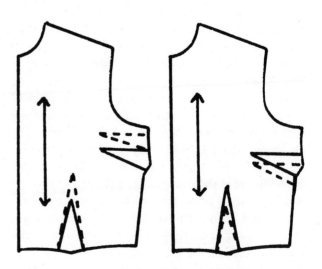

Figure 7.20

Comparison of Methods

Both methods should give identical results if the whole dart was relocated by the slide method. If only the dart point was relocated by the slide method, the dart will be more slanting; however, this extra slant is necessary if an underarm dart must be relocated for a very high bustline.

Waistline darts are usually raised or lowered the same amount that the underarm dart was raised or lowered. Mark a new dart point on the pattern at the desired location. Redraw the center and stitching lines of the dart from this point to the original dart lines at the waistline (Figure 7.20). Note: A low or very full bustline can be softened and made more flattering if you change the waistline darts to tucks or gathers. If gathers are used instead of darts, ease the fullness over a 2- to 3-inch (5- to 7.5-cm) area that is centered over the original waistline dart.

BUSTLINE WIDTH CHANGES

Patterns are created for the average figure, which, on misses' patterns, usually means a bra with a B cup. If you wear a C or D cup or if you purchased a pattern by your high bust measurement, the bustline will need increasing. If you wear a small bra cup size, the bustline may need to be made smaller.

Internal Method

To alter a fitted bodice, first find the bust point by extending the center lines of both the underarm and the waistline darts until they intersect (Figure 7.22). Cut through the center of the waistline dart to the bust point and then diagonally to the notch at the armscye. Make a second cut through the center of the underarm dart, extending the cut almost to the bust point. If the bodice needs lengthening at the center front, make a third cut horizontally from the waistline dart to the center front (Figure 7.23). Without mixing up the pieces, place tissue paper under

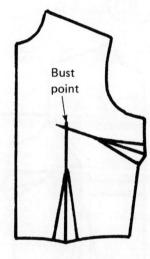

Figure 7.22

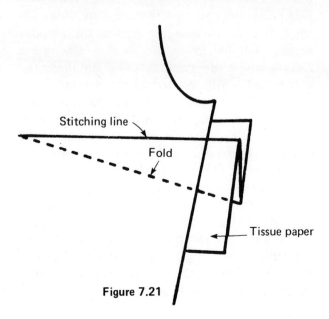

Figure 7.21

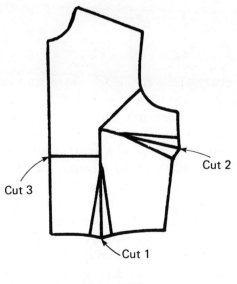

Figure 7.23

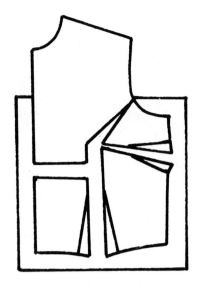

Figure 7.24

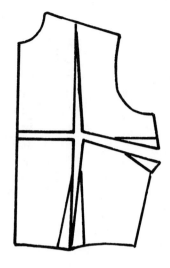

Figure 7.26

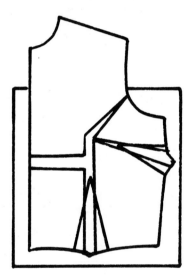

Figure 7.25

the pattern. Tape the upper center front section in place. Extend the center front line and tape the lower center front below the upper section, aligning the center front lines and lengthening the center front of the pattern the amount needed. To *increase* the bustline width, spread the pattern apart at the bust point, adding one half of the total amount needed. Continue this same amount of spread to the base of the waistline dart so that the edges of the vertical cut are parallel. This procedure will cause the diagonal cut and the underarm dart to spread and will increase the dart depth (Figure 7.24). Tape in place. Locate the point of each dart in the center of the spread and redraw the stitching lines by connecting the new points with the original stitching lines at the base of the dart. Connect the cutting lines at the waistline and the side seams (Figure 7.25).

If additional width is needed above as well as around the bustline (e.g. in children's patterns), use this method: Cut the bodice front from the center of the waistline, just to the shoulder seam. Make a second cut horizontally across the bodice front, through the underarm dart if there is one. Tape the upper portion to tissue, spreading the vertical cut the amount needed across the bustline or chest. Tape the lower center-front portion below the upper portion, aligning the center front and lengthening the bodice the amount needed. Tilt the lower side section, closing the vertical cut at the waistline and maintaining the length and width needed in the center of the pattern. Tape in place. Locate the dart point and redraw the stitching lines from the original dart lines at the side seam to the dart point. If the original pattern did not have an underarm dart, create one in the side cut. Use the curved ruler to smooth the waistline edge (Figure 7.26).

To *decrease* the bustline, make cuts 1, 2, and 3 as directed in Figure 7.23, but lap the lower center-front section over the upper to shorten the center front length the amount needed. Lap the side section of the pattern over the front at the bust point, removing one half of the excess

ALTERING BODICES • 45

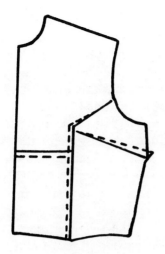

Figure 7.27

amount. Lap the same amount at the base of the waistline dart. This procedure will also cause the diagonal cut to lap and will decrease the dart depth (Figure 7.27). Tape in place. Locate the point of the dart in the center of the lap and redraw the stitching lines by connecting the new points with the original stitching lines at the base of the dart.

Slide Method

To *increase* the bustline width, pin paper under the front pattern. Use the center-front length measurement and alter the front pattern evenly along the waistline seam using the slide method for lengthening. Return the pattern to the original position and pin to the paper. Cut the paper along the center front, neckline, and shoulder cutting lines and down 1/4 inch (6 mm) at the armscye cutting line. Mark the side seam at the bustline and one half of the width needed along the side seam at the bustline (Figure 7.28). Unpin the pattern. Match the shoulder–armscye corner of the pattern to the paper and slide the bustline of the pattern out to the bustline alteration mark, increasing the width. Pin and cut around the armscye and down to the bustline mark. Mark the top stitching line of the underarm dart at the side seam and unpin the pattern. Match the side–waistline corners and slide the pattern so that the underarm is in line with the underarm on the tissue. Mark the lower dart-stitching line (Figure 7.29). Note that the dart is now wider. Return the pattern to its original position, aligning the center fronts, and mark the dart points for underarm and waistline darts. Remove the pattern and draw in the darts (Figure 7.30). Pin the underarm dart as it will be stitched, and finger-press the dart tuck toward the waistline. With a ruler, draw the side cutting line from the underarm to the waistline and cut along the line.

To *decrease* the bustline width, pin paper under the front pattern. Use the center-front length measurement and alter the front pattern evenly along the waistline, making the bodice

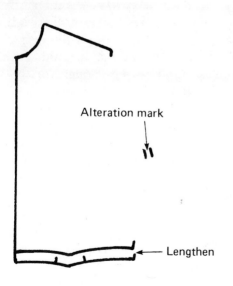

Figure 7.28

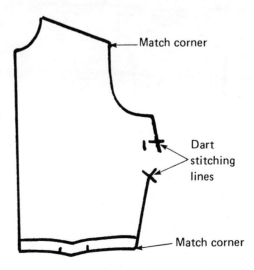

Figure 7.29

46 • COMPARATIVE ANALYSIS OF PATTERN TECHNIQUES

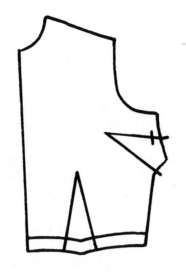

Figure 7.30

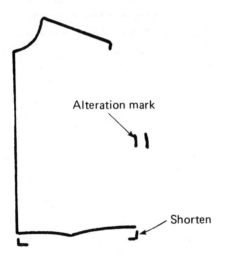

Figure 7.31

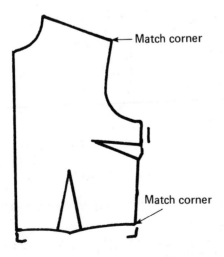

Figure 7.32

shorter. Cut the paper along the center front, neckline, and shoulder edges and down 1/4 inch (6 mm) at the armscye. At the side seam, transfer the original bustline width to the paper. Unpin the pattern and mark one half of the necessary decrease at the bustline (Figure 7.31). Match the shoulder-armscye corner of the pattern to the paper and slide the bustline of the pattern in to the bustline mark, decreasing the width. Pin and cut around the armscye and down to the bustline mark. Mark the top stitching line of the underarm dart at the side seam and unpin the pattern. Match the side-waistline corner of the pattern to the paper and slide the pattern so that the underarm is in line with the underarm of the tissue. Mark the lower dart-stitching line. Note the dart is now narrower. Return the pattern to the original position, aligning the center front, and mark all dart points. Remove the pattern and draw in the darts (Figure 7.32). Pin the underarm dart as it will be stitched, and finger-press the dart tuck toward the waistline. With a ruler, draw and cut the side cutting line.

Comparison of Methods

The slide method and the second internal method (Figure 7.26) increase the width above the armscye notch, and this additional width is needed for figures that are full above the breast and when a bra with a lot of lift is worn. The first internal method does not increase the width above the armscye notch, and the method gives a better fit if the figure has a slight concave curve above the breast. When the bustline width is increased by the slide method, the dart depth is less than when the internal method is used, and darts may not be deep enough for the figure. Generally, if the bustline is increased for the figure with a small frame, a great amount of dart depth is needed. If the bustline width is decreased by the slide method, the underarm dart may become very narrow or may be eliminated. If this occurs, you may desire to move some of the waistline dart depth to the underarm seam. Note that all of the dart depth is increased or decreased in the underarm dart when the slide method is used.

Changing Dart Depth

If only one dart is increased or decreased when the bustline is altered, you may desire to move some of the dart depth from the wide dart to the narrow one. Do this by drawing lines through both darts to locate the bust point (Figure 7.22). Cut on both of these lines from the seamline almost to the bust point. Move the outer, lower portion of the front pattern, narrowing one dart while widening the other. Place tissue under the pattern and tape the darts in place. Locate dart points and redraw the stitching lines (Figure 7.33). Adjust the dart extensions by folding the pattern on the dart stitching lines as instructed under the slide method for raising or lowering darts (Figure 7.21).

If the bustline is very full, create a third dart to distribute the fullness more evenly over the breast. Draw lines through both darts to locate the bust point, and draw a third line where you desire the third dart to be located (Figure 7.34). Cut on all three lines almost to the bust point and shift the dart openings as desired (Figure 7.35). Tape to tissue. Locate dart points and redraw the stitching lines (Figure 7.36). Adjust the dart extensions by folding the pattern on the dart stitching lines (Figure 7.21).

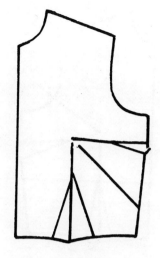

Figure 7.34

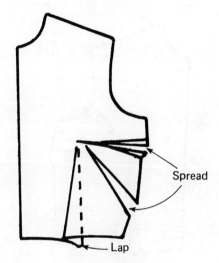

Figure 7.35

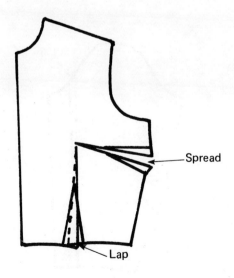

Figure 7.33

Figure 7.36

48 • COMPARATIVE ANALYSIS OF PATTERN TECHNIQUES

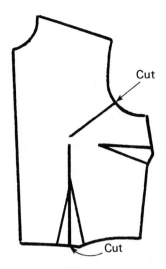

Figure 7.37

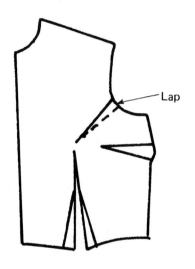

Figure 7.38

ELIMINATE ARMHOLE POUCH

If the front of the bodice gaps at the notch area or a wrinkle of excess fabric forms from the armscye and extends toward the bustline, the armscye is too long for the figure, and wider bustline darts are needed. The amount of alteration needed can be determined by measuring the depth of the wrinkle at the armscye seam.

Internal Method

Locate the bust point on the front pattern (Figure 7.22) Draw a line from the bust point to the armscye notch. Cut on the center line of the waistline dart to the bust point, and make a second cut from the armscye notch almost to the bust point (Figure 7.37). Lap the amount to be eliminated at the armscye (Figure 7.38). This lap will spread the waistline cut, creating a wider dart, which is needed. Locate new dart points and redraw the lower edge.

A similar alteration is needed on the sleeve so that it will fit the armscye. Draw a line from the front notch to the lower edge (Figure 7.39). Cut on this line from the sleeve cap, just to the lower seamline or hem. Lap the same amount at the sleeve cap that you lapped on the bodice front (Figure 7.40). Tape in place.

The internal method is the only method that can be used for this alteration.

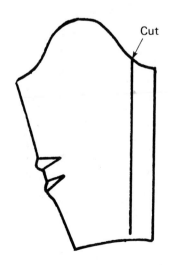

Figure 7.39

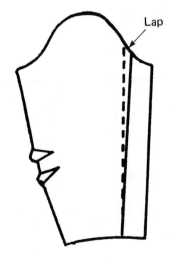

Figure 7.40

ROUND SHOULDERS

If you have round shoulders, you will find that the center back length of the bodice is too short. The back bodice will pull across the shoulders, and the crosswise grainline of the garment will bow upward across the back. Box jackets will stand away from the body at the center back waistline.

Internal Method

Draw a horizontal line across the pattern about five inches (12.5 cm) below the center back neckline. Draw a second line through the shoulder dart to the horizontal line (Figure 7.41). If there is no shoulder dart on the pattern, create one by drawing a slanting line from the center of the shoulder seam to the horizontal line. Cut on these lines from the center back just to the armscye seam and from the shoulder almost to the horizontal cut. Place tissue under the pattern and tape it to the lower portion. Spread the pattern at the center back the amount needed, keeping the center back line straight. This procedure will spread the shoulder cut, creating a dart or widening the existing dart (Figure 7.42). Locate the point of the shoulder dart in the center of the spread with the dart point about 2 inches (5 cm) above the horizontal cut. Redraw the dart by connecting the new point with the original stitching lines, or draw a new dart from the point to the edges of the slash at the shoulder seam. Fold the dart as it will be stitched and redraw the shoulder line. This procedure also alters the dart extension. Do not permit the shoulder dart to become wider than 1 1/4 inches (3.2 cm) at the base. If the dart becomes wider, draw the dart only 1 1/4 inches (3.2 cm) wide. Then ease in the additional back shoulder length when you sew the shoulder seam, or add a second dart at the neckline (Figure 7.43). The point of the shoulder

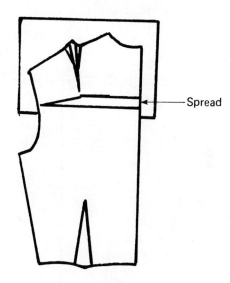

Figure 7.42

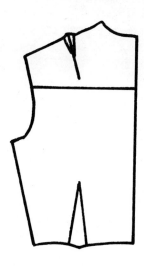

Figure 7.41

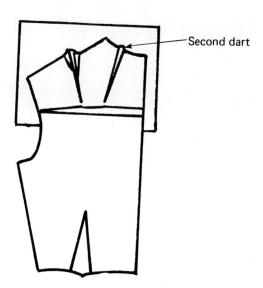

Figure 7.43

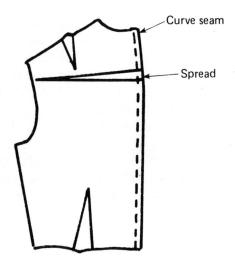

Figure 7.44

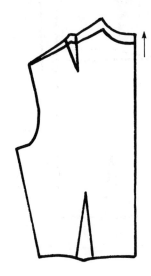

Figure 7.45

dart should be directed toward the fullest part of the shoulder curve, and the dart should end 2 to 3 inches (5 to 7.5 cm) short of the fullest part of the shoulder curve.

If the garment has a center back seam, spread the pattern the needed amount, but allow the center back seam to curve in 1/4 inch (6 mm) at the neckline (Figure 7.44). Redraw the center-back cutting line, creating a smooth curve.

Slide Method

Pin paper under the upper back pattern. Transfer the cutting lines of the neckline, shoulder, and upper portion of the armscye to the paper. Unpin the pattern and slide it up the amount of length needed in the center back. Refer to your pattern measurement chart for the amount needed. Redraw the neckline. Match the neckline–shoulder corners, and slide the pattern to the original shoulder edge at the armscye. Note that the new back-shoulder line is longer than the original. Draw the shoulder cutting line from the neckline to the dart. If the pattern does not have a back dart, create one by drawing a vertical line in the middle of the shoulder. Slide the pattern to the armscye, and draw the shoulder cutting line from the armscye to the dart. Return the pattern to its original position and tape in place (Figure 7.45). Redraw the dart lines, making the dart deeper and wider. If a new dart is created, fit the pattern to the figure and mark the dart point location. Draw the stitching lines from the undrawn shoulder edges to the point. Fold the dart as it will be stitched and redraw the shoulder cutting line. This procedure also alters the dart extension.

Comparison of Methods

The internal method may distort the armscye curve slightly if the maximum round-shoulder spread is used; however, this curve can be easily redrawn and corrected. The internal method allows adequate width and dart depth, which the slide method does not give when used for pronounced round shoulders. Thus the slide method should be used only when a small adjustment is needed.

VERY ERECT BACK

If the pattern is too long at the center back, either crosswise wrinkles will form in the lower back area of the garment or the grainline will droop at the center back. The following alteration is needed.

Internal Method

Draw both lines and cut as directed for round shoulders using the internal method. Lap the pattern at the center back the amount needed, keeping the center back line straight. This operation will lap the shoulder cut, removing some of the shoulder length (Figure 7.46). If the pattern has a back shoulder dart, the lap may remove some or all of the dart. If the dart becomes very narrow, eliminate it and ease in the back fullness when sewing the shoulder seam. If the front shoulder seam becomes slightly longer than the back, ease in the front fullness when sewing the shoulder seam.

Slide Method

Lay tissue paper under the upper back portion. Mark the center neckline, the neckline–shoulder corner, and the shoulder–armscye corner. Slide the pattern down the amount needed at the center back. Draw the neckline of the pattern. Match the neckline–shoulder corners and slide the pattern to the original shoulder edge at the armscye. Draw a new shoulder line. Return the pattern to its original position. Fold down the neckline, exposing the new pattern, and tape in place (Figure 7.47).

Comparison of Methods

The internal method adjusts the back shoulder dart or ease so that the excess fullness is removed between the shoulder blades. As the slide method retains the original dart and back width, the garment will be too full across the shoulders of a very erect back.

BROAD BACK

If you have a broad back, you will find that garments lack sufficient width across the shoulders between the armscye notches. Thus garments will pull and may tear along the back armscye seams.

Internal Method

Draw a line parallel to the grainline arrow, which is located about 1 inch (2.5 cm) from the back armscye notch. Cut on this line from the waistline, just to the shoulder seam. Make a second horizontal cut from the slash to the armscye notch (Figure 7.48). Tape the main part of the pattern to tissue paper. Spread the vertical slash one half of the amount needed at the armscye notch and tape the top section in place. Bring the pattern back together again at the waistline,

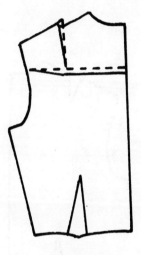

Figure 7.46

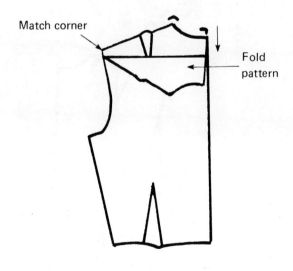

Figure 7.47

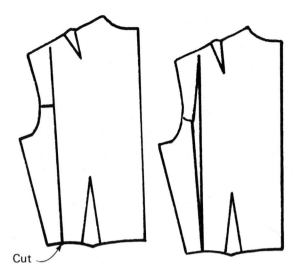

Figure 7.48   Figure 7.49

allowing the short cut to lap. Redraw the shoulder and waistline cutting lines (Figure 7.49).

Slide Method

Lay paper under the side back portion and draw around the shoulder–armscye corner, the armscye, and the side seam cutting lines. At the armscye notch, measure out and mark one half of the amount needed (Figure 7.50). Matching the shoulder–armscye corners, slide the pattern out to meet the alteration mark and draw around the armscye. Matching the underarm corners, slide the pattern back to the original cutting line along the side seam and draw a new cutting line. Return the pattern to the original position and tape in place (Figure 7.51).

Seamline Method

Tape paper under the back armscye of the pattern if the margin in not sufficient. Mark one half of the amount needed (up to a maximum of 1/2 inch, or 1.3 cm) at the armscye, just above the notch. Draw a new cutting line from the mark, tapering to the shoulder and to the underarm (Figure 7.52).

Figure 7.50

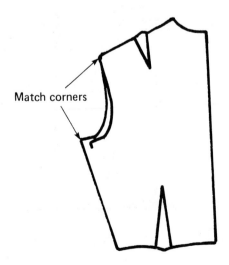

Figure 7.51

Figure 7.52

Comparison of Methods

The seamline method can be used only for small increases, whereas both the slide and the internal methods can be used for any amount. Both the internal and the slide methods increase the back bustline width as well as the shoulder width, with the slide method adding the greatest width across the back bustline. This greater width across the back bustline may be too much for some figures unless the increase across the shoulders is very small.

NARROW BACK

If the pattern is too wide between the armscye, and excess fullness or vertical folds form in back, make the following alteration.

Internal Method

Draw both lines and cut as directed for a broad back using the internal method. Lap the vertical slash one half of the excess amount. Tape in place and redraw the waistline edge (Figure 7.53).

Slide Method

Lay paper under the side back portion and draw around the shoulder–armscye corner, the armscye, and the side seam cutting lines. At the armscye notch, measure in and mark one half of the amount needed (Figure 7.54). Match the shoulder–armscye corners, and slide the pattern in to meet the mark. Cut or draw around the armscye. Match the underarm corners and slide the pattern back to the original cutting line along the side seam. Cut or draw a new cutting line (Figure 7.55). Return the pattern to the original position, and fold in the side portion to expose the new pattern. Tape in place.

Seamline Method

At the armscye, just above the notch, mark one half of the amount to be removed (up to a maximum of ¼ inch or 6 mm). Draw a new cutting line from the mark, tapering to the shoulder and to the underarm (Figure 7.56).

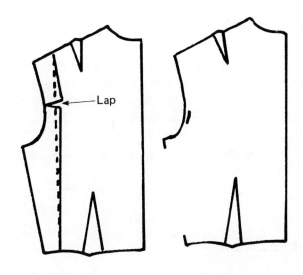

Figure 7.53   **Figure 7.54**

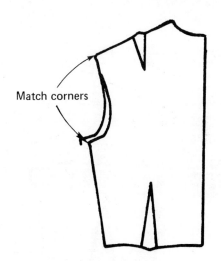

Figure 7.55

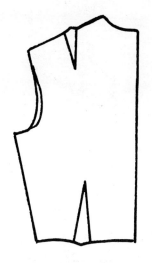

Figure 7.56

Comparison of Methods

The seamline method can be used only for very small decreases in width because larger decreases distort the armscye. Both the internal and the slide methods decrease the back bustline width as well as the shoulder width; however, the slide method decreases the back bustline width too much for most figures and should be used only for very small back changes.

HOLLOW CHEST

If you are hollow in the chest area, you will find the pattern too long between the front neckline and the bustline. Thus horizontal wrinkles may form above the bustline. Before making this alteration, be sure that the bodice is not too tight around the bustline, as the wrinkles that form because of that problem may look similar. Altering for a hollow chest will not correct a pattern that is too tight across the bustline, and that alteration should be made before this one.

Determine the amount of alteration needed by pinning the front and back patterns together at the shoulder and side seams and fitting the pattern on the figure. Pinch out and measure the excess length above the bustline.

Internal Method

Draw a diagonal line from the shoulder-armscye corner to the center front, about 4 inches (10 cm) below the neckline. Cut on this line from the center front, just to the shoulder-armscye corner (Figure 7.57). Place tissue paper under the pattern and tape it to the lower bodice section. Lap the center front the amount needed. Redraw the center front line and, if necessary, the shoulder cutting line (Figure 7.58).

Slide Method

Pin tissue paper under the upper front portion. Mark the center front neckline, the neckline-shoulder corner, and the shoulder-armscye corner. Slide the pattern down the amount needed at the center front. Cut or draw around the neckline on the pattern. Match the neckline-shoulder corners, and slide the pattern to the original shoulder line at the armscye. Cut or draw a new shoulder cutting line. Return the pattern to its original position (Figure 7.59). Fold down the neckline, exposing the new pattern, and tape in place.

Comparison of Methods

Both methods retain the center front and the neckline curve, but the shoulder is squared slightly more with the slide method than with the internal method.

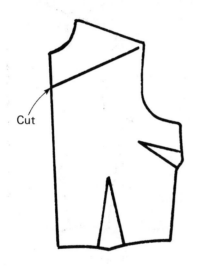

Figure 7.57

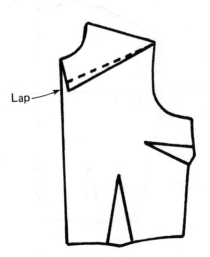

Figure 7.58

ALTERING BODICES • 55

PIGEON CHEST

If you are rounded in the upper chest area, you will find the pattern too short between the front neckline and the bustline. The crosswise grainline will curve upward and the garment will pull above the bustline.

Determine the amount of alteration needed by altering the pattern an assumed amount. Then pin the front and back patterns together and fit them on your figure.

Internal Method

Draw a diagonal line and cut as described for the hollow chest alteration using the internal method. Tape tissue paper under the lower section. Spread the amount needed at the center front and tape in place. Redraw the center front and the shoulder cutting lines (Figure 7.60).

Slide Method

Lay paper under the upper front portion. Mark the center front neckline, the neckline-shoulder corner, and the shoulder-armscye corner. Slide the pattern up the amount needed at the center front. Draw around the neckline on the pattern. Keep the neckline-shoulder corners even, and slide the pattern to the original shoulder line at the armscye. Cut or draw a new shoulder cutting line. Return the pattern to its original position and tape in place (Figure 7.61).

Comparison of Methods

The internal method creates a shallower and wider neckline, whereas the slide method retains the original neckline curve. Both methods retain the neckline circumference. The slide method lengthens the front shoulder line more than the internal method, which may make a second alteration necessary.

NARROW SHOULDERS

If your shoulders are narrow, you will find that the shoulder seam of the pattern is too long and

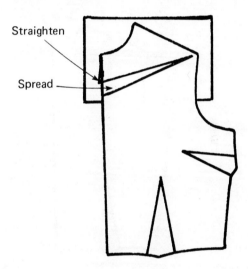

Figure 7.60

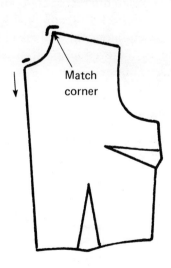

Figure 7.59

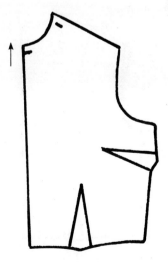

Figure 7.61

56 • COMPARATIVE ANALYSIS OF PATTERN TECHNIQUES

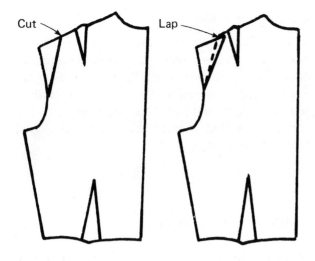

Figure 7.62   Figure 7.63

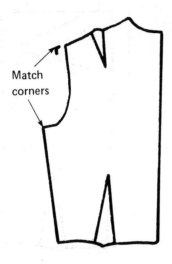

Figure 7.64

Figure 7.65

that the armscye seam will lie beyond the end of the shoulder, drooping off the shoulder.

Determine the amount of excess shoulder length by pinning the front and back pattern pieces together at the shoulder seam. Align the center front of the pattern to your figure, and mark the end of the shoulder on the shoulder seam of the pattern. Measure the excess pattern (not the seam allowance) at the shoulder seam. Identical alterations are usually needed on the front and back pieces, however, this is not always true, and either piece can be narrowed with the adjoining piece eased to fit.

Internal Method

Draw a line from the shoulder seam, 2 inches (5 cm) in from the armscye, to the armscye notch (Figure 7.62). Cut on the line from the shoulder just to the armscye seamline. Lap the pattern at the shoulder seam the amount needed, and tape in place. Redraw the shoulder cutting line (Figure 7.63).

Slide Method

Pin the shoulder-armscye area to tissue paper and mark the shoulder-armscye, underarm, and waistline corners. Cut the neckline and the shoulder along the original cutting lines. Unpin and slide the pattern back along the shoulder line the amount needed to narrow the shoulder. Match the shoulder-armscye corners, and slide the underarm to the original mark. Pin and cut the armscye. Matching the underarm corners, slide the pattern back to its original width at the waistline, and cut along the side seamline. Return the pattern to the original position and cut the waistline edge (Figure 7.64).

Seamline Method

Mark the amount the shoulder needs to be narrowed on the shoulder seam. Draw a new armscye line, tapering to the original above the armscye notch (Figure 7.65). Do not use this alteration for changes over 1/4 inch (6 mm).

Comparison of Methods

The internal method slopes the shoulder seam, which the slide method does not; however, the slide method needlessly lengthens the side seam. The seamline method should be used only for very small alterations, as it changes the armscye circumference.

BROAD SHOULDERS

If you have broad shoulders, the pattern will be too narrow across the shoulders, and garments will be uncomfortable.

Determine the amount of alteration needed by pinning the front and back patterns together at the shoulder seam. Align the center front of the pattern to the figure and measure the length needed (excluding the seam allowance) to bring the armscye seam across the end of the shoulder.

Internal Method

Draw a line and cut as described for narrow shoulders, using the internal method. Tape tissue paper under the larger portion of the pattern, and spread the cut at the shoulder seam the amount needed. Tape in place and redraw the shoulder cutting line (Figure 7.66).

Slide method

Pin tissue paper under the shoulder–armscye area, and mark the shoulder–armscye and the underarm corners. Cut the neckline and shoulder edges. Unpin and slide the pattern out along the shoulder line the amount needed to widen the shoulder. Match the shoulder–armscye corners and slide the underarm to the original mark. Pin and cut or draw along the armscye. Matching the underarm corners, slide the pattern to the original width at the waistline. Cut along the side-seam cutting line. Return the pattern to the original position, and cut the waistline edge (Figure 7.67).

Seamline Method

To broaden the shoulders 1/4 inch (6 mm) or less, mark the amount of increase needed on the pattern margin at the shoulder line. Draw a new armscye cutting line, tapering to the original above the armscye notch (Figure 7.68).

Comparison of Methods

The seamline method distorts the armscye if the alteration is greater than 1/4 inch (6 mm). Neither the internal nor the slide method changes the armscye, but the slide method shortens the side seam.

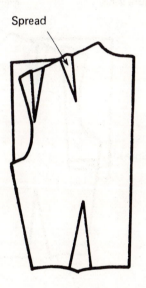

Figure 7.66

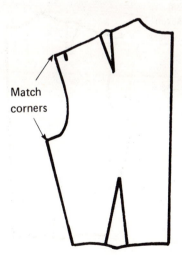

Figure 7.67

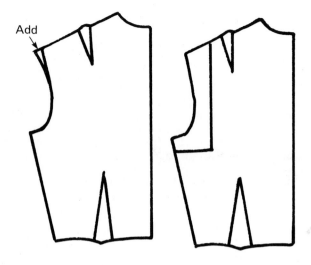

Figure 7.68 **Figure 7.69**

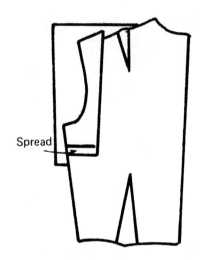

Figure 7.70

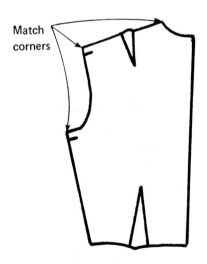

Figure 7.71

SQUARE SHOULDERS

If you have square shoulders, the pattern shoulder line slopes too much for your figure. Garments will pull and wrinkle from the end of the shoulder bone.

Internal Method

Measure in 2 inches (5 cm) from the armscye on the shoulder seam. From this point, draw a line parallel to the grainline arrow down to below the armscye and then across to the side seam. Cut on this line, through both seam allowances (Figure 7.69). Tape tissue paper under the larger section. Move the armscye section up the amount needed and tape in place. Redraw the shoulder and side cutting lines (Figure 7.70).

Slide Method

Pin tissue paper under the pattern, and mark the neck-shoulder corner, the shoulder-armscye corner, the bustline along the side seam, and the waistline. Cut the paper along the original neckline. Unpin. Match the neck-shoulder corners and slide the shoulder-armscye corner up the amount needed to square the shoulder. Cut or draw along the shoulder line. Match the shoulder-armscye corners, and slide the pattern to meet the bustline mark. Cut or draw along the armscye. Match the underarm corners, and slide the pattern to the original waistline. Pin and finish cutting (Figure 7.71).

Comparison of Methods

If altered correctly, patterns altered by both methods should be identical.

SLOPING SHOULDERS

If you have sloping shoulders, the shoulder seam will not slant enough for your figure. Diagonal wrinkles will form from the neckline to the armscye unless the garment is altered.

Internal Method

Draw a line and cut the pattern as described for square shoulders, using the internal method. Move the armscye section down the amount needed. Redraw the shoulder and side cutting lines (Figure 7.72).

Slide Method

Follow the instructions for altering square shoulders, using the slide method, except slide the shoulder-armscye corner down the amount needed. Cut along the shoulder line and continue the instructions for square shoulders (Figure 7.73).

Comparison of Methods

The slide method does not give the needed length along the shoulder seam, and the internal method does. Both methods maintain the neck and armscye curves.

If the figure is small-boned and has either square or sloping shoulders, the following internal method will give a better fit. Draw a line from the shoulder-neck corner down 3 or 4 inches (7.5 to 10 cm) and then across to the armscye (Figure 7.74). Cut on this line from the armscye, just to the seamline at the shoulder neck corner. Spread or lap the cut at the armscye the amount needed to alter the shoulder (Figure 7.75). Place tissue under the cut, if needed, and tape in place. Redraw the armscye edge. Identical alterations are usually needed on the back and front pattern pieces. Use the instructions in Chapter 9, "Altering Sleeves," to lengthen or shorten the sleeve cap a like amount.

LARGE OR SMALL NECKLINE

If your neck circumference is larger or smaller than the average, you will find that a high, round neckline does not fit smoothly at the base of the neck. The neckline of the garment must be made smaller or larger. To determine the amount of

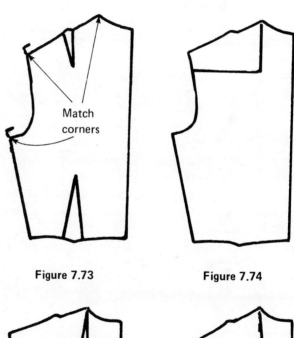

Figure 7.73   **Figure 7.74**

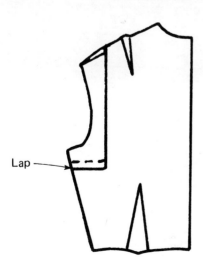

Figure 7.72

Figure 7.75

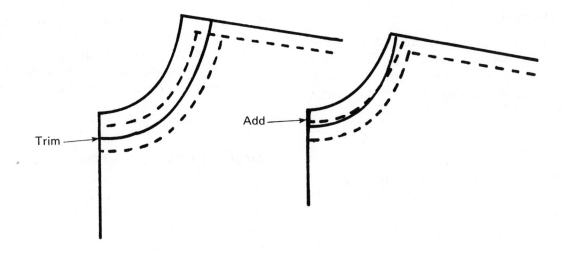

Figure 7.76

alteration needed, pin the back and front patterns together along the shoulder seam. Clip the seam allowance at two or three places so that the pattern lies flat. At several places around the neck, mark where the new neckline seam should lie. Remove the pattern and unpin the seams.

Seamline Method

If necessary, tape tissue paper under the pattern. Use a curved ruler to draw a smooth neck seamline on the front and/or back pattern pieces. Measure out from the seamline, adding a seam allowance (usually 5/8 inch, or 1.5 cm) and draw a cutting line (Figure 7.76). Make identical alterations on the facing patterns. If necessary, add to or cut off the outer edge of the facing to restore the original width (Figure 7.77).

The seamline method is the only method applicable to this alteration, as other methods cannot be used to increase or decrease the circumference of the neckline.

NECKLINE TOO LOW

If a V-shaped or scoop neckline is too low and more revealing than desired, it can be raised at the center front. Determine the amount needed by pinning the front and back patterns together at the shoulder and fitting the pattern on the figure. Measure the amount needed to raise the neckline at the center front.

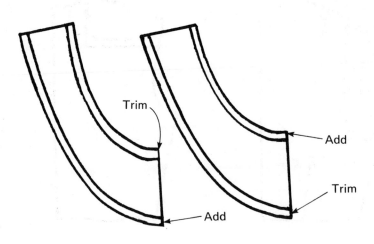

Figure 7.77

Seamline Method

Tape tissue paper under the center front of the neckline. Measure and mark the amount needed above the cutting line at the center front of the neckline. Draw a smooth curve or V shape from the center front mark to the original cutting line at the side of the neckline (Figure 7.78). Make identical alterations on the facing pattern, and restore the width of the facing along the lower edge of the center front (Figure 7.79).

The seamline method is the only method applicable to this alteration.

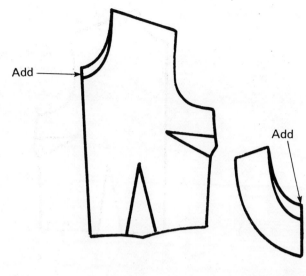

Figure 7.78 **Figure 7.79**

WAISTLINE CHANGES

Adjusting the waistline circumference is necessary on many patterns that are fitted close to the waistline. Determine the amount of change needed by comparing the pattern and your body measurements.

Internal Method

Draw a line from the underarm corner to the waistline, about 2 inches (5 cm) from the side seam. Cut on this line from the waistline just to the underarm. If enlarging the waistline, tape tissue paper under the larger portion of the pattern. Lap or spread the cut one fourth of the amount needed at the waistline, and tape in place (Figure 7.80). Correct the waistline seam by folding the waistline darts as they will be stitched, and redraw the waistline curve. Make identical alterations on the front and back patterns.

Slide Method

Pin tissue paper under the side portion of the pattern. Mark the underarm corner and the side cutting line at the waistline seam. Unpin the pattern, and mark one fourth of the amount of change needed at the waistline. Match the underarm corners of the pattern and tissue, and slide the pattern to the alteration mark. Draw along the side seam. Return the pattern to the original position on the tissue paper and tape in place. If necessary, fold under the side of the

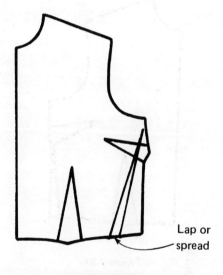

Figure 7.80

pattern, exposing the new side-seam cutting line (Figure 7.81). Make identical alterations on the front and back pattern pieces.

Seamline Method

If the margin is not sufficient, tape tissue paper under the side seam. Mark one fourth of the amount of change needed at the side waistline edge. Draw a new cutting line, tapering from the altered waistline to the bustline (Figure 7.82). Make identical alterations on the front and back pattern pieces.

62 • COMPARATIVE ANALYSIS OF PATTERN TECHNIQUES

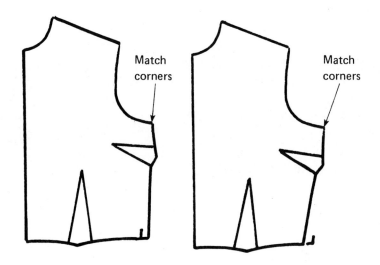

Figure 7.81

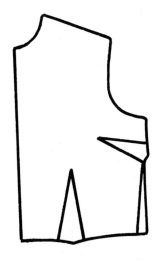

Figure 7.82

Comparison of Methods

The internal method can be used accurately with large or small changes, and it maintains the waistline curve. The slide and seamline methods should be used only for small changes or a maximum of 1/2 inch (1.3 cm) on each pattern piece.

TEST THE FIT

After altering the bodice, see Chapter 9 for altering the sleeves. When the altering is complete, test for fit by sewing the bodice and sleeves in fabric. Use a firm woven fabric such as muslin or a cotton blend for the fitting shell. Sew the complete bodice and attach the sleeves and under collar. You may omit the upper collar and all facings if you desire. Check your fitting shell for comfort and appearance following the guidelines in Chapter 4.

8

Altering Shirts

Altering shirts involves many of the same techniques as altering bodices. Before altering any shirt pattern, be sure to read Chapters 4, 5, and 6 and to take accurate body measurements.

LENGTH CHANGES

Shirts are altered in length by the same techniques as have been described for bodices. Small length adjustments can be made by any method; however, adjustments of more than 1 inch (2.5 cm) will be easiest and most accurate if the internal method is used.

CHEST WIDTH CHANGES

If the shirt fits correctly through the shoulder area, but needs to be increased or decreased in the chest, make the following changes.

Internal Method

At 3 inches (7.5 cm) from the armscye on the shirt front and back pattern pieces, draw a line parallel with the grainline arrow. Cut from the bottom of the shirt just to the stitching line at the yoke seam (Figure 8.1). Spread or lap the pattern one fourth of the amount needed in the chest area. If this alteration makes the bottom of the shirt too wide or too narrow, redraw the side seam, tapering to the original width at the hem (Figure 8.2). Be sure to make alterations on both the back and the front pattern pieces.

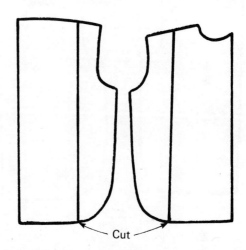

Figure 8.1

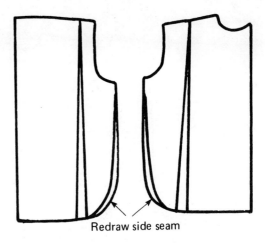

Figure 8.2

64 • COMPARATIVE ANALYSIS OF PATTERN TECHNIQUES

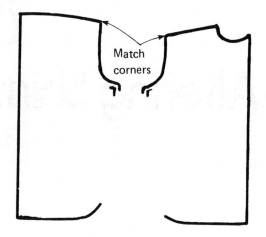

Figure 8.3

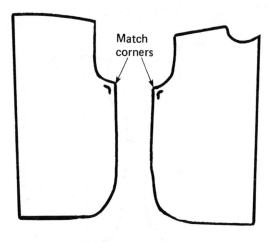

Figure 8.4

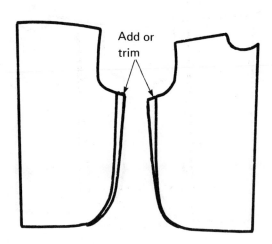

Figure 8.5

Slide Method

Lay tissue paper under the pattern and cut or draw along the bottom of the shirt. Also cut or draw along the center front or back fold and along the yoke edge. On the tissue, mark the underarm corner and the alteration needed. Match the yoke armscye corners and slide the underarm corner to the alteration mark. Pin and cut or draw along the armscye (Figure 8.3). Unpin the pattern. Match the underarm corners, and slide the bottom edge to the original position. Pin and cut or draw along the side seam (Figure 8.4). Unpin the pattern, and return it to the original position. Tape in place. Make identical alterations on the back and front pattern pieces.

Seamline Method

Add tissue paper along the side seam if the margin is not sufficient. Extend or reduce the lower armscye curve up to 1/4 inch (6 mm), giving a total alteration of 1 inch (2.5 cm) in the circumference. Draw a new side cutting line from this point to the bottom of the shirt (Figure 8.5). The shirt sleeve must also be altered so that the armscye seam can be sewn smoothly. Follow the information in the section titled "Increase Sleeve Width," using the seamline method in Chapter 9, "Altering Sleeves."

Comparison of Methods

The internal and slide methods give identical results if the alteration is made correctly. The seamline method increases the shirt width only below the armscye and not across the upper chest. Also, it is not satisfactory for large alterations because it increases the armscye circumference. The seamline method can be used along with the internal method if the shirt width needs to be increased more than 6 inches (15 cm).

ROUND SHOULDERS OR VERY ERECT BACK

If you have round shoulders, you will find that the shirt is too short at the center back and that the crosswise grainline will bow upward across the back. If you have a very erect back, shirts will be too long at the center back.

Internal Method

Draw a horizontal line across the pattern, 3 inches (7.5 cm) below the yoke edge. Draw a vertical line from the first line to the yoke edge, 2 inches (5 cm) from the armscye (Figure 8.6). Cut on these lines from the center back just to the armscye seam and from the yoke edge almost to the horizontal slash. Place tissue under the pattern if altering for round shoulders. Spread (for round shoulders) or lap (for very erect back) the amount needed at the center back, keeping the center back edge straight (Figure 8.7). This round-shoulder alteration will also spread the vertical cut, creating or widening the pleat. The erect back alteration laps both cuts, decreasing the width of the back along the yoke seam. If the back yoke edge becomes slightly longer than the yoke, ease in the fullness of the yoke edge when sewing the seam.

Slide Method

Pin tissue paper under the upper back pattern. Mark around both corners of the upper back edge on the tissue paper. Also mark the amount of alteration needed above or below the upper center-back corner (Figure 8.8). Unpin the pattern. Match the armscye corners, and slide the center back corner to the alteration mark. Pin and cut or draw along the upper edge of the pattern. Return the pattern to the original position. Fold down the upper edge, if necessary, to expose the new pattern, and tape in place (Figure 8.9).

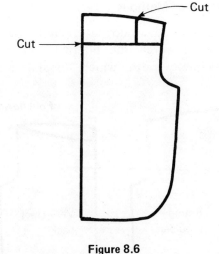

Figure 8.6

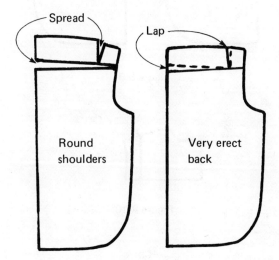

Figure 8.7

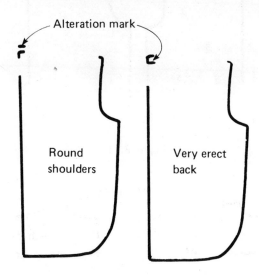

Figure 8.8

Comparison of Methods

Both methods give adequate length for broad shoulders; however, the internal method also gives adequate width, which the slide method does not give. Either method may be used for a very erect back.

NARROW OR BROAD SHOULDERS

If your shoulders are narrow, the yoke pattern will be too long for your body, and the armscye seam will droop off the shoulder. If your shoulders are too broad or wide for the pattern, the armscye seam will not lie at the end of the shoulder, and the shirt will be tight and uncomfortable.

Determine the amount of alteration needed by fitting the yoke piece to your shoulder. Align the center back of the pattern to your body, and mark the end of the shoulder on the pattern. Measure the excess or needed amount (do not include the seam allowance) at the shoulder seam. Alterations will be needed on the yoke, the back, and the front pattern pieces.

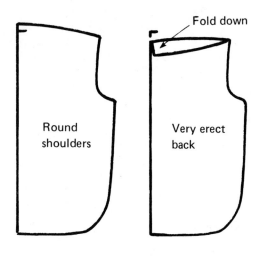

Figure 8.9

Internal Method

On the yoke, draw a line 2 inches (5 cm) from the armscye, and cut the yoke apart on this line. On the back and front pattern pieces, draw a line from the upper edge 2 inches (5 cm) from the armscye, to the armscye notch. Cut on this line from the upper edge just to the armscye seam. Lap or spread the yoke pattern the amount needed, and tape in place (Figure 8.10). Lap or spread the front and back pieces the same amount so that the edges will match when the yoke seam is sewn. Redraw the cutting lines on all pieces (Figure 8.11).

Figure 8.10

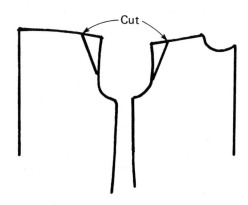

Figure 8.11

Slide Method

Pin the yoke pattern to tissue paper, and draw around the neckline and all four corners. Mark the alteration needed along the back and front armscye corners (Figure 8.12). Match the front neck corners, and slide the armscye corner toward the alteration mark. Cut or draw along half of the front edge. Slide the front edge so that the armscye corners match, and finish cutting the front edge. Match the lower center back corners, and slide the back armscye corner toward the alteration mark (Figure 8.13). Cut or draw along half of the back edge. Match the

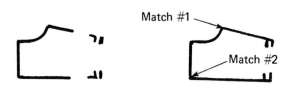

Figure 8.12   Figure 8.13

front and back armscye corners and finish cutting or drawing the back edge and along the armscye (Figure 8.14). Return the pattern to the original position. Fold down the armscye edge, if necessary, to expose the new pattern, and tape in place.

Pin tissue under the upper portion of the front pattern. Draw around the neck yoke corner, the upper armscye corner, and the underarm corner. Also mark the alteration needed at the upper armscye corner (Figure 8.15). Beginning at the center front, cut or draw along the neckline and the first half of the yoke edge. Unpin and slide the upper armscye corner to the alteration mark. Pin and finish cutting the upper edge. Continue to match the armscye corner, and slide the pattern so that the underarm corners match. Pin and cut or draw along the armscye (Figure 8.16). Return the pattern to the original position. Fold down the armscye corner, if necessary, to expose the new pattern, and tape in place. Repeat the steps on the back pattern piece.

Seamline Method

Mark the amount of alteration needed on the yoke, back, and front pieces. Draw a new armscye edge on all pieces, tapering to the original at the notch on the back and front pieces (Figure 8.17). Do *not* use this alteration for changes over 1/4 inch (6 mm).

Comparison of Methods

The internal and slide methods both give adequate results for any amount of change, whereas the seamline method is useful only for very small changes.

SQUARE OR SLOPING SHOULDERS

If you have square shoulders, shirt patterns will have too much slope in the shoulder area, and shirts will form horizontal wrinkles below the back collar. If you have sloping shoulders, shirts will wrinkle diagonally from the neckline to below the armscye. Generally, if you have sloping shoulders, both the shirt front and the shirt

Figure 8.14

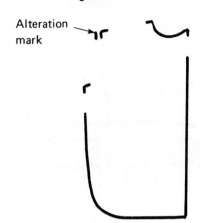

Figure 8.15

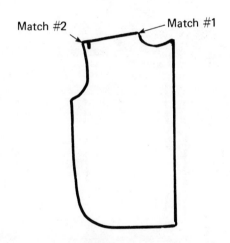

Figure 8.16

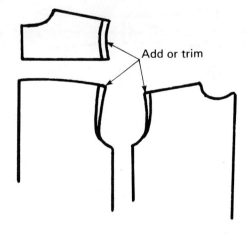

Figure 8.17

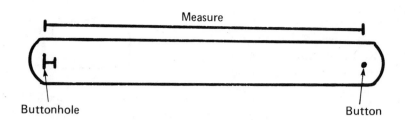

Figure 8.18

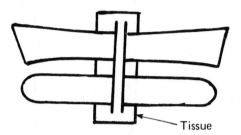

Figure 8.19

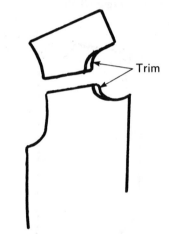

Figure 8.20

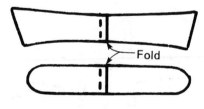

Figure 8.21

"Altering Bodices." Do *not* alter the yoke pattern, only the front and/or back shirt patterns.

COLLAR TOO TIGHT OR LOOSE

Men's dress shirt patterns are usually purchased by the neck measurement, but casual shirts and women's patterns are not. Thus the neck circumference may need altering. Determine the amount of alteration needed by measuring the circumference of the neck, and add 1/2 inch (1.3 cm) of ease. Compare this measurement with the collar-band pattern measurement taken between the button and the buttonhole placement marks at the center front (Figure 8.18).

Internal Method

To *increase* circumference, cut the collar and band patterns apart on the center back line. On tissue paper, draw two parallel lines, making the distance between the lines equal to the increase needed. Tape one portion of the pattern to each line, keeping the cutting edges even. Connect the cutting lines (Figure 8.19). Increase the circumference of the neckline on the shirt front and yoke patterns by drawing a new cutting line. Lower the neckline one fourth of the amount added to the collar and band pieces (Figure 8.20). To *decrease* the circumference on the band and collar patterns, draw two lines, parallel to the center back line, making the distance between the lines equal to the amount of decrease needed. Fold on one line and bring the fold to the second line, creating a tuck. Tape in place and redraw the cutting lines, if needed (Figure 8.21). Also decrease the circumference of the neckline on the shirt front and yoke patterns by

back patterns will need altering; however, if you have square shoulders, alterations may be needed only on the back pattern.

To alter the pattern, follow the information on square and sloping shoulders in Chapter 7,

ALTERING SHIRTS • 69

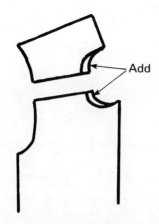

Figure 8.22

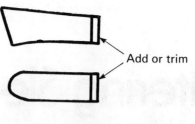

Figure 8.23

drawing a new cutting line. Raise the neckline one fourth of the amount folded out of the collar and band pieces (Figure 8.22).

Seamline Method

If the collar and band pieces are cut on the fold at the center back, add or remove half of the change needed at the center back of each pattern piece (Figure 8.23). Also alter the neckline on the shirt front and yoke patterns by drawing a new cutting line. Raise or lower the neckline one fourth of the amount of alteration needed (Figures 8.20 and 8.22).

Comparison of Methods

Both methods will give identical results if altered correctly. The internal method will be easier to use if full band and collar patterns are given, whereas the seamline method is easier if both patterns are "laid on the fold" at the center back.

WAISTLINE CHANGES

To increase or decrease the waistline circumference of the pattern, follow the information in Chapter 7, "Altering Bodices."

TEST THE FIT

For sleeve alterations, refer to Chapter 9, "Altering Sleeves." Once the pattern is altered, you are ready to cut and sew the shirt in fabric. After sewing, try on the shirt and check the fit for comfort and appearance. Use the information in Chapter 4 for evaluating the fit of the shirt.

9
Altering Sleeves

Sleeves must be altered to fit the length, width, and contour of the arm, as well as to fit smoothly into the armscye of the bodice or shirt. Like the proceeding chapter, this one discusses several body characteristics and suggests three methods of altering for each characteristic. Before attempting any alteration, be sure to read Chapter 6, "Pattern Alterations: General Techniques," and to take accurate body and pattern measurements.

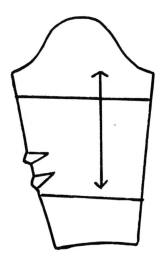

Figure 9.1

LENGTH CHANGES

Length alterations can be made above or below the elbow or at both locations, depending on where the arm varies from the pattern. Measure the arm as directed in Chapter 5, and refer to the measurement worksheet (Appendix) for information on where your personal adjustment is needed.

Internal Method

Most fitted-sleeve patterns have a printed line or length-adjustment guide above and below the elbow, whereas loose-sleeve patterns and shirt patterns have only one line or guide. If your pattern has neither, draw a line across the pattern, 2 to 3 inches (5 to 7.5 cm) above the elbow and/or a line 2 to 3 inches (5 to 7.5 cm) below the elbow. Make the lines at right angles to the grainline arrow (Figure 9.1). To *lengthen*, cut the pattern apart on one of the length-adjustment lines. On tissue paper, draw two parallel lines, making the distance between the lines equal to the amount you want the pattern lengthened in that portion of the sleeve. Tape the upper part of the pattern to one of these lines. With a ruler, extend the grainline arrow onto the tissue paper. Tape the lower part of the pattern to the second line, matching the grainline arrow (Figure 9.2). Redraw the side cutting lines. If the sleeve is to be altered both above

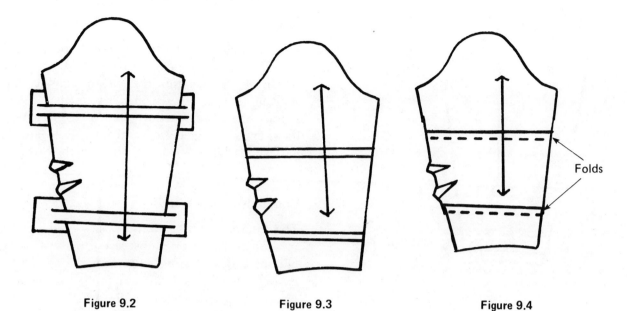

Figure 9.2   Figure 9.3   Figure 9.4

and below the elbow, repeat these operations. When the sleeve is altered in two locations, the dart positions are more apt to correspond to the elbow.

To *shorten* the sleeve length, draw a second line across the pattern, parallel to each original length-adjustment line. Make the distance between these lines equal to the amount of alteration needed in that portion of the sleeve (Figure 9.3). Fold along one line and bring the fold to the second line, creating a tuck. Tape the tuck in place and redraw the side cutting lines. If the sleeve is to be altered both above and below the elbow, repeat these operations (Figure 9.4).

Slide Method

Pin tissue under the lower edge of the pattern. Cut through the tissue along the lower edge and for about 1/4 inch (6 cm) up both sides (Figure 9.5). Transfer all pattern markings to the tissue. Unpin and slide the pattern *up* the amount needed to *lengthen* (Figure 9.6) the sleeve or *down* the amount needed to *shorten* the sleeve (Figure 9.7). Pin and check your measurements to see that the alteration is equal on both sides of the pattern. Tape the pattern to the tissue and redraw the side cutting lines. Also redraw any placket or vent lines.

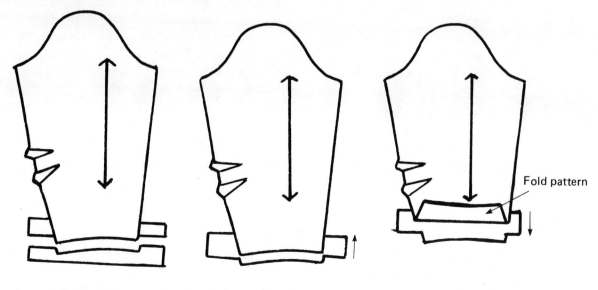

Figure 9.5   Figure 9.6   Figure 9.7

72 • COMPARATIVE ANALYSIS OF PATTERN TECHNIQUES

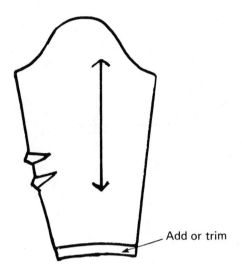

Figure 9.8

Seamline Method

Pin tissue paper under the lower edge of the pattern if the margin is not sufficient. Measure up or down the amount needed to lengthen or shorten the pattern (Figure 9.8). With a ruler, redraw the lower cutting line, the side cutting lines, and any placket or vent lines. Relocate all pattern markings along the bottom of the pattern.

Comparison of Methods

The internal method is the easiest of the three methods for changing most sleeve patterns, as it eliminates transferring pattern markings, and it is the only satisfactory method for making changes above the elbow. Full or shirt-sleeve patterns may be altered correctly by any of these three methods; however, if the length change is greater than 1 inch (2.5 cm), it may be less accurate to use the seamline method.

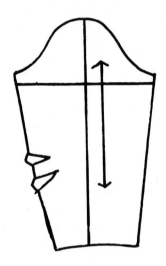

Figure 9.9

INCREASE SLEEVE WIDTH

If your sleeve feels tight in the upper arm area and wrinkles form around the sleeve, more width is needed across the sleeve pattern. To determine the amount of adjustment needed, see the information in Chapter 5 on measuring the upper arm and refer to the measurement worksheet (Appendix). After altering the pattern, pin the underarm seam allowances together and try on the sleeve. Check to see if it is large enough, with a minimum of 2 inches (5 cm) of ease around the arm.

Internal Method

Draw a line across the sleeve pattern 1 inch (2.5 cm) below the underarm seam allowance and a vertical line down the center of the sleeve, parallel with the grainline arrow (Figure 9.9). Cut on the vertical line from the lower edge, just to the seamline at the top of the sleeve. Cut on the horizontal line from the center of the vertical cut, in both directions, just to the side seamlines. Lay tissue under the pattern and spread the upper portions of the pattern until the amount

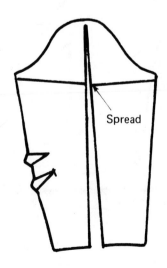

Figure 9.10

ALTERING SLEEVES • 73

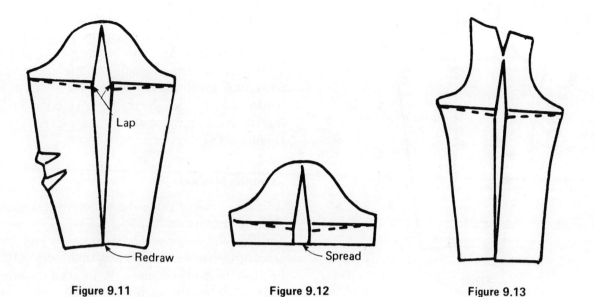

Figure 9.11
Figure 9.12
Figure 9.13

needed is added at the horizontal cut (Figure 9.10). Pin and tape the upper portion in place. Lap the horizontal cuts, and bring the lower edges of the sleeve pattern together (Figure 9.11). Redraw the lower edge to correct the curve or hemline. If the sleeve is short, additional width will be needed at the hemline. In this case, spread the vertical cut at the lower edge the amount of additional width needed (Figure 9.12). Tape the alteration securely, and straighten the lower edge of the pattern. Raglan sleeves are altered by the same techniques (Figure 9.13).

Slide Method

Pin tissue under the entire sleeve pattern, and cut or draw along the bottom edge of the sleeve. On the tissue, mark the shoulder dot at the cap and around both underarm corners. Also mark one half of the additional width needed at each underarm corner (Figure 9.14). Match the shoulder dot of the pattern and the tissue, and slide one underarm corner to the alteration mark. Pin and cut or draw along that side of the sleeve cap. Match the underarm corners and slide the lower edge to the hemline (Figure 9.15). Pin and cut or draw along the underarm cutting edge. Unpin

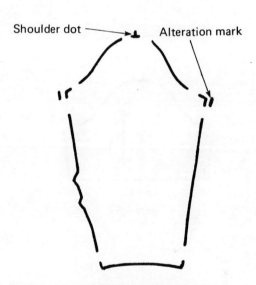

Figure 9.14

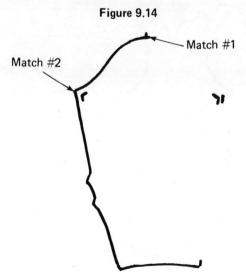

Figure 9.15

74 • COMPARATIVE ANALYSIS OF PATTERN TECHNIQUES

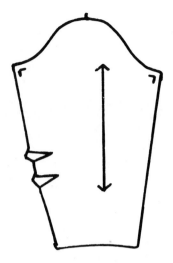

Figure 9.16

and repeat these steps on the other side of the sleeve (Figure 9.16). Return the pattern to the original position, and tape in place. Long sleeves are tapered to the original circumference at the wrist, but short sleeves usually need additional width across the sleeve hem (Figure 9.17). Raglan sleeves are altered by the same techniques (Figure 9.18).

Seamline Method

Add tissue paper along the underarm seam edge if the margin is not sufficient. Extend the lower armscye curve up to 1/2 inch (1.3 cm) on both sides of the sleeve. Draw a new underarm cutting line from this extension to the original underarm edge, close to the bottom of the sleeve (Figure 9.19). Ease this under-the-arm fullness into the seam when sewing. For short sleeves, the width around the hem may also need to be increased. Accomplish this by adding one half of the desired width at each side of the hemline, and redraw the underarm edges from the armscye

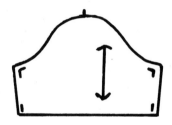

Figure 9.17

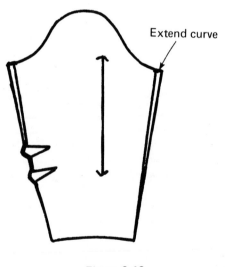

Figure 9.19

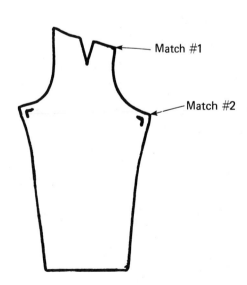

Figure 9.18

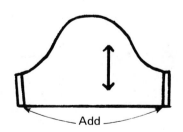

Figure 9.20

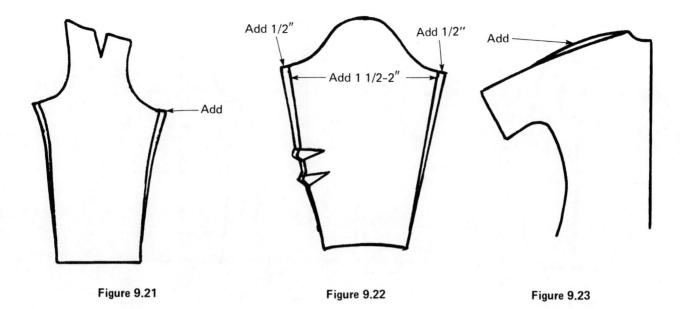

Figure 9.21 Figure 9.22 Figure 9.23

extensions to the hem marks (Figure 9.20). Also extend the lower cutting edge to the side hem marks. Raglan sleeves can be altered by the same techniques (Figure 9.21).

Comparison of Methods

The internal and slide methods give identical results in the sleeve cap if the alteration is made correctly; however, the slide method slightly increases the underarm sleeve length. The seamline method is recommended for use only in combination with another method to obtain maximum width for people with very large upper arms.

To alter for very large upper arms, use the internal or slide method to increase the sleeve width up to 2 inches (5 cm). Then use the seamline method for an additional 1 inch (2.5 cm) of width (Figure 9.22).

Note: Kimono sleeves can be altered only by the seamline technique. Tape tissue along the shoulder edge if the margin is not sufficient. Draw a new shoulder edge, increasing where necessary (Figure 9.23). Make identical alterations on the back and front patterns.

DECREASE SLEEVE WIDTH

If you have thin arms, vertical wrinkles may form in the sleeve, indicating that the sleeve is too full for your arm. The most satisfactory method for finding the amount of alteration needed is determined after the sleeve is sewn in fabric. Determine the amount of excess fabric by pinning a vertical tuck in the sleeve. Measure the depth of the tuck (both sides) and alter the pattern the same amount.

Internal Method

Draw a vertical line down the center of the pattern parallel to the grainline arrow. Cut on the line from the sleeve cap, just to the seamline or hem at the lower edge (Figure 9.24). Lap the

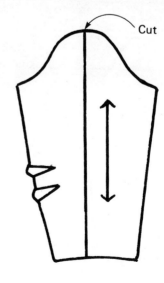

Figure 9.24

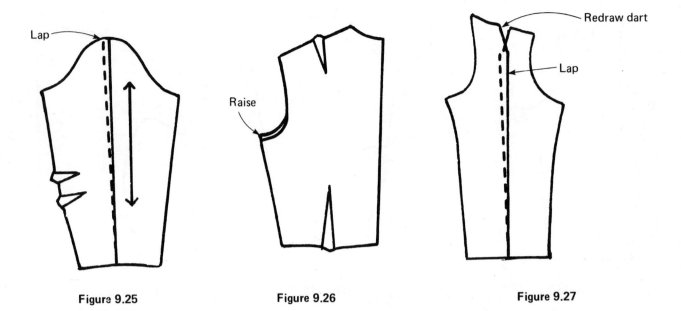

Figure 9.25　　　　Figure 9.26　　　　Figure 9.27

sleeve cap the amount needed, and tape in place (Figure 9.25). If the lap is greater than 1/2 inch (1.3 cm), redraw the underarm curves on the back and front pattern pieces, raising them one half of the amount of the lap. Raise the armscye notches on the front and back patterns the same amount (Figure 9.26). Raglan sleeves are altered by the same techniques, except no change is needed on the front and back pattern pieces (Figure 9.27).

Slide Method

Pin tissue under the entire sleeve pattern and cut or draw along the bottom edge of the sleeve. On the tissue, mark the shoulder dot at the sleeve cap and around both underarm corners. Also mark one half of the alteration needed at each underarm corner (Figure 9.28). Match the shoulder dot of the pattern and the tissue, and slide one underarm corner to the alteration mark. Pin and cut or draw along that side of the sleeve cap. Repeat on the other side of the sleeve (Figure 9.29). Match the underarm corners and the lower hem corners on one side of the sleeve. Pin and cut or draw along one underarm seam edge, and repeat on the other side of the pattern (Figure 9.30). Return the pattern to the original position, and tape in place, folding down the

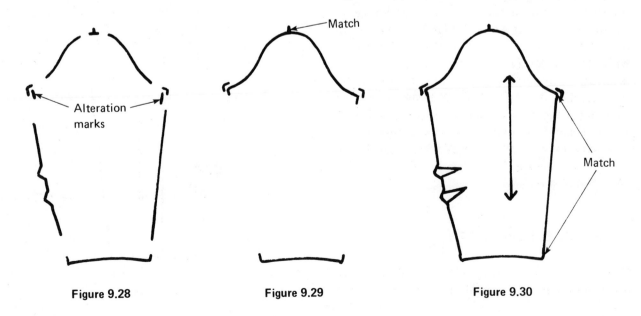

Figure 9.28　　　　Figure 9.29　　　　Figure 9.30

underarm corners. Raglan sleeves are altered by the same techniques (Figure 9.31).

Comparison of Methods

Both methods should adequately reduce the sleeve width when a small alteration is needed. If the pattern is altered more than 3/4 inch (2 cm), the slide method is not satisfactory, as the circumference of the sleeve cap must be reduced, and the armscye on the front and back pieces will need to be altered.

Note: Kimono sleeves are altered by the seamline method. Remove fullness on the back and front pattern pieces by redrawing both the shoulder and the underarm edges (Figure 9.32).

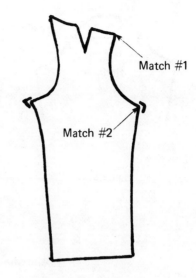

Figure 9.31

SLEEVE CAP ALTERATIONS

When fitting a garment, observe whether diagonal wrinkles form from the underarm to the top of the sleeve. If the wrinkles are due to excess fullness in the sleeve cap and the figure has sloping shoulders, the sleeve cap is too long. If the wrinkles are due to strain, the cap is too short because the person has square shoulders and/or fleshy upper arms.

Determine the amount of alteration needed after the garment is sewn, by ripping the top of the armscye seam. Pull the sleeve up or down until it is smooth and comfortable. Measure the gap or lap (excluding the seam allowance) between the sleeve and the bodice. This alteration is rarely needed on shirt sleeves.

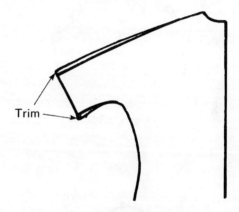

Figure 9.32

Internal Method

To *lengthen,* draw a line across the sleeve cap above the notches. Also draw two vertical lines for matching (Figure 9.33). Cut the pattern apart on the horizontal line. On tissue paper, draw two parallel lines, making the distance between the lines equal to the amount of alteration needed. Tape the upper sleeve section to one of these lines. With a ruler, extend the vertical lines onto the tissue paper. Tape the lower sleeve section of the pattern to the second line, matching the vertical lines. Tape in place and connect the cutting lines (Figure 9.34).

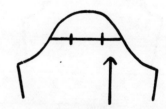

Figure 9.33

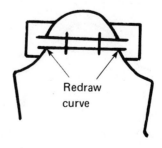

Figure 9.34

78 • COMPARATIVE ANALYSIS OF PATTERN TECHNIQUES

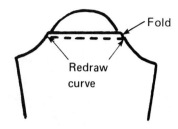

Figure 9.35

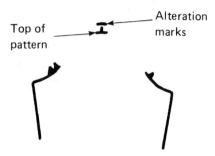

Figure 9.36

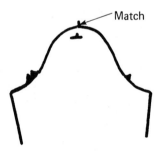

Figure 9.37

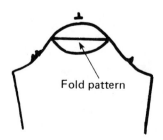

Figure 9.38

To *shorten* the sleeve cap, draw two lines across the sleeve cap above the notches. Make the distance between the lines equal to the amount of alteration needed. Fold along one line, and bring the fold to the second line, creating a tuck. Tape in place, and straighten the cutting lines (Figure 9.35).

Slide Method

Pin tissue under the sleeve cap. Mark the top of the sleeve above the shoulder dot and the underarm curve below the notches. Also mark the alteration needed above or below the shoulder dot (Figure 9.36). Unpin the pattern. Match the top of the sleeve to the alteration mark, and slide the armscye notch on one side to the original cutting edge. Pin and cut or draw that side of the sleeve cap. Repeat on the other side (Figure 9.37). Return the sleeve to the original position, folding down a portion of the cap if necessary, and tape in place (Figure 9.38).

Comparison of Methods

Alterations using either method should be identical; therefore the choice depends on which you find more convenient and easier to use.

Note: If the sleeve cap is shortened 1/2 inch (1.3 cm) or less, no alteration is needed on the front and back bodice patterns, as the ease in the sleeve cap is reduced. However, if the sleeve is shortened a greater amount or is lengthened *any* amount, or if shoulder pads are desired, the following alterations will be needed on the back and front bodice patterns.

Draw a line from the shoulder-neck corner down 3 to 4 inches (7.5 to 10 cm) and then across to the armscye (Figure 9.39). Cut on this line from the armscye, just to the seamline at the shoulder-neck corner. Spread or lap the cut at the armscye the same amount that the sleeve was lengthened or shortened (Figure 9.40). Place tissue under the cut, if needed, and tape in place. Redraw the armscye edge. Make identical alterations on the back and front pattern pieces.

ALTERING SLEEVES • 79

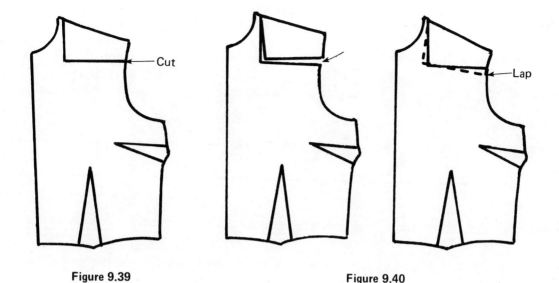

Figure 9.39

Figure 9.40

LARGE OR TIGHT ARMSCYES

If your arm is larger than the average, the armscye of a sleeveless garment may bind and pull under the arm. If the arm is small, the armscye may be too large and gaping. To determine the amount of alteration needed, pin the pattern together at the shoulder seam and at the lower half of the underarm seam. Clip the pattern at the armscye notch so that it lies flat, and fit it on the figure. At several places, mark where the new armscye seamline should lie. Remove the pattern and unpin the seams.

Seamline Method

Use the armscye sloper (Appendix) to draw a smooth armscye seam on the front and/or back pattern piece. Measure out from the seamline, adding a seam allowance (usually 5/8 inch, or 1.5 cm), and draw a cutting line (Figure 9.41). Make identical alterations on the facing patterns. If necessary, add or trim the outer edge of the facing to restore the original width (Figure 9.42).

The seamline method is the only method applicable to this alteration, as other methods do not change the armscye circumference.

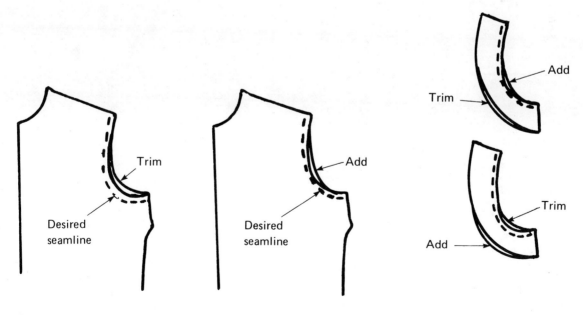

Figure 9.41

Figure 9.42

TEST IN FABRIC

Now that your have altered the sleeves of your garment, you are ready to test the fit in fabric. Cut the sleeves from the fabric you used for the bodice or shirt, and sew them into the garment. Check the fit of the sleeves for smoothness and comfort, following the guidelines in Chapter 4.

10
Altering Skirts

Skirts involve fewer alterations than many other garments, and for this reason, they are a good beginning project. Like bodices, skirt patterns must be adjusted to fit each individual so that the garments made from them are both aesthetically pleasing and comfortable.

This chapter discusses several characteristics and suggests three methods for altering each characteristic. Thus you can learn various alteration techniques and evaluate each method.

Before attempting to use any method, be sure to read Chapter 6, "Pattern Alterations: General Techniques," and to take accurate body and pattern measurements. Make alterations only where changes are needed, remembering that when body curves vary from those on the pattern, changes may be needed in both the length and the width of the pattern.

LENGTH CHANGES

Because the fashion in skirt lengths changes so rapidly, you must measure or fit every pattern before sewing; otherwise the finished skirt may be too short or too long. It is unwise to cut every skirt several inches too long with the idea of correcting the length just before hemming, as this method wastes expensive fabric and may distort style features such as vents and slits.

Internal Method

Most patterns have a printed line or guide below the thigh area that indicates where the length adjustment should be made. If not, draw a length-adjustment line across the front and back pieces just below the thigh area at a right angle to the grainline arrow (Figure 10.1).

To *lengthen,* cut the pattern apart on the length-adjustment line. On tissue paper, draw two parallel lines, making the distance between the lines equal to the amount of additional length needed. Tape the upper part of the pat-

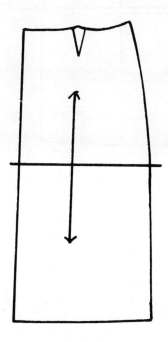

Figure 10.1

82 • COMPARATIVE ANALYSIS OF PATTERN TECHNIQUES

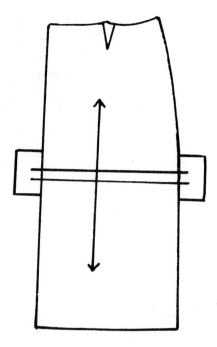

Figure 10.2

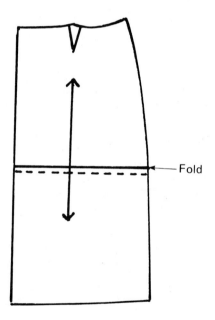

Figure 10.3

to make identical changes on the front and back skirt patterns.

To *shorten*, draw a second line across the pattern, parallel to the original length-adjustment line, making the distance between the lines equal to the amount of alteration needed. Fold the pattern along one line, and bring the fold to the second line, creating a tuck (Figure 10.3). Tape the tuck in place, and redraw the cutting lines at both sides of the pattern. Be sure to make identical changes on the front and back skirt patterns.

Slide Method

Either to lengthen or to shorten the skirt pattern, pin tissue paper under the lower edge. Cut through the tissue paper following the bottom edge of the skirt and for about 1/4 inch (6 cm) up both sides. Unpin the pattern. To *lengthen*, slide the pattern up the additional length needed, measuring at both side seams to ensure that the added amount is even. Tape the tissue to the pattern. With a ruler, redraw the side cutting lines from the hem edge to the hipline (Figure 10.4).

tern to one of these lines. With a ruler, extend the grainline arrow onto the tissue paper. Tape the lower part of the pattern to the second line, aligning the grainline (Figure 10.2). Redraw the cutting lines at both sides of the pattern. Be sure

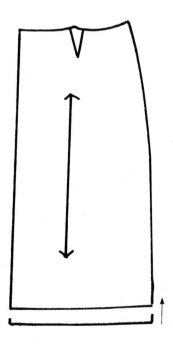

Figure 10.4

To *shorten,* pin tissue under the pattern and cut following the hem edge as instructed for lengthening. Unpin the pattern and slide it down the amount needed. Pin the pattern to the tissue paper, and recheck the length. If it is correct, fold up the lower portion and tape in place (Figure 10.5). With a ruler, redraw the side cutting lines from the hem edge to the hipline.

Seamline Method

Pin tissue paper under the lower portion of the pattern if the margin is not sufficient. Extend the grainline arrow to the bottom of the tissue paper. Measure up or down the amount needed to lengthen or shorten the pattern (Figure 10.6). Be sure that the measurement at each side of the pattern is the same distance from the grainline arrow as the original pattern so that the hem width is not changed. With a ruler, redraw the side cutting lines. Recheck the pattern width, by measuring the new and the original patterns across the hem. This step is especially important if the skirt is flared.

Comparison of Methods

Patterns altered correctly with any of these three methods should be identical; however, it is more difficult to maintain the curve of the hemline when using the seamline method.

HIP AND THIGH WIDTH ALTERATIONS

Skirts are easiest to alter when purchased according to the hip measurement; however, as they are often part of a dress or suit pattern, alterations are commonly needed. Before altering the hip or thigh width, divide the amount of alteration needed by 4, because the alteration will be made on both side seams and on the back and front pattern pieces. Measure down the side of the body from the waistline to the widest point of the hip or thigh to determine at what point the alteration is needed. On the pattern, measure the same distance down from the waistline seam and mark the pattern so that hip or thigh adjustments can be made at this location.

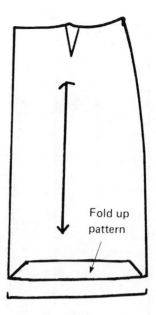

Figure 10.5

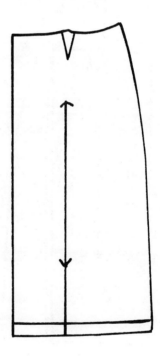

Figure 10.6

Internal Method

Draw a line parallel to the grainline from the waistline to the bottom of the skirt at about 2 inches (5 cm) from the side seam. Cut from the hem along this line to the waistline seam. At the

84 • COMPARATIVE ANALYSIS OF PATTERN TECHNIQUES

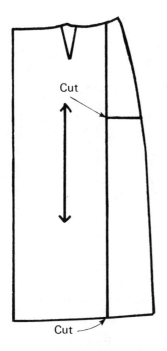

Figure 10.7

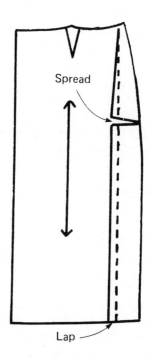

Figure 10.9

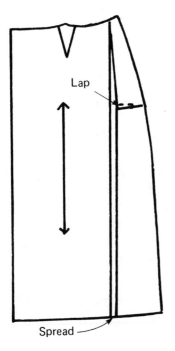

Figure 10.8

fullest part of the hip or thigh, cut horizontally from the vertical cut to the side seam (Figure 10.7). To *increase,* tape tissue paper under the larger portion of the pattern along the vertical cut. Spread the vertical cut the amount needed at the fullest part of the hip or thigh, and tape the upper side portion in place. The lower side portion of the skirt may be laid so that the vertical opening is parallel from the hip or thigh to the hem (Figure 10.8) *or* the vertical cut may be brought back together again at the hemline, lapping the horizontal cut. The latter tapers or pegs the skirt, a style that is unbecoming to a figure with heavy hips and thighs. Correct the hemline, and if a sharp curve or bulge forms at the hip area of the side seam, redraw the cutting line, creating a smooth curve. Make identical alterations on both the back and the front pattern pieces.

To *decrease* the hip or thigh circumference, cut as directed for increasing. Lap the vertical cut the amount needed at the hip or thigh area, and tape the upper side portion in place. Lap the lower side portion of the skirt so that the vertical opening is parallel from the hip or thigh to the hem (Figure 10.9), or if a wider hem width is desired, bring the vertical cut together again at the hemline. Correct the hem curve, and smooth the side cutting line at the point of adjustment if it is indented. Make identical alterations on both the back and the front pattern pieces.

Slide Method

Pin tissue paper under the outer portion of the side seam area, extending from above the waistline to below the hem. On the tissue, trace the lower side corner, the side-waistline corner, and the hip or thigh area. Also mark the amount of change needed in the hip or thigh area and an equal amount at the hemline (Figure 10.10).

Cut the tissue that extends above the waistline, following the pattern and for about 1/4 inch (6 mm) down the side seam. Unpin the pattern. Match the side waistline corners, and slide the pattern to meet the desired hip or thigh mark. Pin and cut, following the pattern from the waistline to the hip or thigh area. Unpin the pattern, and match the hip and thigh marks, sliding the pattern so that the lower portion of the side seam is parallel to the original side cutting line (Figure 10.11). Finish cutting the side seam. Unpin and return the pattern to its original position (matching the original marks along the side seam), and tape in place. Be sure to make identical alterations on the back and the front skirt patterns.

Seamline Method

Mark the change needed (one fourth of the increase or decrease) on the pattern, attaching

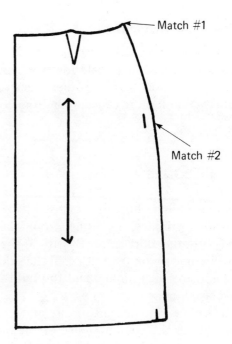

Figure 10.11

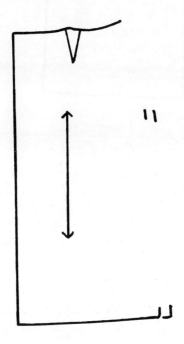

Figure 10.10

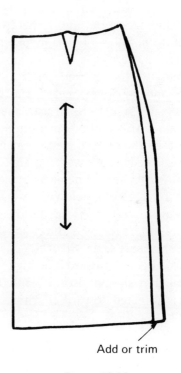

Figure 10.12

additional tissue if necessary. Using a curved ruler, redraw the hip and thigh curve, tapering to the original at the waistline. Below the thigh area, draw the alteration line parallel to the side seam of the skirt (Figure 10.12).

Comparison of Methods

Patterns altered correctly with any of these three methods should be identical; however, you may prefer one method over the others because you personally find it more efficient and/or accurate.

HIGH HIP BONES

If you have a high hipbone(s) close-fitting skirts will form wrinkles, radiating from the hipbones(s). If the skirt is loosely fitted, the hemline will curve up on the sides, and the skirt may be snug at the high hipline and too full through the average hip area.

Determine the amount of alteration needed by measuring the circumference of the body at 3 and 5 inches (7.5 and 12.5 cm) below the waistline as well as at the usual waist and hiplines. To the body measurements, add 1 1/3 and 2 inches (3.6 and 5 cm) of ease, respectively, and divide each total by 4. Lap and pin the skirt front and back patterns together on the stitching lines and measure the circumference at 3 and 5 inches (7.5 and 12.5 cm) below the waistline seam. Double these pattern measurements, and compare them with your body measurements. Do not add ease to the pattern measurements. Note the changes needed as well as any possible change in the average hipline measurement (7 to 9 inches, or 18 to 23 cm, below the waistline).

After the alteration is made, restore the waistline circumference by adding a short, curved dart close to the side seam. Slant the dart so that the point is directed toward the high hipbone. The original dart should also be slanted so that the point is directed toward the high hipbone (Figure 10.13).

Internal Method

Draw a vertical line, parallel with the side seam, from the waistline to below the hipline and then horizontally to the side seam. Cut on this line from the waistline, just to the side seam. Make horizontal cuts at 3 and 5 inches (7.5 and 12.5 cm) below the waistline seam, from the side seam to, but not through, the vertical cut. Spread the horizontal cuts to produce the desired curve

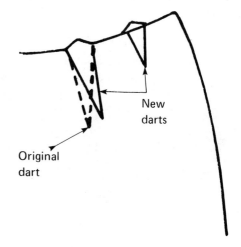

Figure 10.13

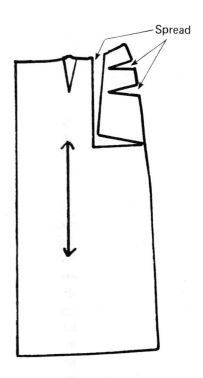

Figure 10.14

(Figure 10.14). Correct the waistline and side seam curves. Repeat to make the identical curve on the front and back pattern pieces. Restore the original waistline circumference by creating a short, curved dart in the waistline spread.

Slide Method

Lay tissue paper under the upper side portion of the pattern, and trace the original side edge from the waistline to below the hipline. Mark the

ALTERING SKIRTS • 87

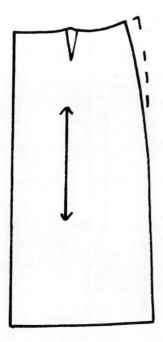

Figure 10.15

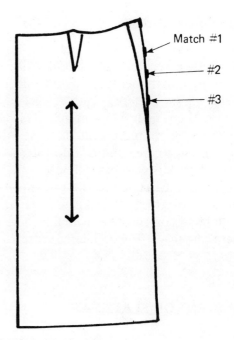

Figure 10.16

changes needed at 3, 5, and 7 inches (7.5, 12.5, and 18 cm) below the waistline seam (Figure 10.15). Match the side of the pattern and the first alteration mark, and slide the pattern horizontally until the waistline is increased in width and the waistline cutting edge is smooth. Draw along the upper side–waistline corner and down 3 inches (7.5 cm). Continue to match the first alteration mark and slide the side of the pattern to the second alteration mark. Draw between the marks. Repeat the technique between the second and third alteration marks, and again between the third mark and the hemline (Figure 10.16). Return the pattern to the original position and tape in place. Reposition the waistline dart(s), and create a short, curved dart close to the side seam (Figure 10.13). Make identical alterations on the front and back patterns.

Seamline Method

Lay tissue paper under the upper side edge if the margin is not sufficient. Measure and mark the changes needed at 3, 5, and 7 inches (7.5, 12.5, and 18 cm) below the waistline seam. Use a curved ruler to extend the waistline edge, increasing the waistline width the same amount as the increase needed 3 inches (7.5 cm) below. Then join the marks along the side seam, taper-

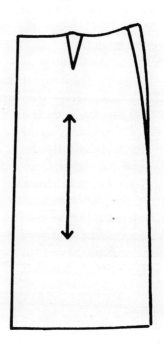

Figure 10.17

ing to the original cutting edge below the hipline (Figure 10.17). Restore the original waistline circumference by creating a short, curved dart close to the side seam, and slant the original dart toward the high hip-bone (Figure 10.13). Make identical alterations on the back and front pattern pieces.

88 • COMPARATIVE ANALYSIS OF PATTERN TECHNIQUES

Comparison of Methods

If altered correctly, all three methods should be identical; however, the slide and seamline methods may be more acceptable, as they do not involve cutting the pattern.

Note: Many figures are uneven, and one hip is higher and more prominent than the other. If the hemline is uneven on one side only, separate right and left skirt patterns will need to be made. Be very careful not to overfit garments in the hip area, as overfitting can call more attention to high hipbones or an uneven hipline than when garments are made from unaltered patterns.

PROMINENT OR FLAT SEAT

If you have a prominent seat, the skirt may wrinkle across the seat, and the hemline will be short in back. If you are very flat in back, the skirt will be too full across the seat, and the hemline will droop in back.

To determine the amount of width needed, fasten a tape around the body at the fullest part of the seat. Measure across the back along the tape between the normal side seam locations and add at least 1 1/2 inches (3.8 cm) of ease. Then divide this measurement by 2, as the pattern covers only one half of the back. Measure and note the distance between the waistline and the fullest part of the seat. You will find it easier to estimate the length change needed if you sew the skirt in fabric first or try on a similar skirt and determine the change needed for the hemline to hang evenly at the center back.

Internal Method

Draw a line parallel to the grainline through the center of the dart (if there are two back darts, draw the line through the one closest to the center back) and a horizontal line across the pattern at the fullest part of the seat (Figure 10.18). To *increase,* cut the pattern apart on the vertical line, and cut on the horizontal line from the center back just to the side seam. Lay tissue under the pattern and spread the vertical cut the amount needed, equally from waistline to hem. Pin in place. Spread the horizontal cut the amount needed at the center back, tapering to

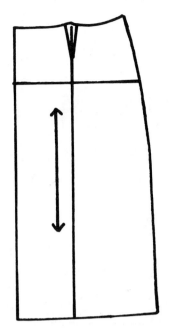

Figure 10.18

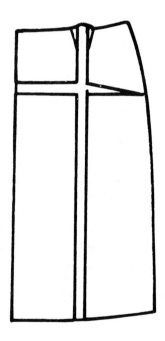

Figure 10.19

nothing at the side seam. Pin in place. Recheck your measurements, and tape the pattern in place (Figure 10.19). Use a ruler to straighten the center back edge of the pattern. Redraw the dart, and correct the waistline cutting edge (Figure 10.20). If the dart is quite wide, divide the depth into two darts as described following the comparison of methods.

ALTERING SKIRTS • 89

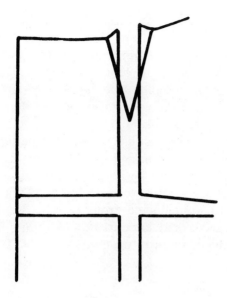

Figure 10.20

To *decrease,* draw a second vertical line parallel to the first line, making the distance between the lines equal to the amount of alteration needed. Fold the pattern on one line, and bring the fold to the second line, creating a tuck. Tape in place. Cut the pattern on the horizontal line from the center back just to the side seam. Lap the cut at the center back the amount needed and tape in place (Figure 10.21). Use a ruler to straighten the center back edge of the pattern.

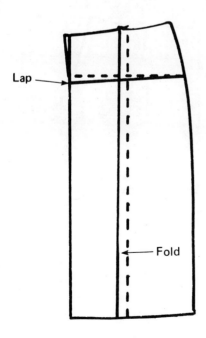

Figure 10.21

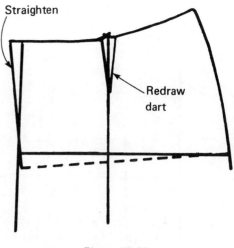

Figure 10.22

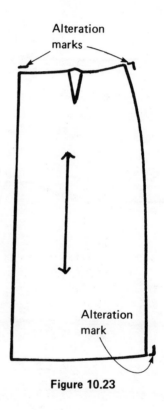

Figure 10.23

Redraw the dart, and correct the waistline edge (Figure 10.22).

Slide Method

Pin the pattern to tissue and mark the side corners at the hem, the waistline, and the center-back waistline corner. Mark the width increase or decrease needed at the side waistline and hem edges, and mark the length increase or decrease needed at the center back waistline (Figure 10.23). Slide the pattern horizontally to match

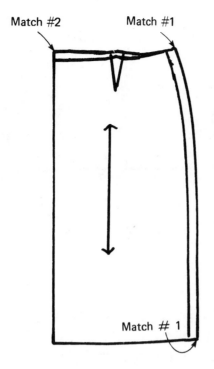

Figure 10.24

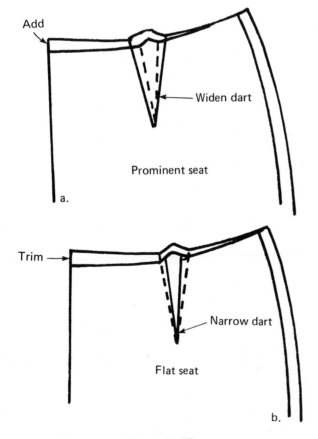

Figure 10.25

both alteration marks at the side edge. Beginning at the hem, cut or draw along the side edge of the pattern, and continue around the waistline corner for 1/4 inch, or 6 mm (Figure 10.24, Match #1). Keeping the waist side corners matched, slide the center back to the alteration mark (Figure 10.24, Match #2). Pin and cut or draw along the waistline. Return the pattern to the original position, and tape in place. Restore the original waistline width by increasing or decreasing the dart by the same amount that was added to or deducted from the side waistline (Figure 10.25). If the dart becomes quite large, divide the depth into two darts.

Seamline Method

Pin tissue under the side and waistline edges of the pattern if the margin is not sufficient. Mark the width change needed at several places along the side seam, and mark the length alteration needed above or below the center back edge of the pattern (Figure 10.26). Using a ruler, join the marks along the side seam. Also draw a new waistline edge from the alteration mark at the center back to the original side-waistline corner

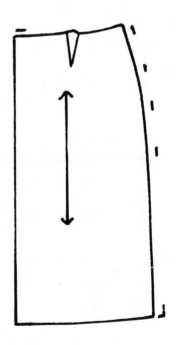

Figure 10.26

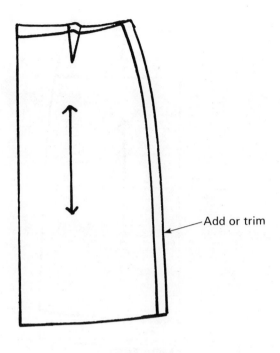

Figure 10.27

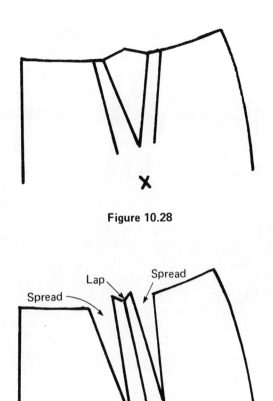

Figure 10.28

Figure 10.29

(Figure 10.27). Restore the original waistline width by increasing or decreasing the dart by the same amount that was added or deducted from the side waistline (Figure 10.25). If the dart becomes quite large, divide the depth into two darts.

Comparison of Methods

If used correctly, all three methods give similar results; however, the slide method is generally the most accurate. If the back pattern needs to be increased more than 1 1/2 inches (3.8 cm) on each side, use both the internal and the slide methods. Use each method to adjust the pattern for half of the increase needed. This technique prevents making all of the increase at one place and distorting the pattern.

Dividing Darts

Generally, when one large dart needs to be divided at the waistline seam, it is more aesthetically pleasing to create two smaller darts on each side of the original. First, fit the pattern to the figure and mark the fullest part of the hip curve.

Draw two lines where the new darts should be located. Be sure to slant the lines toward the fullest part of the hip curve. Generally these lines are positioned 1/2 inch (1.3 cm) on each side of the original dart-stitching lines at the waistline and about 1 1/2 inches (3.8 cm) apart at the points (Figure 10.28). Cut through the center of the original dart, beyond the point, to the fullest part of the hip curve. Also cut on the lines for the new darts to below the points and then angle to the end of the first cut. Do not cut completely through the pattern, but keep all of these sections joined at the fullest part of the hip curve. Close the original dart by taping one stitching line on top of the other at the waistline; thus spreading the new darts. Position the new darts so that the spread is equal, or unequal if desired, and tape in place (Figure 10.29). Again, fit the pattern to the figure to locate the new dart points. Two darts are often shorter in length

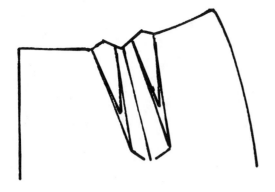

Figure 10.30

than one. Draw the stitching lines from the edges of the spread to the dart points (Figure 10.30). Determine the dart extensions by folding and cutting as instructed in Chapter 7, "Altering Bodices."

SWAYBACK

If you are swaybacked, snug-fitting skirts will wrinkle below the back waistline, indicating that the garment is too long between the waist and the hips. Loose-fitting skirts will droop at the center back, and the side seams will swing forward at the hemline.

You can determine the most satisfactory method for finding the amount of adjustment needed after you have sewn the skirt in fabric or if you try on a similar skirt. Correct the fit by pinning a horizontal tuck below the back waistline, tapering to nothing at the side seams. Measure the depth of the full tuck (both sides) at the center back.

Internal Method

Draw a horizontal line across the back pattern piece between the waistline and the hipline. Cut on this line from the center back just to the side seam (Figure 10.31). Lap the center back seam the depth of the horizontal tuck, tapering to nothing at the side seam. Tape in place, and redraw the center-back cutting edge (Figure 10.32). If necessary, redraw the back-dart stitching lines so that the dart point is directed to the fullest part of the seat.

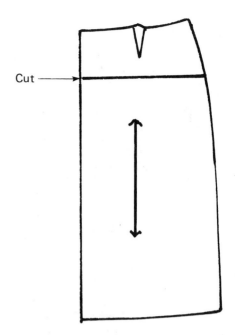

Figure 10.31

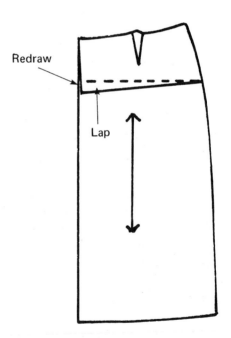

Figure 10.32

Slide Method

Pin tissue under the upper back pattern. On the tissue, mark the original center and side waistline corners. Also mark the depth of the horizontal tuck below the original center back waistline corner (Figure 10.33). Unpin the pattern. Match the side waistline corners, and slide the center

ALTERING SKIRTS • 93

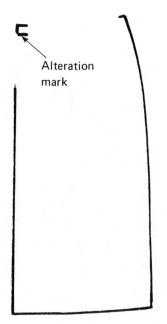

Figure 10.33

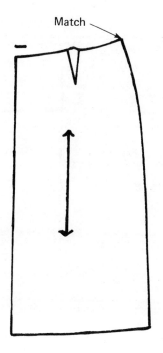

Figure 10.34

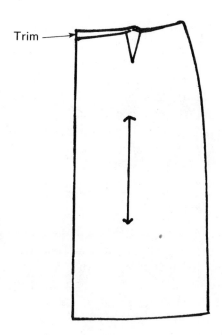

Figure 10.35

Seamline Method

Mark the depth of the horizontal tuck below the center back waistline. Using a curved ruler, redraw the waistline edge from the alteration mark at the center back to the original edge near the side seam. Cut off the excess pattern and straighten the dart stitching lines (Figure 10.35).

Comparison of Methods

The internal method is the quickest to complete; however, all three methods give similar results if used accurately.

PROMINENT STOMACH

If your stomach is large, skirts will be tight below the waistline across the stomach. The hem will ride or curve upward in the center front, and the skirt will flare out at the hemline. Thus the front pattern piece must be increased in both width and length.

To determine the amount of width needed, fasten a tape around the body at the fullest part of the stomach. Measure the front of the body, along the tape, between the normal side-seam locations, and add at least 1 inch (2.5 cm) of

waistline corner down to the alteration mark. Pin and cut or draw along the waistline edge (Figure 10.34). Unpin and return the pattern to the original position. Fold down the pattern's center waistline edge, and tape the tissue in place.

ease. Then divide this measurement by 2, as the pattern covers only one half of the front. Measure and note the distance between the center front waistline and the fullest part of the stomach. You will find it easier to find the length adjustment needed after sewing the skirt in test fabric or by trying on a similar skirt and estimating the length needed to make the hemline hang evenly in front.

Internal Method

Draw a line parallel to the grainline through the center of the dart (if there are two darts, draw through the one closest to the center front) and a horizontal line across the pattern at the fullest part of the stomach (Figure 10.36). Cut the pattern apart on the vertical line, and cut on the horizontal line from the center front just to the side seam. Lay tissue under the pattern and spread the vertical cut the amount of additional width needed, equally from the waistline to the hem. Pin the pattern to the tissue. Spread the horizontal cut the amount of additional length needed at the center front, tapering to nothing at the side seam. Pin in place. Recheck your measurements, and tape the pattern in place (Figure 10.37). Use a ruler to straighten the center-front cutting edge. Redraw the dart, and

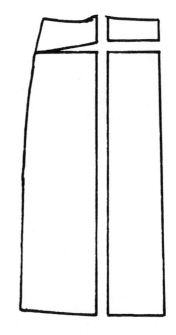

Figure 10.37

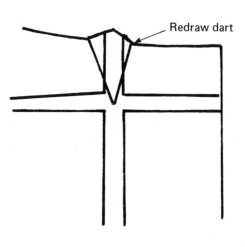

Figure 10.38

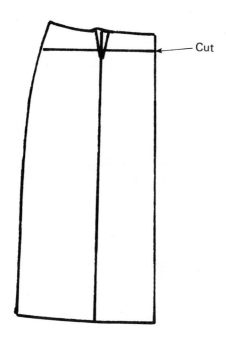

Figure 10.36

correct the waistline edge (Figure 10.38). If the dart becomes quite large, divide it into two darts.

Slide Method

Pin the pattern to tissue and mark the side corners at the hem, the waistline, and the center-front–waistline corner. Mark the width increase needed at the side waistline and the hem edges, and mark the length increase needed above the center front waistline (Figure 10.39). Slide the pattern horizontally to match both side altera-

ALTERING SKIRTS • 95

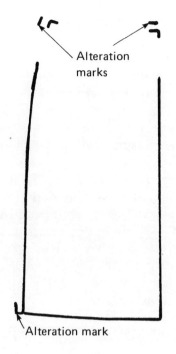

Figure 10.39

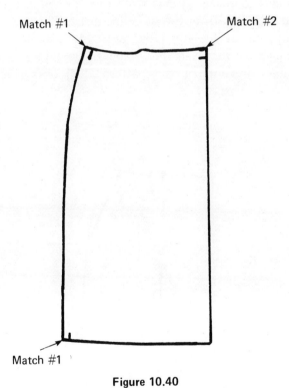

Figure 10.40

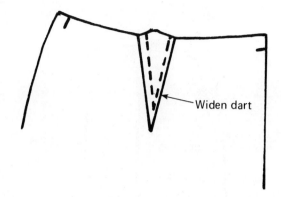

Figure 10.41

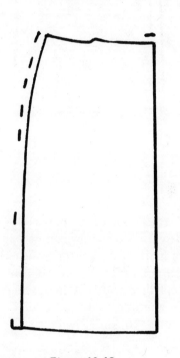

Figure 10.42

tion marks. Beginning at the hem, cut or draw along the side edge of the pattern and continue around the waistline corner for 1/4 inch, or 6 mm (Figure 10.40, Match #1). Keeping the side corners matched, slide the center front to the alteration mark (Figure 10.40, Match #2). Pin and cut or draw along the waistline. Return the pattern to the original position, and tape in place. Restore the original waistline width by increasing the dart by the same amount that was added to the side seam (Figure 10.41). Divide the dart if it becomes quite large.

Seamline Method

Pin tissue under the side and waistline edges of the pattern if the margin is not sufficient. Mark the width increase needed at several places along the side seam and the length increase needed above the center front edge (Figure 10.42). Using

96 • COMPARATIVE ANALYSIS OF PATTERN TECHNIQUES

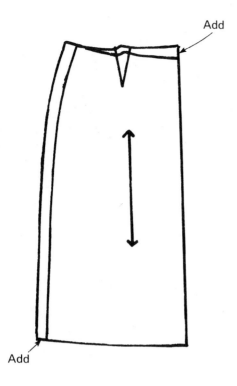

Figure 10.43

a curved ruler, join the marks along the side seam. Also draw a new waistline edge from the alteration mark at the center front to the original side waistline corner (Figure 10.43). Restore the original waistline width by increasing the dart by the same amount that was added to the side seam (Figure 10.41). Divide the dart if it becomes quite large.

Comparison of Methods

If used correctly, all three methods give similar results; however, the slide method is generally the most accurate. If the front pattern needs to be increased more than 1 1/2 inches (3.8 cm) on each side, use both the internal and the slide methods. Use each method to adjust the pattern for half of the increase needed. This procedure prevents making all of the increase at one place and distorting the pattern.

WAISTLINE ALTERATIONS

Adjusting the waistline circumference is often necessary whether the skirt pattern was purchased by your hip measurement or by your bust measurement. Determine the amount of change needed by comparing the pattern and your body measurements and dividing the increase by 4. Often you can make small changes of less than 1 inch (2.5 cm) by stitching the darts (change at least four darts) narrower or wider to adjust the circumference. Alterations are usually made on both the back and the front pattern pieces, but they can be made on only one piece if preferable. For example, only the front pattern may need altering if you have a prominent stomach.

Internal Method

Draw a line from the side hipline to the waistline, about 2 inches (5 cm) from the side seam. Cut on this line from the waistline just to the stitching line at the hip (Figure 10.44). If you are enlarging the waistline, tape tissue under the larger portion of the pattern. Lap or spread

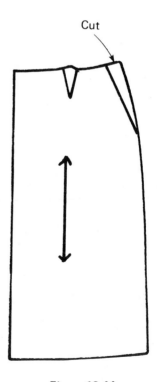

Figure 10.44

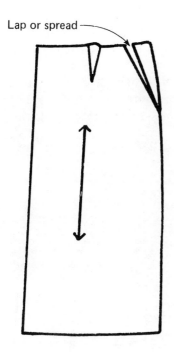

Figure 10.45

the cut one fourth of the amount needed at the waistline and tape in place (Figure 10.45). Redraw the side edge at the hipline, creating a smooth curve.

Slide Method

Pin tissue paper under the upper side portion of the pattern. Mark the side hipline and both waistline corners. Also mark one fourth of the change needed at the side waistline (Figure 10.46). Match the side hip edges of the pattern and the tissue, and slide the pattern to the alteration mark. Cut or draw along the side seam. With the side hiplines still matched, return the pattern to the original position, and tape in place (Figure 10.47). If necessary, fold under the side of the pattern, exposing the new side cutting-line.

Seamline Method

If the margin is not sufficient, tape tissue paper under the upper side edge of the pattern. Mark one fourth of the amount of the change needed at the side waistline edge. Draw a new cutting line, tapering it from the mark to the original hipline (Figure 10.48).

Comparison of Methods

All three methods should give adequate results for changes up to 3/4 inch (2 cm) on each pattern piece. If a greater change is needed, follow

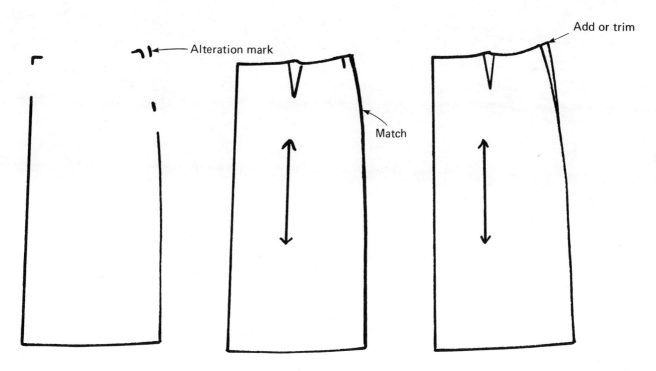

Figure 10.46   **Figure 10.47**   **Figure 10.48**

one of the above methods and narrow (or widen) the darts. If more than a 4 inch (10 cm) increase in circumference is needed, alter the side seam with one of the three methods, narrow the darts, and use either the slide or the seamline method to increase the waistline width at the center front or back (or both the center front and the center back) as needed. If increased width is needed because of a prominent stomach, make most of the alteration on the front pattern piece. Likewise make larger increases on the back pattern piece for figures with a high, rounded seat.

SKIRTS WITH YOKES

When altering patterns with yokes, pin the two pieces together (back yoke to back pattern or front yoke to front pattern), matching the seamlines (Figure 10.49). Follow the instructions given in this chapter to alter the pattern for waist, hip width, and thigh width changes. Swayback alterations are usually made on the skirt back below the yoke.

Width changes for a prominent stomach or a prominent or flat seat should also be made following the instructions in this chapter after the yoke is pinned to the corresponding pattern. You can make length changes for a prominent stomach or a prominent or flat seat by adding to the seamlines of the lower yoke and the upper

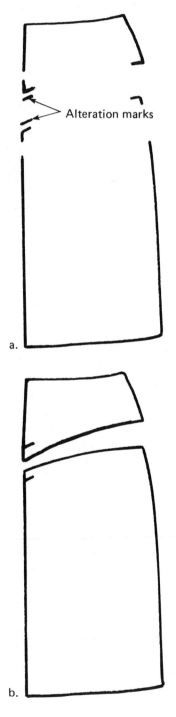

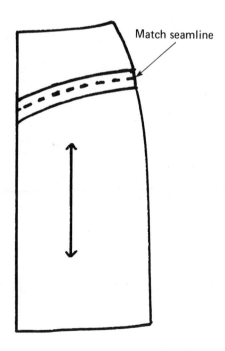

Figure 10.49

Figure 10.50

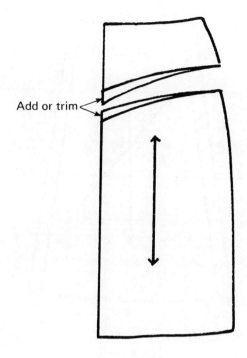

Figure 10.51

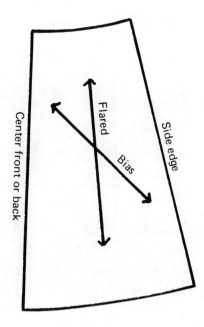

Figure 10.52

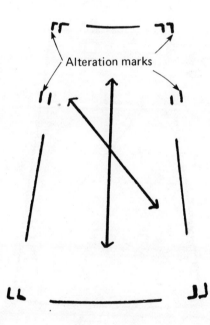

Figure 10.53

back or front patterns, using the slide (Figure 10.50) or seamline method (Figure 10.51). Make the changes equally on the yoke and the back or front patterns unless doing so distorts the design curve drastically. If distortion occurs, make the change on either the yoke or the corresponding pattern, whichever gives the most pleasing design. Remember that if your body curves very much from the average, a skirt with a yoke placed close to this curve will make this characteristic more noticeable.

FLARED AND BIAS SKIRTS: WIDTH ALTERATIONS

Flared and bias skirts (Figure 10.52) without darts can be altered in width if you add or decrease along both side seams. Thus width changes are divided by 8 instead of by 4, as they can be made on both sides of four pieces. This method allows the fullness to hang evenly, so that there is less possibility of an uneven hemline. Usually the slide or seamline method is used because the alteration is small.

Slide Method

Pin tissue under the pattern and mark all four corners and the edge along the hip or thigh area. With tracing paper, transfer the grainline arrow to the tissue. Also mark needed changes at the six places. Make the changes at the hem the same as those needed in the thigh area (Figure 10.53). Unpin the pattern. Slide the pattern to

100 • COMPARATIVE ANALYSIS OF PATTERN TECHNIQUES

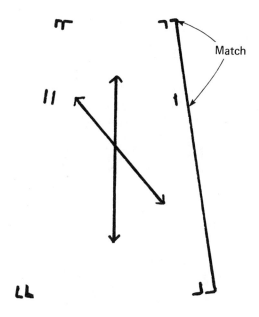

Figure 10.54

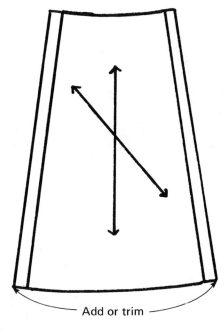

Figure 10.56

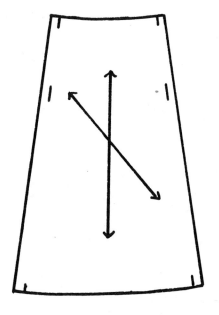

Figure 10.55

one side, matching the hem and the thigh alteration marks. Cut or draw from the hem to the thigh area. Keeping the thigh area matched, slide the pattern to the waistline mark, and continue cutting the side seam to the waistline (Figure 10.54). Repeat these steps along the other side seam. Center the waistline between the alteration marks at the waistline, and cut or draw along the waistline edge (Figure 10.55).

Seamline Method

Tape tissue under the pattern if the margins are not sufficient. Mark the needed changes at the waist, the hip, the thigh, and the hemline. Make the hemline change the same width as the thigh alteration. Using a ruler, draw a new side cutting-line (Figure 10.56). Repeat on the other side of the pattern.

Comparison of Methods

The seamline method is the more convenient method because tissue paper seldom needs to be attached; however, alterations made by either method should be identical.

FLARED AND BIAS SKIRTS: SEAT AND STOMACH ALTERATIONS

Make the width alterations for a prominent stomach and all seat changes using one of the above alterations. Length adjustments should be made at the waistline by one of the methods described below.

Slide Method

Lay tissue under the waistline edge and mark both side corners at the waistline. Also mark the length adjustment needed above or below the center front or back (Figure 10.57). Keeping the side corners of the pattern and the tissue matched, slide the center of the pattern to the alteration mark. Draw or cut along the waistline edge (Figure 10.58). Return the pattern to the original position and tape in place.

Seamline Method

Add tissue to the waistline edge, if needed. Mark the length change needed above or below the center waistline (Figure 10.59). Draw a new waistline from the alteration mark, tapering to the original cutting line near the side seam (Figure 10.60).

Comparison of Methods

Both methods give identical results if used correctly. Choose the one most convenient for you.

A FITTING SHELL

Now you have altered your pattern and are ready to test the fit in fabric. Use firm woven fabric

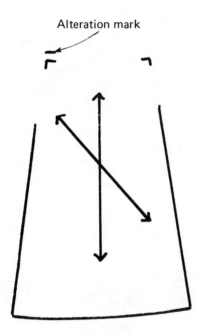

Figure 10.57

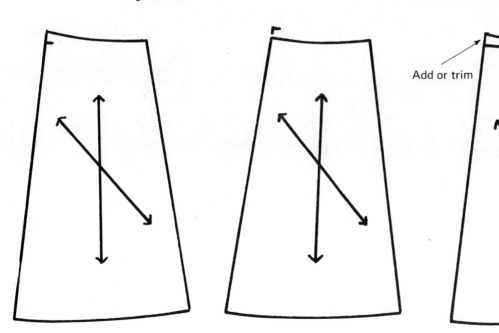

Figure 10.58 **Figure 10.59** **Figure 10.60**

such as muslin or a cotton blend to make the fitting shell. Sew the skirt together and attach the waistband; however, you may omit the zipper if you desire. Check your fitting shell for comfort and appearance following the guidelines in Chapter 4.

11
Altering All-in-One Dresses

Once you have learned to alter bodices, sleeves, and skirts, you are ready to advance to various types of dresses. This chapter discusses altering the all-in-one dress, which includes the sheath, shift, A-line, princess, raglan, and kimono styles. Be sure that you understand the basic alteration techniques and the figure characteristics to which every technique applies before attempting to alter these styles.

LENGTH CHANGES

The skirt portion of an all-in-one dress can be lengthened or shortened with any of the three methods outlined in Chapter 10, "Altering Basic Skirts." To change the length of the bodice portion, draw a line across the front and back pattern pieces (and across the side front and the side back pieces of princess styles) just above the waistline. Follow the instructions for making length alterations, using the internal method found in Chapter 7, "Altering Bodices," as it is the only method applicable to altering an all-in-one dress above the waistline. Note: The waistline is indicated on most all-in-one patterns by a short line that is perpendicular to the center back and front seams. Usually this line is labeled *waistline*.

RAISING OR LOWERING THE BUSTLINE

If your bustline is higher or lower than the average, the curve of a princess seam must be raised or lowered to fit your figure. Draw a horizontal line across the pattern above the upper bust notch and a second horizontal line below the lower bust notch on both the front and the side front patterns. If the upper line on the side front extends into the armscye, slant it to the side seam. On both pieces, draw a third line below the *upper* line if you desire to raise the bustline, or draw it below the *lower* line if you desire to lower the bustline. Make the distance between this and the corresponding line the amount of the alteration needed. Fold along one line and bring the fold to the other line, creating a tuck (Figure 11.1). Restore the original length of the front pieces by cutting on the other lines and spreading both patterns by the same amount that was folded into the tucks. Tape to the tissue, and redraw the cutting lines where needed. Note that a tuck below the bustline lowers the curve and that a tuck above the bustline raises it.

Underarm and waistline darts may be raised or lowered by any of the methods discussed in Chapter 7, "Altering Bodices." Angled darts that extend from the side seam at the hip or the waistline and armscye darts are easier to raise

103

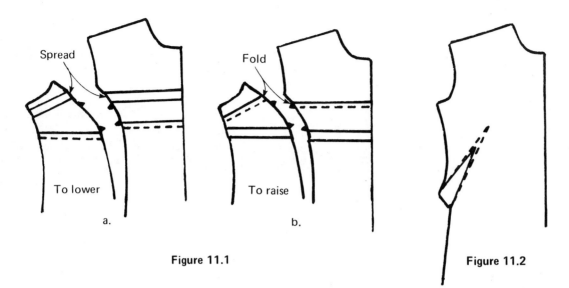

Figure 11.1

Figure 11.2

or lower by the slide rather than the internal method. In the slide method, you relocate the dart point and draw new stitching lines from the original dart lines at the side seam (Figure 11.2).

BUSTLINE WIDTH CHANGES

If your pattern was purchased by the high bust measurement, or if you wear less than a B cup bra size, the bustline will need altering.

Sheath, Shift, And A-Line Dresses

Internal method. On sheath, shift, and some A-line styles, cut the pattern apart at the waistline. Alter as you would a basic bodice, but do not maintain an equal amount of lap or spread along the side bustline. Instead, position the lower side-bodice section so that the original waistline width is restored (Figure 11.3).

On an A-line style with an angled dart, or if you want to add an angled dart, use the following method. Cut through the angled dart (or the place where you want one) to the bust point and to, but not through, the shoulder seam. Cut through the center of the underarm dart to the bust point and across to the center front (Figure 11.4). Lap or spread the amount needed at the bust point.

Slide method. First lengthen or shorten the dress the amount needed at the hemline on the front

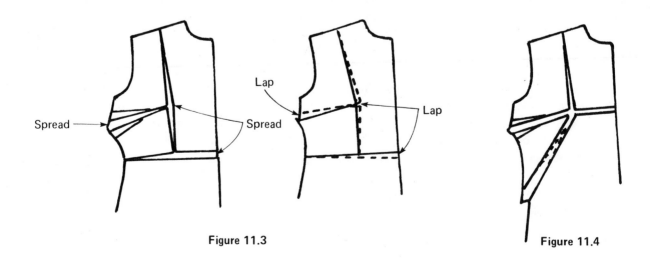

Figure 11.3

Figure 11.4

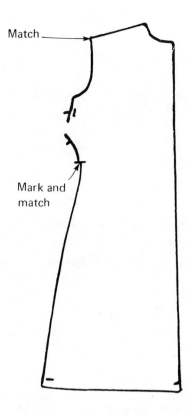

Figure 11.5

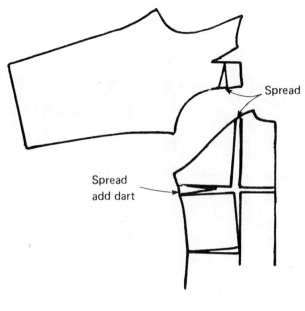

Figure 11.6

pattern, as a smaller or larger bustline curve dictates both a width and a length change. Do not be concerned that the front pattern no longer matches the back along the side seam because you will later change the dart width so that the two patterns match. With the pattern positioned at the desired length (not the original length), mark the waistline at the side seam. Then return the pattern to the original position and proceed as directed for a basic bodice, using the slide method (Figure 11.5).

Comparison of methods. Both methods change the bustline width. The internal method, which increases the dart depth more than the slide method, is more desirable if the bustline width is increased more than a pattern size. When using the slide method, be sure to mark the side waistline at the desired length and then use this mark when drawing the cutting line below the underarm dart.

Raglan Styles

Internal method. On raglan styles, cut as already directed for the internal method, but extend the vertical cut through the front raglan seam on the pattern and through the front portion of the sleeve pattern to the shoulder-dart stitching line. When altering, make sure that the spread or lap is identical at the seamline on both the front and the sleeve patterns (Figure 11.6). The internal method is the only acceptable one for altering the bustline width on raglan patterns.

Kimono Styles

Internal method. Cut kimono patterns apart at the waistline. Proceed as for basic bodices, but extend the cut above the bust point to the neck shoulder corner instead of the shoulder seam (Figure 11.7). If the bustline has been increased and the pattern does not contain an underarm dart, create one in the underarm spread. If the bustline has been decreased, the back bodice can be eased onto the front at the bustline.

Slide method. Proceed as directed for the slide method on sheath, shift, and A-line dresses, but

106 • COMPARATIVE ANALYSIS OF PATTERN TECHNIQUES

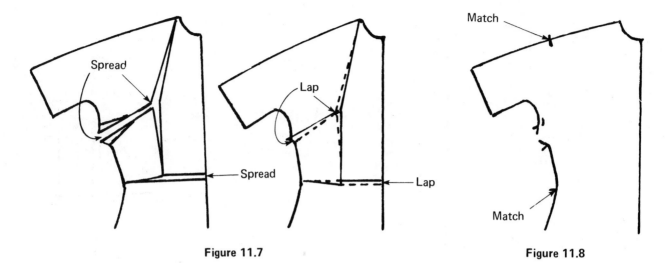

Figure 11.7

Figure 11.8

first locate the shoulder length on the pattern. Use your shoulder length measurement (see the measurement worksheet in the Appendix), and measure that amount from the neckline along the shoulder seam. Use this location as the shoulder armscye corner (Figure 11.8).

Seamline method. On kimono styles, add or trim the pattern along the underarm curve. Use a curved ruler to create a smooth line, and extend the dart stitching lines to the new side seam (Figure 11.9).

Comparison of methods. Usually the alteration needed is small, as kimono styles seldom fit close to the body at the bustline; therefore all alteration methods are acceptable. However, the internal method can give adequate width and dart depth if a large alteration is needed. Because the slide method changes the angle of the shoulder seam, patterns designed for matching stripes and plaids in this area will be askew.

Princess Styles

Internal method. On the side front pattern, cut across the pattern from the bust curve (between the bustline notches) just to the side seam. Make a second cut from the first cut just to the center of the armscye or shoulder seam (depending on the curve and location of the princess seam). Make a third cut from the first cut to the waistline and then across the pattern just to the side front seam (Figure 11.10). On the front pattern, cut across the pattern at the bustline. From the center of this cut, make a cut just to the seam at the neck–shoulder corner. Make a third cut from the first cut to the waistline and across

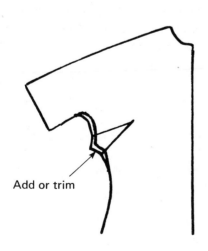

Figure 11.9

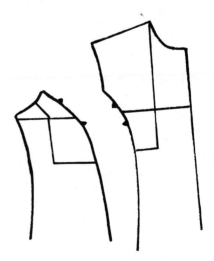

Figure 11.10

just to the side front seam. Spread or lap all cuts making the needed bustline alteration (Figure 11.11). Tape to tissue. Use a curved ruler to redraw the cutting lines.

Seamline method. Add or trim one fourth of the amount needed from the bustline curve on both the front and side front patterns (Figure 11.12). Use a curved ruler to create a smooth line.

Comparison of methods. Because the alteration is made at four locations, regardless of the method used, the amount of change is small, and both methods give similar results.

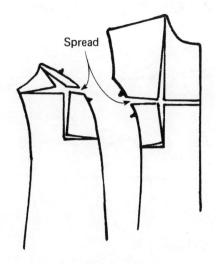

Figure 11.11

HOLLOW OR PIGEON CHEST

Internal Method

Cut and alter as you would a basic bodice, regardless of the dress style. On raglan styles, pin the front and sleeve patterns together along the upper raglan seam before making the cut. Then extend the cut across the front bodice and the front sleeve to the corner of the shoulder dart. Princess styles in which the princess seam extends to the shoulder should also be pinned together in the upper chest area before cutting. Mark the shoulder length on kimono styles before altering (Figure 11.13).

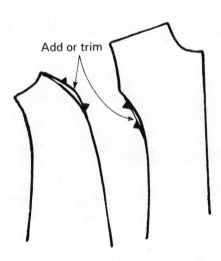

Figure 11.12

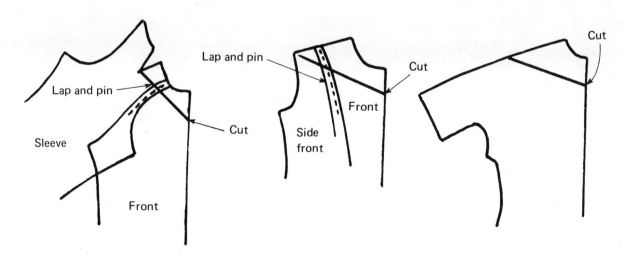

Figure 11.13

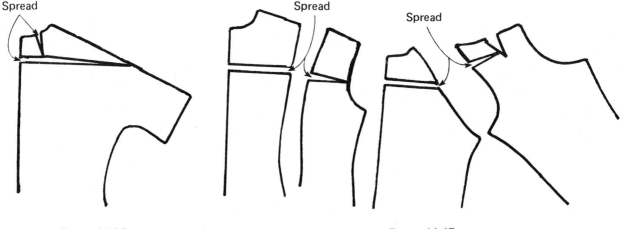

Figure 11.14   Figure 11.15

Slide Method

Pin raglan and princess styles together as described above for the internal method. Locate the shoulder length on kimono styles and use this point as the shoulder–armscye corner. Alter the pattern as you would a basic bodice, regardless of the style.

Comparison of Methods

The internal method reshapes the neckline, as needed for this figure characteristic, whereas the slide method changes only the center front length.

ROUND SHOULDERS

Internal Method

Use the following helps with the internal method, as described in Chapter 7, "Altering Bodices." Extend the horizontal line on kimono styles across the garment to the shoulder seam, and add a neckline dart (Figure 11.14). Raglan and princess styles with seams extending to the shoulder seam need only the horizontal cut, as the raglan or princess seam eliminates the need for a dart (Figure 11.15). However, if the figure problem is severe, a back neckline dart may be needed.

Slide Method

Follow the instructions given for altering a basic bodice, with these additional suggestions. Before beginning to alter a kimono style, locate the shoulder length, and use this point as the shoulder–armscye corner (Figure 11.16). Pin princess and raglan seams together before drawing the shoulder cutting line.

Comparison of Methods

The slide method does not give enough darting or width for sheath, shift, A-line, and princess styles. It is acceptable for most kimono and raglan styles, as these styles do not fit as closely to the body. The internal method is acceptable for all styles.

VERY ERECT BACK

Either the internal or the slide method may be used. If the style's seam extends to the neck or the shoulder area, pin the seam together as it will be stitched, and alter the pattern as you would alter a basic bodice. The internal method adjusts the darts or the curve of a seam (the dart's equivalent) as well as the back bodice length and the shoulder seam angle. The slide

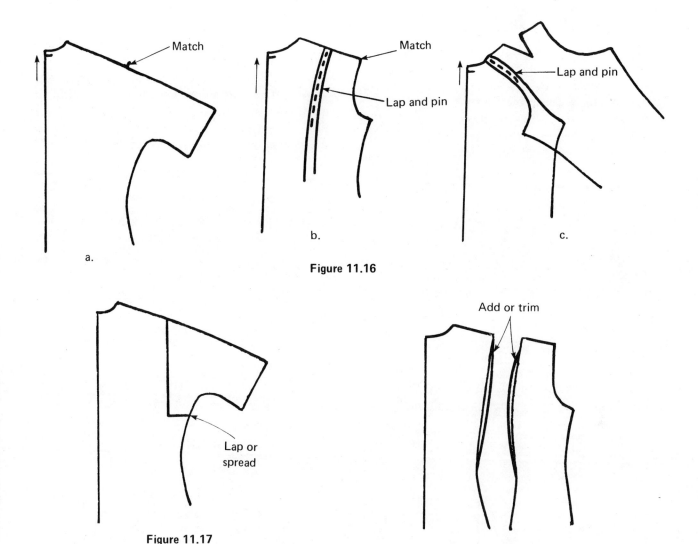

Figure 11.16

Figure 11.17

Figure 11.18

method changes only the back length and the angle of the shoulder seam; thus, it will not fit as smoothly as the internal method.

BROAD OR NARROW BACK

Internal and Slide Methods

Pin together any seam that extends to the neck or the shoulder area. Follow the basic bodice instructions for either method with the following exception: when altering kimono styles using the internal method, cut across the pattern from the underarm to a point below the shoulder blade and vertically just to the shoulder seam; lap or spread the pattern at the underarm (Figure 11.17). Redraw the underarm cutting line.

Seamline Method

Sheath, shift, and A-line patterns are altered in the same way as basic bodices. Alter princess styles that have the princess seam extending to the shoulder by adding or trimming one fourth of the width needed along the princess seam allowance on the back and the side back patterns (Figure 11.18).

110 • COMPARATIVE ANALYSIS OF PATTERN TECHNIQUES

Comparison of Methods

The internal and slide methods alter all styles satisfactorily, regardless of the amount of alteration needed. The seamline method is recommended only for princess styles in which the princess seam extends to the shoulder and for very small alterations on sheath, shift, and A-line dresses. Raglan and kimono styles are not successfully altered by the seamline method; however, the alteration is seldom needed because these styles do not fit closely to the body in the shoulder area.

NARROW AND BROAD SHOULDERS

Internal Method

Alter sheath, shift, A-line, and princess styles as you would a basic bodice. On kimono styles, cut from the shoulder length mark just to the underarm seam, and lap or spread the amount needed at the shoulder (Figure 11.19). On raglan styles, cut through the upper portion of the sleeve pattern and down the front and/or the back pattern to a line parallel with the sleeve notch. Then cut across the pattern just to the seamline at the notch (Figure 11.20). Lap or spread the sleeve pattern the amount needed at the shoulder dart. Lap or spread the front and/or the back pieces the same amount, so that the edges match when the raglan seam is sewn.

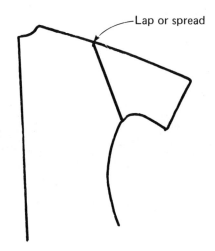

Figure 11.19

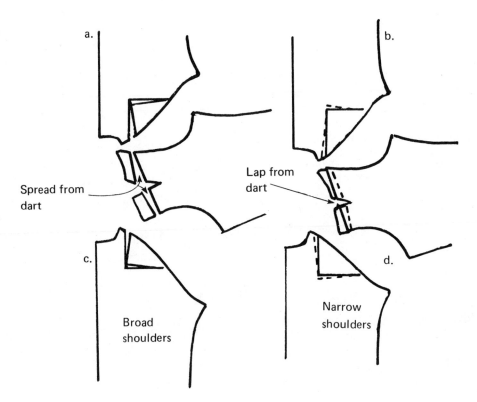

Figure 11.20

Slide Method

Alter sheath, shift, A-line, and princess styles as you would a basic bodice. On kimono styles, lay tissue under the sleeve portion, and mark the shoulder length and the bustline. Cut or draw along the neckline and for 1/4 inch (6 mm) down the shoulder seam. Slide the pattern along the shoulder seam the amount of alteration needed. Finish cutting or drawing the shoulder seam. Match the sleeve shoulder corner and slide the underarm to the original bustline mark. Continue cutting around the sleeve (Figure 11.21). Return the pattern to the original position and tape in place.

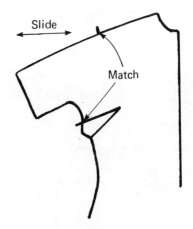

Figure 11.21

Comparison of Methods

Both methods change the shoulder length; however, on sheath, shift, A-line, and princess styles, the slide method also changes the length of the side seam. Kimono styles altered by either method are similar. Raglan styles can be altered only by the internal method.

SQUARE AND SLOPING SHOULDERS

Sheath, shift, A-line and princess styles can be altered by either the internal or the slide method for basic bodices. Kimono styles can be altered by any method listed below, and raglan sleeves can be altered only by the seamline method.

Internal Method

Alter kimono styles by cutting the pattern from the shoulder-length mark to the underarm curve. Raise the sleeve portion for square shoulders, and lower it for sloping shoulders (Figure 11.22). Redraw the shoulder and the underarm cutting lines.

Slide Method

Pin tissue under the shoulder and the sleeve portions of the pattern. Cut or draw along the neckline and for 1/4 inch (6 mm) down the shoulder edge. Mark the bustline, the shoulder-length

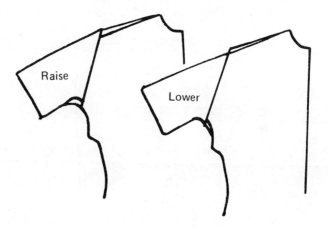

Figure 11.22

point, and the amount of alteration needed above or below the shoulder-length point. Unpin the tissue. Match the neck–shoulder corner, and slide the shoulder-length point to the alteration mark. Cut or draw along the shoulder edge between these points (Figure 11.23). Keep the shoulder-length marks matched, and slide the bustline to the original mark. Cut or draw around the sleeve to the bustline. Return the pattern to the original position, and tape in place.

Seamline Method

Redraw the cutting line, raising or lowering the shoulder from the neckline to the shoulder-length

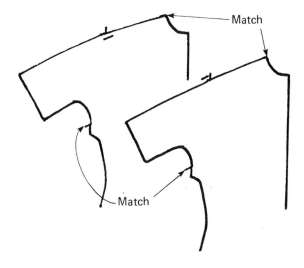

Figure 11.23

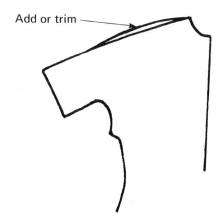

Figure 11.24

Figure 11.25

mark (Figure 11.24). Use a curved ruler to draw a smooth cutting line. On raglan styles, make the alteration by lengthening or shortening the shoulder dart (Figure 11.25).

Comparison of Methods

All methods adequately change the depth of the armscye when you are altering for square shoulders. If the shoulder seam is straight instead of curved, the slide and seamline methods distort the line of the shoulder seam when you are altering for sloping shoulders. Therefore the internal method should be used on these patterns. The internal and slide methods also raise or lower the whole sleeve, an operation that may be desirable if you are matching stripes or plaids.

WAISTLINE CHANGES

Before making waistline alterations consider changing the width of the waistline darts. Figures that are heavier through the waistline in comparison with the bust and hip measurements need narrower darts and less curve at the side seam. The opposite is true of figures that are small through the waist. In close fitting garments, these figures need wider darts and more curve at the side seam.

The following instructions are written for making the complete alteration at the side seam; however, on a princess style, the alteration may be made equally at the side and princess seams. Thus, if the waistline alteration is to be made only at the side seam, divide the alteration needed by 4, but if it is to be made equally at the side seams and at the front and back princess seams, divide by 12.

Internal Method

To alter the waistline on any style that does not have a waistline seam, use the techniques you learned when altering bodices as well as skirts. Cut horizontally from the side waistline for about 2 inches (5 cm). Then cut diagonally just to the seamlines at the underarm and the hipline (Figure 11.26). Spread or lap the diagonal cuts, altering the waistline width as desired.

ALL-IN-ONE ALTERING DRESSES • 113

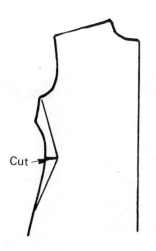

Figure 11.26

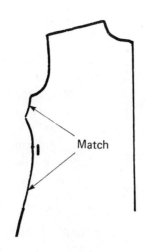

Figure 11.27

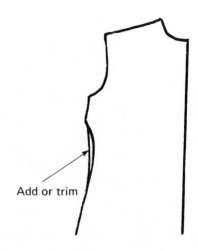

Figure 11.28

Slide Method

Place tissue under the side waistline area, and mark the bust, the waist, and the hipline on the tissue. Also mark the desired waistline alteration. Match the hipline, and slide the waistline to the alteration mark. Cut or draw the lower side cutting line. Keeping the waistline marks matched, slide the bustline to the original mark (Figure 11.27). Cut or draw between these points. Return the pattern to the original location, and tape in place.

Seamline Method

Add tissue if the margin is insufficient. Mark the width change needed at the waistline. With a curved ruler, reshape the waistline curve, tapering it to the original cutting line at the bustline and the hipline (Figure 11.28).

Comparison of Methods

All methods give similar results, especially when the alteration is small. Be sure to combine one of the above methods with a change in the dart width.

HIPLINE CHANGES

Alterations in the hip and the thigh area can be made by any method given for basic skirts, Chapter 10, with this addition. When using the internal method for A-line styles, cut from the hem to about 4 inches (10 cm) below the waistline and across through the side seam (Figure 11.29). Spread or lap the lower side portion equally from hipline to hem and redraw the side seam at the waistline.

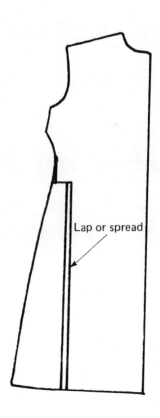

Figure 11.29

114 • COMPARATIVE ANALYSIS OF PATTERN TECHNIQUES

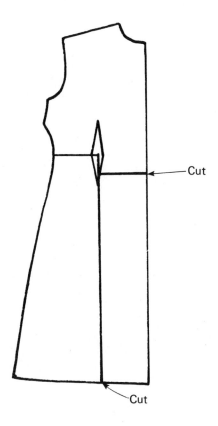

Figure 11.30

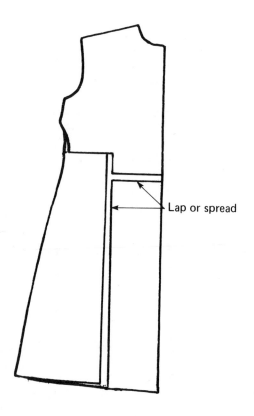

Figure 11.31

PROMINENT OR FLAT STOMACH

Before using any of the following methods on dress patterns without waistline seams, consider whether redesigning the darts would correct the fit of the garment. Darts must both be directed toward the fullest part of the curve and be made short enough to stop before reaching the fullest part of the curve. Fuller stomach curves necessitate deeper or wider darts. If your stomach curve varies from the average, styles that fit loosely through the waistline and stomach area will be more pleasing than close-fitting styles.

Internal Method

Make a cut parallel with the center front from the hem to the waistline through the waistline dart and then across to the side seam. Also cut across the pattern from the first cut to the center front at the fullest part of the curve (Figure 11.30). Shorten or lengthen the center front the amount needed, and lap or spread the vertical cut (Figure 11.31). Redraw the side seam at the waistline, and correct the hemline. Redraw all dart lines. On princess styles, the center front pattern should be lengthened, and the side front pattern should be altered as instructed above (Figure 11.32).

Slide Method

Lengthen the center front hemline the amount needed, and mark the original bust, the waist, and the side hemline. Also mark the alteration needed at the side waistline, parallel with the stomach curve. Match the side hem corners and slide the pattern to the alteration mark. Cut or draw along the lower side cutting-line. Keep the alteration marks matched, and slide the pattern to the bustline mark (Figure 11.33). Cut or draw between these points. Return the pattern to the original position, and tape in place. On princess styles, the length must be changed on the front and side front patterns, and the width change is made on the side front.

Seamline Method

Add tissue if the margin is insufficient. Mark the width change needed along the side cutting line.

ALL-IN-ONE ALTERING DRESSES • 115

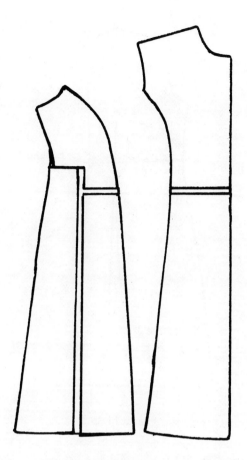

Figure 11.32

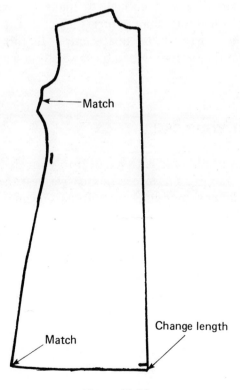

Figure 11.33

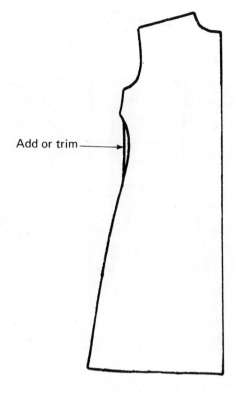

Figure 11.34

With a curved or shaped ruler, redraw the side cutting line, tapering it to the original at the bustline and the hemline (Figure 11.34).

Comparison of Methods

Any method can be used if the increase is small and if no length alteration is necessary. The seamline method changes only the width, whereas the other two methods also alter the length. The seamline method may be the easiest to use on princess styles because a small alteration can be made at six locations: at both front side seams and at all four edges of the princess seam. The internal method is the easiest to use if large length and width alterations are needed on sheath and A-line styles.

PROMINENT OR FLAT SEAT

Use one of the methods given for altering a prominent or flat stomach, but use the dress back pattern (and the side back for princess

116 • COMPARATIVE ANALYSIS OF PATTERN TECHNIQUES

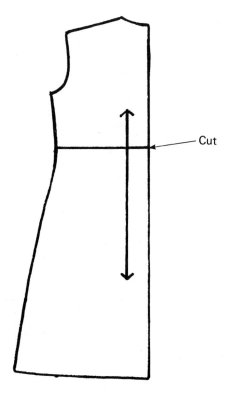

Figure 11.35

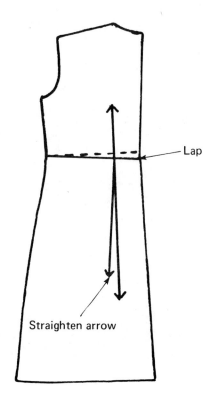

Figure 11.36

styles), and make the alteration at or parallel to the fullest part of the seat curve.

SWAYBACK

Internal Method

Cut across the back pattern and the side back pattern on princess styles below the waistline from the center back just to the side seam (Figure 11.35). Lap the center back the amount needed, tapering to nothing at the side seam. As this alteration shifts the skirt portion off-grain, straighten the grainline arrow and the dart stitching lines (Figure 11.36). This is the only method applicable to this alteration. If the figure problem is severe enough to make the needed alteration more than 1 inch (2.5 cm), the hang of the skirt will be unattractive. In this case, design the pattern with a back waistline seam.

TEST YOUR SKILL

After altering the pattern, fit it to your figure. If the alterations have been extensive, test the pattern in muslin or gingham before using an expensive fabric.

12

Altering Pants

Know your figure characteristics and body measurements before making any alterations. As pants are generally fitted very closely to the body, and as few pattern pieces are used to cover large areas, correct altering techniques are critical. After the pattern is altered and the fabric is cut, all alterations must be handled through seams and darts. Also the crotch area cannot be raised a large amount without the pants' becoming too short.

Various figure characteristics and two or three methods of altering for each characteristic are discussed in this chapter, from which you can learn various alteration techniques and evaluate each method.

Before attempting to use any method, be sure to read Chapter 5, "Measurements, Proportions, and Body Curves," which explains how to take pattern and body measurements and how to recognize figure characteristics. Alterations should be made only where changes are needed, and both the pattern and the paper used for the alteration must be kept flat; otherwise the alteration will not be accurate.

CROTCH DEPTH ALTERATIONS

The first adjustment made on a pants pattern should be the alteration of the crotch depth, if it is needed, as several other alterations depend on having the crotch depth measurement correct. Even though the total pants length (full side length) may be the same as the length indicated on the pattern, your figure may have a longer or a shorter crotch-depth measurement than the pattern. It is possible for two people to wear pants that are 33 inches (84 cm) in length one of whom has a short body (needing a short crotch depth) and long legs and the other of whom has a long body and short legs. Of course, the final patterns for these two people would be different.

To determine the needed amount of crotch depth adjustment for women, measure as directed in Chapter 5. To this measurement add the following amounts of ease. If your hip measurement is less than 35 inches (89 cm), add 1/4 inch (6 mm) ease. If it is between 35 and 38 inches (89 and 96.5 cm), add 1/2 inch (13 mm) ease. For hips between 38 and 40 inches (96.5–102 cm), add 3/4 inch (2 cm) ease, and if the measurement is over 40 inches (102 cm), add 1 inch (2.5 cm) of ease. The crotch depth on the *front* pattern piece should be the same as this total. If it is not, the difference indicates the amount of alteration needed.

For men, the crotch depth is not measured as it is for women's pants. Because men do not have the sharply defined waistline that women have, they can wear their pants with the waistband at various places below or even above the waistline. Determine the body measurement by measuring for the desired location of the waistband seam to the table top and add 1/2 inch (13 mm) of ease. Determine the body measurement by measuring from the desired waistband seamline to the crotch line. If these two measurements are not the same, the difference is the amount of pattern alteration needed.

Another method for obtaining the men's body measurement is to measure a well-fitting pair of pants that have a similar cut. Measure the side seam from the bottom of the waistband to the hem, and the inseam from the crotch point to the hem. The difference between these two measurements should be the same as the crotch depth measurement on the pattern. If it is not, the difference is the amount of pattern alteration needed.

Internal Method

Most patterns have a printed line or guide across the hip area that indicates where crotch depth adjustments should be made. If this line does not appear on your pattern, draw an adjustment line across the front and back pieces just above the hipline at a right angle to the grainline arrows (Figure 12.1). Be sure to determine the amount of adjustment needed by measuring the *front* pattern piece, regardless of the pattern alteration method used.

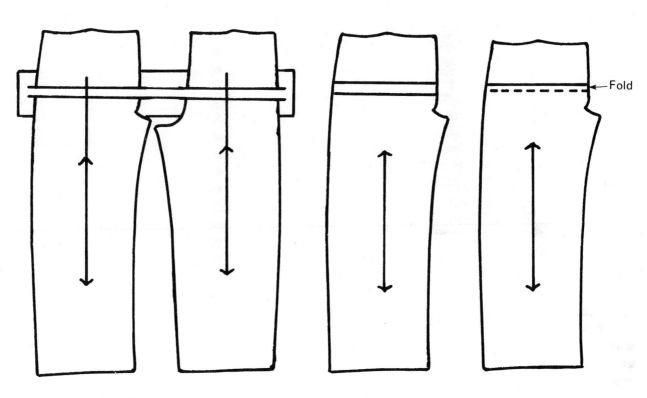

Figure 12.1

Figure 12.2

Figure 12.3

Figure 12.4

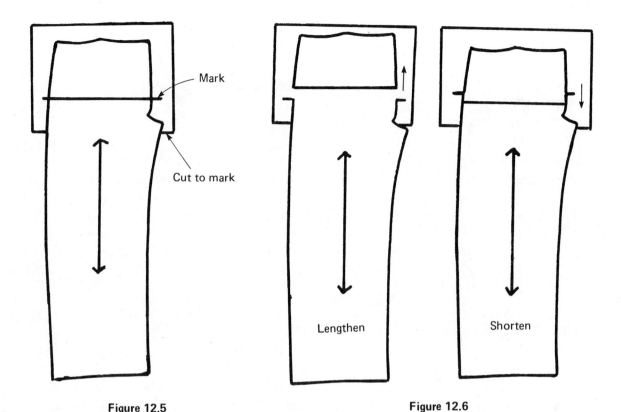

Figure 12.5

Figure 12.6

To *lengthen* the crotch depth, cut the pattern apart on the length-adjustment line. On tissue paper, draw two parallel lines, making the distance between the lines equal to the amount of additional length needed. Tape the upper part of the pattern to one of these lines. With a ruler, extend the grainline arrow onto the tissue paper. Tape the lower part of the pattern to the second line, matching the grainline arrow (Figure 12.2). Redraw the cutting lines at the side and the center back or front seams. Be sure to make identical changes on the front and back pattern pieces. For example, if the front pattern needs to be lengthened 1/2 inch (1.3 cm), also lengthen the back pattern 1/2 inch (1.3 cm).

To *shorten*, draw a second line across the pattern, parallel to the original crotch-depth adjustment line, making the distance between the lines equal to the amount of alteration needed (Figure 12.3). Fold along one line, and bring the fold to the second line, creating a tuck. Tape the tuck in place, and redraw the cutting line at the side and the center front or back seams (Figure 12.4). Be sure to make identical changes on the front and back pattern pieces.

Slide Method

If the pattern does not have a crotch-depth adjustment line, draw a line across the front and back pattern pieces just above the hipline and at right angles to the grainline arrows. Pin tissue paper under the upper portion of the pattern. Cut the tissue paper along the side and the crotch cutting-lines of the pattern to the crotch-depth alteration line. Mark the ends of the alteration line on the tissue paper (Figure 12.5). Unpin the pattern and slide it *up* the amount needed *to lengthen* the crotch depth or *down* the amount needed *to shorten* the crotch depth (Figure 12.6). Repin and cut the tissue paper along the upper crotch, side, and waistline cutting-lines of the pattern. Transfer the dart markings to the tissue paper. Unpin and return the pattern to the original position. Tape in place (Figure 12.7).

Seamline Method

Pin tissue paper under the upper portion of the pattern if the margin is not sufficient. Measure up or down the amount needed from the waist-

120 • COMPARATIVE ANALYSIS OF PATTERN TECHNIQUES

line cutting line and draw a new waistline (Figure 12.8). Draw the center and side cutting lines and the dart stitching lines the same width as the original pattern.

Comparison of Methods

Patterns altered correctly with any of these three methods should be identical. However, if the crotch depth change is greater than 1 inch (2.5 cm), it may be difficult to maintain waistline shape and width by the seamline method. The internal method is the easiest of the three methods for shortening the crotch depth, but it is slightly more time consuming for lengthening. You may also prefer a particular method over another because you find it more efficient and/or accurate.

LEG LENGTH ALTERATIONS

Altering the leg length is an easy alteration, and it can be made at any point after the crotch depth alteration is completed. Recheck the length measurement along the side seam by measuring the full length of the pants and deducting the seam

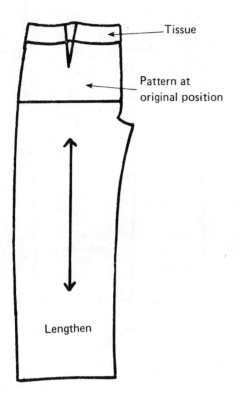

Figure 12.7

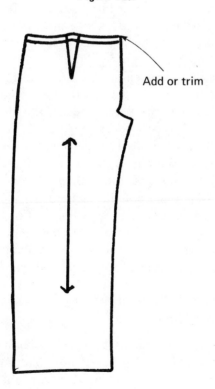

Figure 12.8

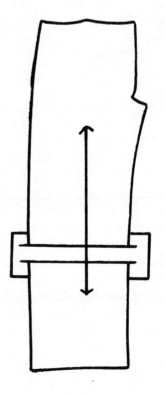

Figure 12.9

allowances and the hem depth. Compare this measurement with the body measurement, and alter accordingly.

Internal Method

Use the length-adjustment markings on the pant leg, or draw a line across the leg at right angles to the grainline arrow, just below the knee area on flared, straight, or tapered styles. Above-the-knee styles should be altered just above the hemline, and bell bottoms may need altering above and below the knee, depending on where the figure differs from the pattern. To *lengthen,* cut the pattern apart on the length-adjustment line. On tissue paper, draw two parallel lines, making the distance between the lines equal to the amount of additional length needed. Tape the upper part of the pattern to one of these lines. With a ruler, extend the grainline arrow onto the tissue paper, and tape the lower part of the pattern to the second line, aligning the grainline arrow (Figure 12.9). Draw in the cutting lines along the side and the inseam. Be sure to make identical changes on the front and back pattern pieces.

To *shorten,* draw a second line across the pattern, parallel to the original length-adjustment line, making the distance between the lines equal to the amount needed to shorten the pattern. Fold along one line, and bring the fold to the second line, creating a tuck. Tape the tuck in place and redraw the cutting lines at both sides of the leg pattern (Figure 12.10). Make identical changes on the front and back pattern pieces.

Slide Method

Either to lengthen or to shorten the leg length, pin tissue paper under the hem of the pants. Cut through the tissue paper, following the bottom edge of the pants and for about 1/4 inch (6 mm) up both sides. Unpin the pattern. To *lengthen,* slide the pattern *up* the additional length needed, measuring at both side seams to ensure that the added amount is even. Tape the tissue to the pattern. With a ruler (use a curved ruler for bell bottoms and for flares), redraw the side cutting lines from the hem edge to the knee area (Figure 12.11).

To *shorten,* pin tissue under the pattern, and cut, following the hem edge as instructed for lengthening. Unpin the pattern and slide it *down* the amount needed. Pin the pattern to the tissue

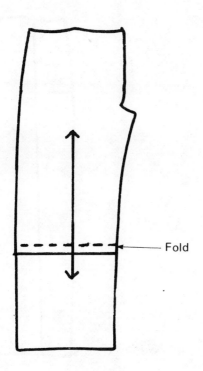

Figure 12.10

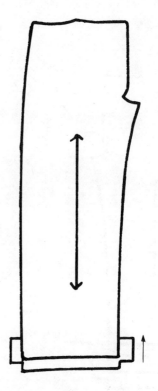

Figure 12.11

paper, and recheck the length. If correct, fold up the lower portion, and tape in place (Figure 12.12). With a ruler (use a curved ruler for bell bottoms and flares), redraw the side cutting lines from the hem edge to the knee area.

Seamline Method

Pin tissue paper under the lower portion of the pattern if the margin is not sufficient. Extend the grainline arrow to the bottom of the tissue paper. Measure up or down from the bottom edge to lengthen or shorten the pattern (Figure 12.13). Draw a new cutting line following these measurements. Be sure that the measurement at each side of the pattern is the same distance from the grainline arrow as the original marking so that the leg width is not changed. With a ruler, redraw the side cutting lines. Check the pattern width by remeasuring the new and the original patterns across the hem. This step is especially important if the pants style is tapered, flared, or belled.

Comparison of Methods

Patterns altered correctly with any of these three methods should be identical; however, it is more difficult to maintain the leg shape for tapered, flared, or belled styles if the seamline or slide method is used. If you want to shorten straight pants legs, the internal and seamline methods are easier than the slide method.

HIP AND THIGH WIDTH ALTERATIONS

Pants patterns are easiest to alter when purchased according to the hip measurement; however, alterations are sometimes needed. The weight and extendability of the fabric (crosswise stretch) also varies the amount of the hip and thigh adjustment needed. Most patterns should be altered and tested in firm fabric so that the pattern is made as large in circumference as needed. Stretchy fabrics with less firmness can be fitted closer to the hip and thigh area later, when the garment is sewn.

Before altering the hip or thigh width, divide the amount of change needed by 4, as the alteration will be made on both side seams and on both the back and the front pattern pieces. Measure down the side of the body from the waistline to the widest point of the hip or thigh to determine at what point the alteration is needed. On the

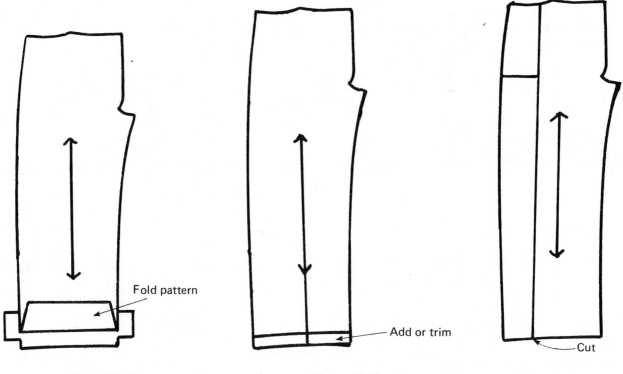

Figure 12.12   Figure 12.13   Figure 12.14

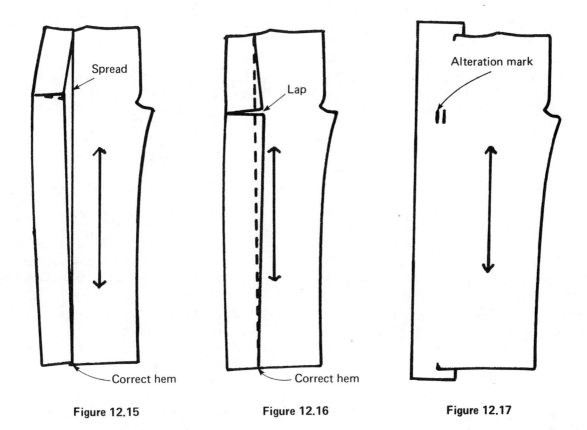

Figure 12.15 **Figure 12.16** **Figure 12.17**

pattern, measure the same distance down from the waistline seam, and mark so that hip or thigh adjustments can be made at this location.

Internal Method

Draw a line parallel to the grainline from the waistline to the bottom of the pants at about 2 inches (5 cm) from the side seam. Cut from the hem along this line to the waistline seam. At the fullest part of the hip or thigh, cut horizontally from the vertical cut to the side seam (Figure 12.14). To *increase,* tape tissue paper under the larger portion of the pattern along the vertical cut. Spread the vertical cut the amount needed at the fullest part of the hip or thigh and tape the upper side portion in place. Bring the vertical cut back together at the bottom of the pants. This procedure permits the horizontal cut to lap, shortening the side section (Figure 12.15). Correct the hemline by adding the needed length to the side section. If a sharp curve or bulge forms at the hip area of the side seam, round off the side cutting line. Make identical alterations on both the back and the front pattern pieces.

To *decrease* the hip or thigh circumference, cut the pattern as directed for increasing. Lap the vertical cut the amount needed at the hip or thigh area, and tape the upper side portion in place. Return the bottom of the vertical cut to the original hem width, spreading the horizontal cut (Figure 12.16). Correct the hemline by trimming off the excess length on the side section. If the side seam is indented at the horizontal slash, redraw the side cutting line to create a smooth curve. Make identical alterations on both the back and the front pattern pieces.

Slide Method

Pin tissue paper under the outer portion of the side seam area, extending from above the waistline to below the hem. On the tissue, mark the pattern cutting line at the lower edge, the side-waistline corner, and at the fullest part of the hip or thigh area. Also mark the amount of increase or decrease needed in the hip or thigh area (Figure 12.17).

Cut the tissue that extends above the waistline, following the pattern and for about 1/4 inch (6 mm) down the side cutting line. Unpin the pattern. Match the side waistline corners, and slide the pattern to meet the desired hip or thigh mark. Pin and cut following the pattern from the waistline to the hip or thigh mark. Unpin the pattern and match the hip or thigh marks and the original side cutting line at the hem of the pants. Finish cutting the side seam (Figure 12.18). Unpin and return the pattern to its original position. Tape in place. Be sure to make identical alterations on both the back and front pattern pieces.

Seamline Method

Mark the change needed (one fourth of the increase or decrease) on the pattern, attaching additional tissue if necessary. Using a curved ruler, redraw the hip and thigh curve, tapering to the original cutting line at the knee and at the waistline. Be sure to make identical alterations on the back and front pattern pieces (Figure 12.19).

Comparison of Methods

Patterns altered correctly with any of these three methods should be identical; however, the slide method may be the easiest and the most accurate because the original side cutting edge of the pattern is used.

Note: If a pants alteration needs to be made for a high hip bone or for hip curves that vary noticeably on each side, use the alteration techniques for this figure characteristic described in Chapter 10, "Altering Basic Skirts."

STOMACH OR SEAT ALTERATIONS

If you have a large stomach, pants will be tight below the waist, across the stomach. The waistline will pull down at the center front, and the side seams will pull toward the front. Thus the front pants pattern needs to be increased in both width and length.

If you have a large seat, the pants will wrinkle across the back, and the side seams will pull toward the back. Both the length and the width of the back pants pattern must be increased. If you have a small seat, the pants will sag across the back and look baggy.

Determine the length of the alteration needed for a prominent stomach or seat by comparing

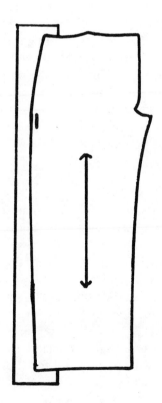

Figure 12.18

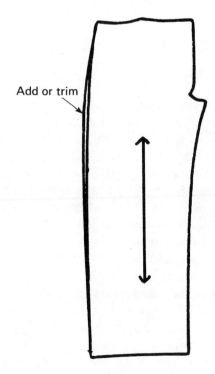

Figure 12.19

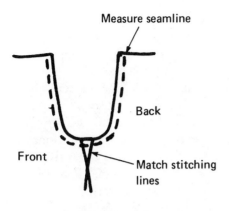

Figure 12.20

the total crotch length of the pattern with the body measurement. Pin the pattern together at the crotch point, matching the leg stitching lines, and measure by holding the tape on edge following the seamline (Figure 12.20). Measure from the front-waist stitching line around the crotch seam to the back-waist stitching line. The pattern measurement and the total crotch-length measurement should be identical. If the body measurement is greater, look at your figure from a side view to see if your stomach or your seat is the most prominent or if the curves are about equal. Note the amount of increase needed and whether it should be added to the front or the back pattern piece. If your body measurement is less than the pattern measurement, recheck these measurements as well as the crotch depth alteration.

For men's pants, it is easier to determine the total crotch length needed by comparing the pattern's total length measurement with the crotch measurement of a favorite pair of pants. Use a pair of pants that are similar in style and that have a comfortable crotch length. Measure the crotch seam on the inside of the pants from the waistband seam in front, around the crotch, and up to the waistband seam in back. This measurement should be the same as the pattern measurement; otherwise an alteration is needed.

Determine the *width* adjustment needed by measuring the figure from side seam to side seam across the fullest part of the stomach or seat curve. Also measure how low the curve is on the body by measuring the prominent stomach curve from the center front waistline to the fullest part of the curve (the point where the width measurement was taken). Measure the length location of a flat or prominent seat by measuring from the back waistline, midway between the side and center seams, to the fullest part of the seat curve. Take corresponding measurements on the pattern, remembering that ease must be added to the figure's width measurement. Do *not* add ease to any pattern measurements.

Internal Method

Draw a vertical line parallel to the grainline through the center of the dart (or if there are two darts, draw the line through the dart closest to the center seam) from the waist to the hemline. For a prominent stomach, draw a horizontal line from the center seam to the side, 3 inches (7.5 cm) below the waistline on the front pattern piece. For a flat or prominent seat, draw a horizontal line just above the hipline where the seat is fullest on the back pattern piece. Cut on the vertical line from the waist to the stitching line at the hemline and on the horizontal line from the center front or back to the side seam (Figure 12.21).

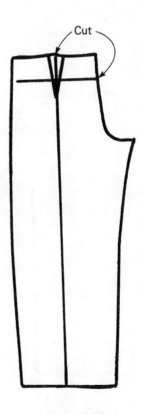

Figure 12.21

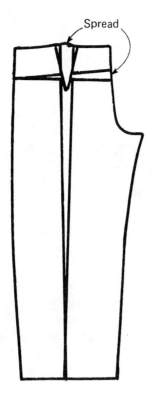

Figure 12.22

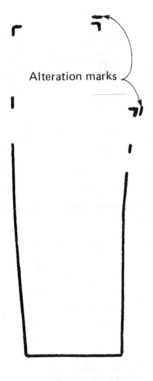

Figure 12.23

Spread or lap the vertical cut at the fullest part of the stomach or the seat, half of the needed width. Also spread or lap the horizontal cut the total amount needed at the center front or back seam. Tape the pattern, using tissue paper if needed, and correct the cutting lines at the center and side seam edges (Figure 12.22). Redraw the darts, or add an additional dart close to the side seam to correct the waistline measurement. Correct the grainline, if necessary, in the upper portion of the pattern.

Slide Method

Pin tissue paper under the upper portion of the pants pattern, extending from the waistline to below the crotch point. On the tissue, mark the pattern cutting line at the side hipline, the side-waistline corner, the center-waistline corner, the crotch point, and the inseam at the lower edge of the tissue. Also mark these alterations on the tissue—half of the length alteration needed above or below the center waistline and the other half of the length alteration needed at the crotch point (Figure 12.23).

Match the side waistline corners, and slide the pattern up or down to the length alteration mark at the center front or back; pin. Cut or draw along the waistline cutting edge and down the center-seam cutting edge for 1/4 inch (6 mm). Unpin the pattern. Match the crotch corner to the crotch alteration mark, and slide the center waistline corner to the center seam edge. Pin and cut or draw along the center seam edge to the crotch point. Match the crotch points and slide the pattern to the inseam edge. Pin and cut or draw the upper leg inseam edge (Figure 12.24). Return the pattern to its original position, and tape in place. Correct the dart stitching lines to restore the waistline measurement. If the width of the waistline dart is increased greatly, divide the amount and create an additional dart.

Seamline Method

Increase or decrease the length of the center back or front pattern piece half of the amount needed at the waistline, tapering to the original cutting line at the side seam. Increase or decrease the

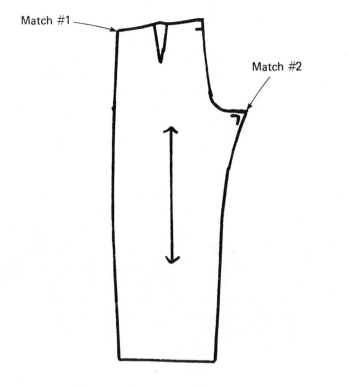
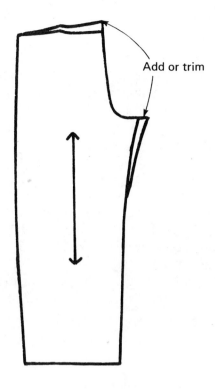

Figure 12.24 **Figure 12.25**

other half needed at the crotch point by increasing or decreasing the pattern width. Taper the new cutting line to the original inseam, midway between the crotch point and the knee area (Figure 12.25). If increased or decreased width is needed in the seat area, draw this change along the side seam as instructed for increasing the hip or thigh area, tapering to the original at the crotch curve. If increased width is needed for a prominent stomach, follow the directions given for increasing the waistline in Chapter 10, "Altering Basic Skirts."

Comparison of Methods

If correctly done, the slide and seamline methods should be identical; however, be careful not to lower or raise the crotch point when making the prominent stomach or seat alteration. Excessive lowering of the crotch point prevents the pattern from fitting the adjoining piece along the inseam, and raising the crotch point excessively creates wrinkles along the inseam. The internal method is usable for a high, prominent stomach, but it greatly changes the waistline circumference when you are altering for a prominent or small seat, creating an additional dart or waistline problem. The internal method also increases width in the thigh and hip areas, which may not be needed.

Note: The crotch curve is lower in back than in front because the body curves lower under the seat than under the stomach. Thus, the front inseam will be approximately 1/2 inch (1.3 cm) longer than the back inseam. When sewing, stitch the seams together from the hem to the knee; then stretch the back inseam to match the front inseam from the knee to the crotch.

SWAYBACK

On figures with a swayback or a flat back, pants wrinkle horizontally between the waistline and the seat. If the pants are quite loose, this horizontal wrinkle may drop below the seat, giving a droopy look. The pattern length between the waistline and the seat must be shortened. Follow the information given in Chapter 10, "Altering Basic Skirts," for swayback alteration techniques.

DROPPED SEAT

Flesh deposits shift as a person ages, creating a dropped or lowered seat. This figure characteristic may also accompany a swayback. Pants on figures with a dropped seat form diagonal wrinkles from the back of the leg above the knee to the side seam or the side seat area.

Correct by restitching the back crotch curve, making the seam allowance 1/4 inch (6 mm) deeper (scoop out) at the curve (Figure 12.26) and tapering to the original seamlines at the crotch point and above the back crotch curve. Trim the excess seam allowance and try on the pants for fit. A second 1/4 inch (6 mm) may also be removed if necessary. Most figures with a dropped seat must also have a pattern alteration for swayback.

HOLLOW PUBIC AREA

If vertical or cupping wrinkles form along the front crotch curve, excess fabric needs to be removed because of a hollow pubic area. Correct by restitching the front crotch curve, making the seam allowance deeper (more squared) above and at the crotch curve. Taper this stitching to the original seamlines at the waistline and at the crotch point (Figure 12.27). Trim the excess seam allowance and try on the pants for fit. Repeat the alteration if necessary. This alteration must be made before a fly zipper is inserted.

WAISTLINE ALTERATIONS

Adjusting the waistline circumference is often necessary if pants patterns were purchased by the hip measurement. Make alterations following the techniques given in Chapter 10, "Altering Basic Skirts." Pants patterns for men have an extra-wide seam allowance at the center back for waistline adjustments. This feature may eliminate the need for altering the waistline.

CULOTTES AND HOSTESS PANTS

Culottes and hostess pants are altered by the same techniques as described in this chapter for basic pants. Besides the obvious style differences

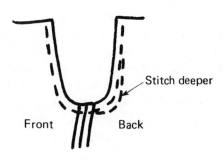

Figure 12.26

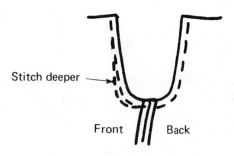

Figure 12.27

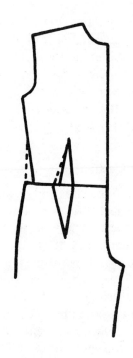

Figure 12.28

of flare and additional width at the hipline, culottes and hostess pants may have a longer crotch depth.

JUMPSUITS

A jumpsuit combines a bodice and a pants pattern with or without a waistline seam. Alter by using the techniques described in this chapter for the pants and the alterations described in Chapter 7, "Altering Basic Bodices," for the top. If the pattern does not have a waistline seam, cut it apart at the waistline and alter each part separately. Then retape the pattern. After altering, if the top and pants are not the same width at the waistline, adjust the darts of both patterns (Figure 12.28). Be sure each section is labeled as to back and front, above and below the waistline before cutting in order to avoid joining a front top pattern to a back pants pattern.

A MASTER PATTERN

Once you have altered a basic pants pattern, cut and sew it in firm fabric. If a commercial pattern for knits was used, make a fitting garment in stable knitted fabric. If a pattern suitable for woven fabric was used, stitch it in firm, closely woven fabric. Fit the garment to your figure, checking for comfort and appearance when walking, sitting, and bending. Use the fitting information in Chapter 4 for evaluating the garment.

After the fit has been refined, transfer each adjustment to the paper pattern. Test the pants pattern in another fabric to check the fit. After the fit is refined as much as possible, make a master pattern in one of the commercial pattern fabrics. This master pattern should not be used for fitting, but it is very useful when you are evaluating the alterations needed on various commercial patterns. Just place the commercial pattern on top of the master pattern, matching the crotch lines and keeping the grainlines parallel. Measure and note the alterations needed in each area.

Also save the fitting garment, as it should be useful for determining whether your figure has changed. Try on the fitting garment before making each additional pair of pants to see if there has been a weight change or a change in your body curves. If the change warrants additional alterations, alter the master pattern, and sew another fitting garment.

The master pattern can also be used to make style variations: tapered, flared, or belled legs; yokes; and pants of various lengths. Study the design possibilities in Chapter 19, and change the basic pattern accordingly. Also observe the design possibilities in ready-to-wear garments for ideas. Continue to experiment, enjoy yourself and keep learning.

Part Three
Drafting Your Own Basic Pattern

13
General Drafting Techniques

Both the enthusiasm and the creativity of the beginning pattern maker are often curtailed when the opening lines of the instructions say, "start with a pattern that *fits you well.*" If you have achieved the fit you desire in a commercial pattern using the alteration techniques described earlier, this pattern may be transformed into a block basic and used for designing. But do not be discouraged if you do not seem to fit the model developed by pattern companies! Persons with fitting problems created by shape, posture, or both can often save hours of alterations, basting, and fitting on garments by drafting a basic pattern from personal measurements. Seldom does a person with significant figure irregularities find individualized fit in a commercial pattern based on averages.

In pattern drafting, you will use comprehensive measurements. These measurements must be precisely taken as described in Chapter 5. They are used to establish the desired pattern lines.

The techniques of pattern drafting presented here are based on body proportions. For ease of presentation and understanding, a model figure with the following measurements has been used: height—64 inches, 5'4" (162.5 cm); chest—36 inches (91.5 cm); bust—38 inches (96.5 cm); waist—26 inches (66 cm); hip—38 inches (96.5 cm). For persons preferring to work with the metric system of measurement, a conversion table is provided in the Appendix. This table gives centimeter equivalents to the inch measurements to the nearest tenth.

As you begin drafting, be sure to use *your measurements* rather than the 5'4" figure selected for illustrative purposes. Substituting your measurements in the drafting instructions involves the use of fractions. The math involved may be simplified if you convert the parts of an inch to decimal equivalents. You can then use a calculator for substituting your measurements. A chart of decimal equivalents of parts of an inch is provided in the Appendix.

SUPPLIES AND EQUIPMENT

You will need a quantity of paper for drafting. This paper must be strong and transparent and must have a slick surface. Suitable paper can often be purchased in quantity from office suppliers, blueprint or architectural firms, or medical supply houses. The width of a roll should be a minimum of 20 inches (51 cm), preferably wider to eliminate the need for splicing in the pattern drafts. Comparative shopping for quality and price is recommended.

For the fitting shell to be made from the drafts, a firm *woven* fabric is recommended. Fabrics including muslin, broadcloth, or gingham are good choices. These fabrics have the obvious grainlines needed to check fit. You will want to select a plain color of medium to light value so that the reference lines you place on the shell can be easily seen. If using gingham, select a yarn-dyed fabric rather than one with the checks

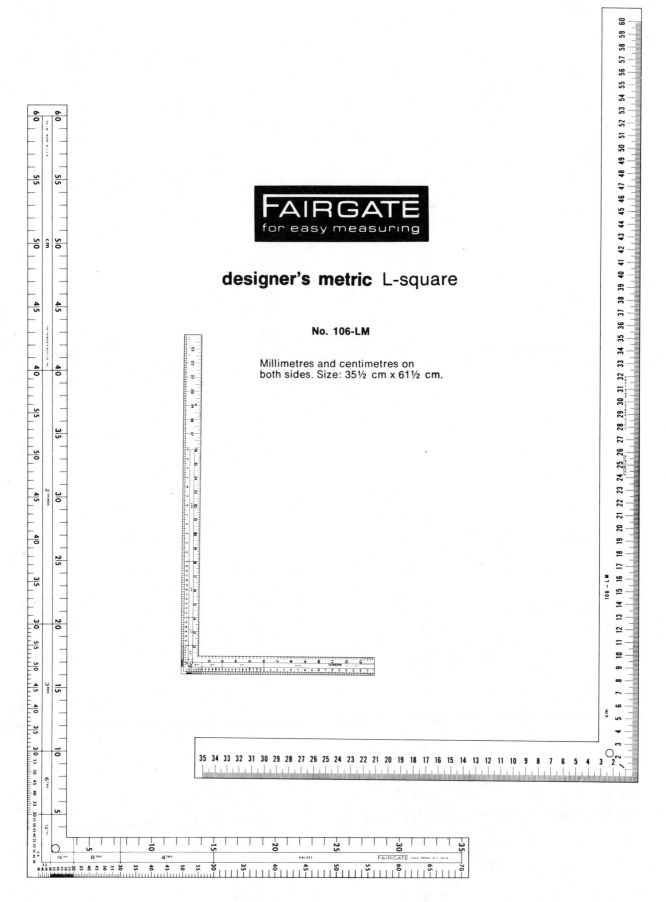

Figure 13.1 Designer L-square

printed on the fabric, so that you can achieve grainline perfection in your fitting.

The sloper (permanent basic pattern) requires a medium-weight poster board. Some students have found it helpful to reproduce their basic drafts on manila folders. The slopers are thus easily folded and more compact for carrying to class and storing. Markings must be visible on the sloper so medium to light colors are suggested.

As in any skilled craft, the tools you work with are very important to the success of your projects. Because good drafting tools represent a sizable investment, it is recommended that you invest in the basic pieces first and add to your collection as you become familiar with the characteristics of the tools and can select those with the features you desire. Tempered-aluminum measuring tools are the most widely used in pattern drafting. Wood, plastic, and heavier metals are also available.

First on your tool list should be a designer's L square. The preferred size is 24" × 14." Size 12" × 20" is also acceptable (see Figure 13.1). These are available in both inches and metric (35.5 × 61.5 cm). Professional designers often use a half-scale L square, which allows them to work in small scale such as half-size with 1/2 inch equaling 1 inch (see Figure 13.2).

For special contours, a tool called a *curve stick* is very helpful. This tool can be used for shaping collar lapels, elbow seams, and hipline seams in skirts and pants. The curve stick is available in both inches and metric (see Figure 13.3).

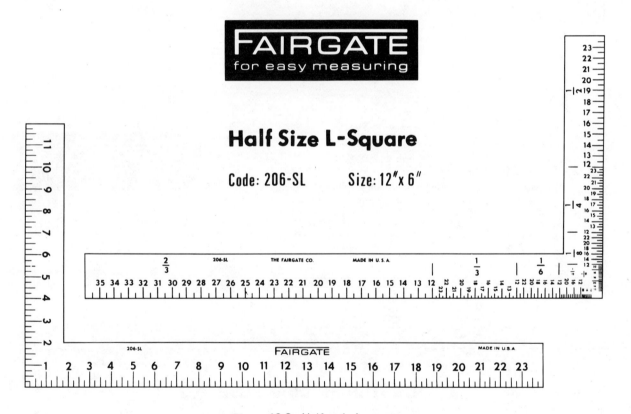

Figure 13.2 Half scale L-square

Figure 13.3 Curve stick

vary form curve

Draw any curve. Just keep turning it.
Create smooth even flowing lines
with a curve that really lasts.
RULE with it. CUT with it.
It's made of metal. Calibrated
in 8ths on both sides.

No. 102-CA **No. 102-CB** **No. 102-CC**
Size: 23"   Size: 18"   Size: 12"

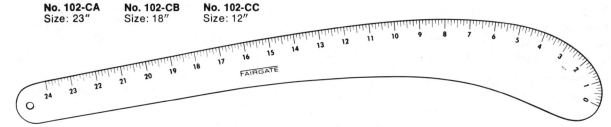

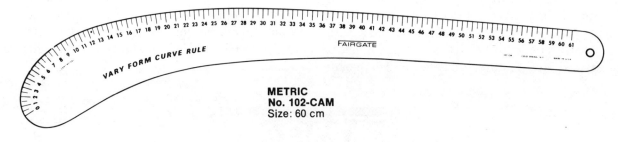

METRIC
No. 102-CAM
Size: 60 cm

Figure 13.4 Vary form curve

center-finding rules

Eliminates guessing • Eliminates math • Eliminates dividers

Get where you're going fast, with a center-finding rule.
Calibrated in 32nds and 16ths. To find the center of any
2 or 3 dimensional object, simply place the CENTER-
FINDING RULE on the "object" so the same measurement
appears to the left of the "O" mark as appears to the
right of the "O" mark. The arrow on the rule now points
to the exact center.

No.	Size	No.	Size
C-6	6" x ¾"	C-24	24" x 1¾"
C-12	12" x 1¾"	C-36	36" x 1¾"
C-18	18" x 1¾"	C-48	48" x 1¾"

ALL METRIC
No. MM-C16   Size: 16cm x 19 mm. Calibration millimeters

Figure 13.5 Center-finding rule

To create smooth, even-flowing lines with a curve, the *vary form curve* is recommended. This tool is made in both inches and metric (see Figure 13.4).

Another drafting aid used by the authors is called an *armscye sloper*. You can make this sloper from the pattern included in the Appendix. Use the same poster board selected for your basic drafts, and keep this sloper with your set of drafts. Detailed information on its use in shaping the armscye is found in Chapter 14, "Drafting Bodices."

Include in your tools a straight-edge ruler in either 12-inch (30.5 cm) or 18-inch (46 cm) length. Soft-lead No. 2 pencils are satisfactory for drafting. In addition, you will need standard sewing equipment, including scissors, a seam ripper, a tape measure, pins, marking equipment, thread, and transparent tape.

As you progress in your drafting skills, you may wish to add tools to your collection. A center-finding rule is useful for locating buttonholes and garment-finishing details. To use this rule, you place it on the draft so that the same measurement appears to the left of the "0" mark as appears to the right of the "0" mark. The exact center is now indicated by the arrow on the rule (see Figure 13.5). For precise sleeve-length measurements, an underarm sleeve rule may be used (see Figure 13.6). Cuff-width-marking rules are also available in different widths for accurate measuring of cuffs (Figure 13.7).

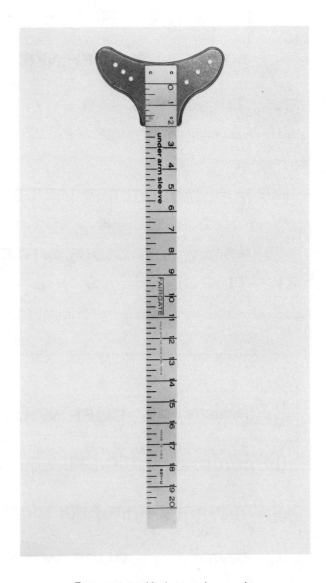

Figure 13.6 Underarm sleeve rule

TERMS AND PROCEDURES

Any new learning experience requires the study of the vocabulary used in the field. Pattern drafting is no exception, and therefore the terms may be unfamiliar as you begin your study. The method of pattern drafting presented in this book is based on body proportions. The procedures involve using these body proportions to establish *lengths* (vertical body divisions) and *widths* (horizontal body divisions). Within these perimeters, the pattern is designed according to the individual's measurements.

The body proportions underlying this drafting method are as follows:

1. The armspread (from the tip of the longest finger on the left hand to the tip of the longest finger on the right hand) is equal to the height.
2. The shoulder height is three sixty-fourths of the height less 1/2 inch (1.3 cm). The shoulder height increases and decreases approximately 1/16 inch (1.5 cm) for every inch added to or subtracted from the 5'4" (162.5 cm) figure.
3. The armscye circumference equals half of the chest measurement.
4. The depth from the shoulder height to the scye line (high chest measurement from underarm to underarm) equals one third of the armscye circumference.

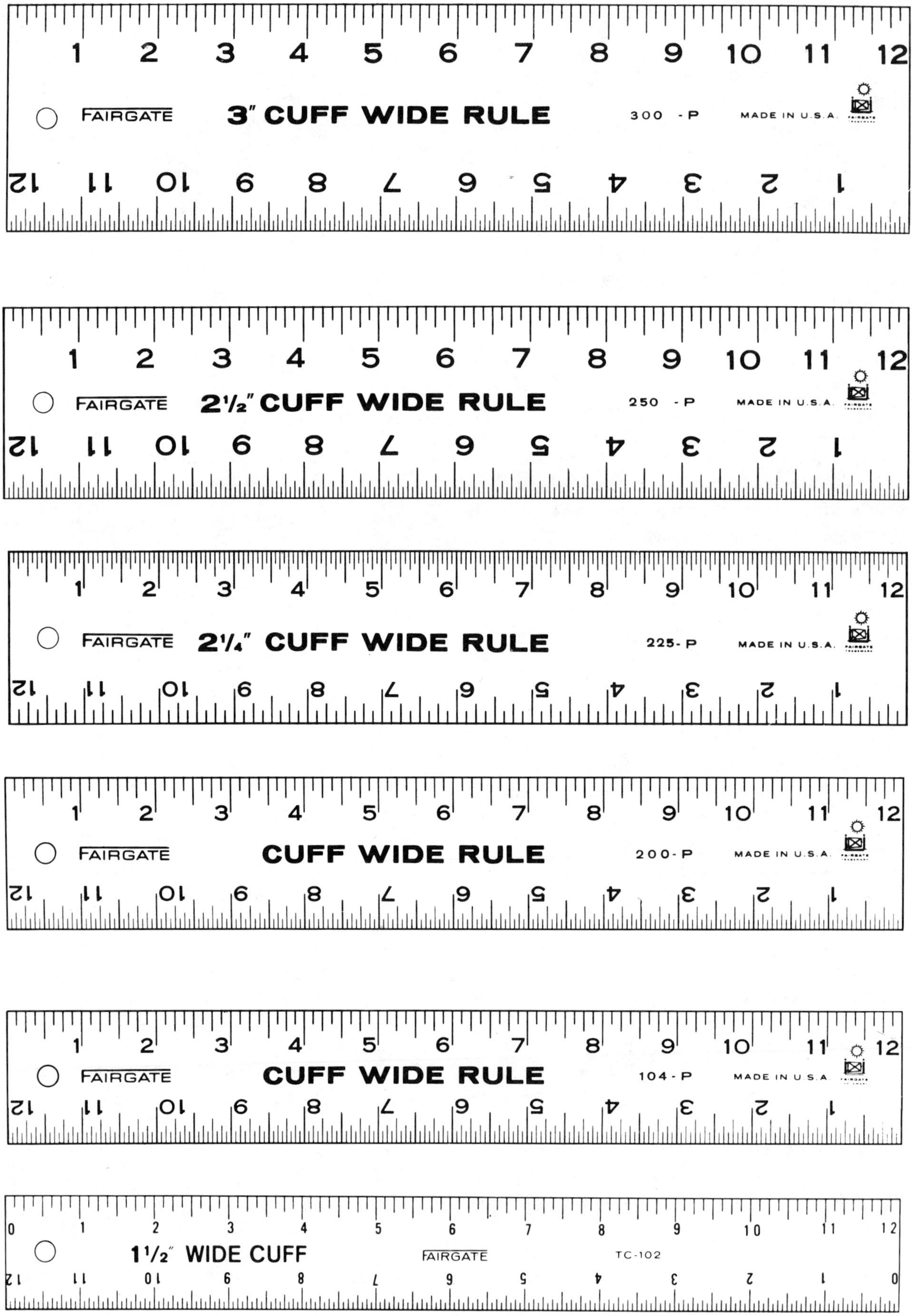

Figure 13.7 Cuff wide rule

5. The back waist length is one fourth the height less 1 inch (2.5 cm).
6. The sleeve inseam equals one fourth of the height less 1 inch (2.5 cm).
7. The hip length is one eighth the height less 1 inch (2.5 cm).

Using these proportions, you begin the drafting procedure by establishing the lengths, or vertical body divisions. Initially the bodice lengths are established. For the skirt draft, a hemline length will be added. For pants, both a knee and a hem length will be added.

PROCEDURES FOR ESTABLISHING LENGTHS AND WIDTHS

Unroll sufficient drafting paper for your back waist measurement plus your waist-to-hip measurement, and include about 6 inches (15 cm) extra for changes and notations you may make. Place the designer's L square in front of you with the short arm at your right hand extending away from you. The long arm of the designer's L square should extend toward your left hand along the edge of the paper. A phrase used frequently will be "square out and down." This means to draw a pencil line along the outside edge of the short arm (square out) and then to draw a pencil line along the outside edge of the long arm (square down) toward your left hand. Refer to Figure 13.8 as you begin drafting by establishing the lengths and widths.

Top Horizontal

Begin by squaring out and down. The line drawn along the short arm of the L square is called the *top horizontal*. Other vertical lengths are established with this top horizontal used as a reference point.

Neck Run or Base of Neck

This reference point is called by either of these terms. The terms refer to the base of the neck at the center back. To establish this point, square down 1 inch (2.5 cm) from the top horizontal.

I. Establishing lengths and widths for bodice back draft

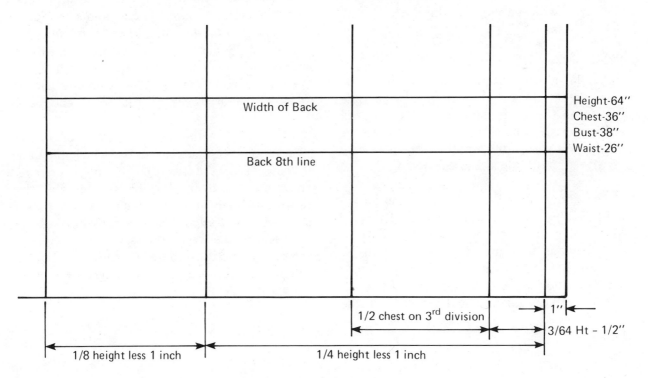

Figure 13.8

Square out from this point and label the line you have drawn.

Shoulder Height

This vertical division is very important to a garment's fit and is often a spot where alterations are required in commercial patterns. The shoulder height is established as three sixty-fourths of the height minus 1/2 inch (1.3 cm) down from the neck run. Square out from this point and label the line.

Scye Line

This line corresponds to the high chest measurement, which is the chest circumference taken under the arms and above the fullest part of the bust. Establish the scye line by squaring down *from the shoulder height line* one half of the chest divided by 3. Square out from this point, and label the line.

Waistline

Square down *from the neck run* one fourth the height less 1 inch (2.5 cm). Double-check yourself to be sure the back waist-length measurement agrees with the length of this line.

Hipline

Square down and out from the waistline one eighth the height less 1 inch (2.5 cm). When working on the skirt and pant drafts, you will need to consider whether this length corresponds to the fullest part of the hip. It may be necessary to draft with both hip measurements.

The above describes the procedure for establishing the bodice vertical lengths. This procedure will be repeated with each bodice draft. It is essential that the terms and lengths be understood. The body must also be divided into widths, or horizontal divisions for drafting. In drafting patterns for men and for children, the same principles of establishing lengths and widths are applicable. The important factor is the use of the individual's own measurements in establishing the perimeters for drafting.

Width of Back

Using the scye line established above, square out half the chest measurement plus ease, usually 1 inch (2.5 cm); divide by 2 as your draft will be for half of the back (or one fourth of the bodice pattern). The amount of ease to use is discussed in Chapter 14. Once you have defined this point, square up and down from this point. The line you have drawn is called the *width of the back line*. This point established on the syce line is the meeting point for the front and back side seamlines at the base of the armscye. This line is necessary for the drafting of the front and back side seams.

Eighth Lines

Using the width of the back line as the starting point, establish the eighth lines on the scye line by squaring back (toward you) half the chest measurement divided by 8 and by squaring forward (away from you) from the width of back line the same amount. These points represent the *back eighth line* and *front eighth line*, respectively. Square up and down from these points, and label the eighth lines. These lines are used in drafting the shoulder seamlines and in shaping the armscyes of the front and back bodice.

Additional terms will be introduced in the instructions for those drafts to which they are specific (e.g., the sleeve). The term *slope* is frequently used in drafting to describe the downward slant of a line. The term *armscye* is a synonym for *armhole*. However, in drafting, the relationship between the scye line and the armscye is so critical to understanding the bodice draft that the term *armscye* has been used throughout the text.

14
Drafting Bodices

The development of a basic bodice pattern using your personal measurements is the first step in pattern drafting. Once the bodice draft is complete, a fabric fitting shell is made from the pattern you have drafted. After you have checked the fit of your pattern in fabric, any changes you have made are recorded on your original pattern draft. Once you have made these corrections, it is advisable to make a cardboard copy of your draft to be used in creating different designs. These cardboard patterns, called *blocks,* give you a precise record of the correct fit of your bodice. Although the blocks may need revision from time to time to correspond with body changes, they provide a convenient outline of your bodice, and you will not need to redraft the bodice each time you wish to create a new pattern design. Design features such as style lines, seams, and darts can be varied with your block pattern, but the fit of the garment remains the same as that of your corrected draft. As you continue through the text, you will draft a set of block patterns for a bodice, a sleeve, a shirt, a skirt, and pants. You will then be able to create an endless variety of styles with personalized fit. You will also find these blocks helpful in identifying problems and making alterations in commercial patterns.

The drafting instructions presented here have been tested in classroom teaching. Followed carefully, these instructions have helped both college students and adults achieve good fit. Two suggestions for success in your drafting are to follow the sequence as given in the instructions and to attempt to understand the relationships with which you are working. Remember that your work must be precise and your measurements exact to achieve good fit. You do not need to memorize the drafting procedures. If you try instead to understand why one step follows the next, the procedures will come naturally with experience. Always use *your own measurements* in the drafts. The measurements used in the instructions are only illustrations of how your personal measurements are to be used in the calculations.

Pattern drafts are always made without seam allowances. Allowances are added to the final patterns once the demands of the design and the fabric are known. In the early stages of drafting, it is much easier to work without seam allowances.

Wearing ease is added only where specific amounts are given in the instructions. The fit of the draft will be snug, but later designs will be more satisfactory if the initial draft fits close to your body. This close-fit is desirable since figure characteristics can be more easily seen and dealt with in the fitting shell.

PROCEDURE FOR DRAFTING BODICE BACK

Establishing Bodice Back Lengths

1. Top horizontal. Unroll your drafting paper and place it parallel to the edge of the table.

142 • DRAFTING YOUR OWN BASIC PATTERN

You will need enough paper to allow for your back waist length plus 6 inches (15 cm). You will work from right to left on the paper. Place your L square at the edge of the paper with the long arm of the L square extending the length of the paper and the short arm extending away from you. Square out and down along the L square. This vertical line will be the center back of the bodice (Figure 14.1).

2. **Neck run or base of neck.** Square down 1 inch (2.5 cm) from the top horizontal and out from this point.

3. **Shoulder height.** Establish the shoulder height line by squaring down from the *neck run* three sixty-fourths of the *height* minus 1/2 inch. Thus, for a person 64 inches tall (5'4" or 162.5 cm), the shoulder height would be placed at 3 inches (7.5 cm) minus 1/2 inch (1.3 cm) or 2 1/2 inches (6.3 cm) from the neck run (Figure 14.1). Square out from this point.

4. **Scye line.** Square down from the shoulder height line half the chest measurement divided by 3. A person measuring 36 inches (9.15 cm) would come down 6 inches or 15.25 cm (36 ÷ 2 = 18 ÷ 3 = 6 inches or 91.5 ÷ 2 = 45.75 ÷ 3 = 15.25) and square out from this point. Note that this measurement corresponds to the high chest and not the fullest part of the bust. The scye line goes around the body from underarm to underarm and is a critical line for achieving good fit.

5. **Waistline.** This line is established from the *neck run* and is equal to one fourth of the height minus 1 inch (2.5 cm). Therefore a person 64 inches (162.5 cm) in height would come down 15 inches or 38 cm (16 - 1 inch or 40.5 - 2.5 cm) from the neck run and square out from this point.

6. **Hip length.** From the waistline established in Step 5, square down one eighth of the height minus 1 inch (2.5 cm) and out from this point. For the 64-inch (162.5 cm) figure, the measurement would be 7 inches or 18 cm (8 - 1 inch or 20.5 - 2.5 cm). This line will not be needed in the drafting of the bodice block but is needed

I. Establishing lengths and widths for bodice back draft

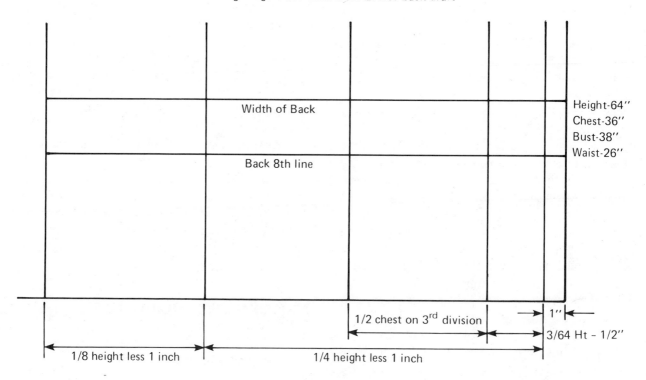

Figure 14.1

when you are designing bodices that extend below the normal waistline.

Once the lengths are established, you have determined the vertical fit of your bodice. You will then continue the draft by establishing widths. The widths determine the horizontal fit of the garment.

Establishing Bodice Back Widths

7. Width of back. The width of the back is established on the scye line. Square out on the scye line half the chest plus 1 inch (2.5 cm) ease divided by 2. Square up and down from this point. If your measurements are based on a 36-inch (91.5 cm) chest, the width-of-back line would be placed 9 1/2 inches (24.1 cm) from the center back (36 ÷ 2 = 18 + 1 = 19 ÷ 2 = 9 1/2 inches or 91.5 ÷ 2 = 45.75 + 2.5 = 48.25 ÷ 2 = 24.1 cm). See Figure 14.2 for the width of the back. The person with an extremely full bust may prefer to add 2 inches (5 cm) ease, but caution should be observed lest the fit be altered more than desired. Later the fabric fitting shell might indicate a need for additional ease. The

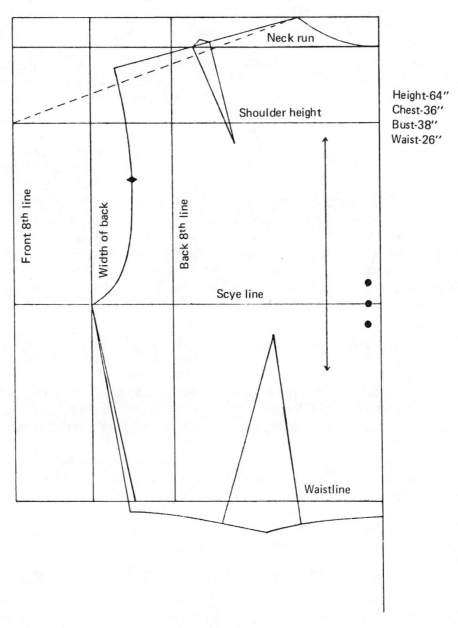

Height-64"
Chest-36"
Bust-38"
Waist-26"

Figure 14.2

basic draft may be changed more successfully when the exact amount of additional ease needed is known. The width-of-back line is the reference line for placing the side seams. The side seams will begin at the point where the scye line and the width-of-back line meet (Figure 14.2).

8. Eighth lines. Both the back and front eighth lines are placed in reference to the width-of-back line established in Step 7. For the back eighth line, square in (toward you) from the width-of-back line half the chest measurement divided by 8. Square up and down from this point. For the 36-inch (91.5 cm) chest, the back eighth line would be placed 2 1/4 inches (5.7 cm) from the width-of-back line (36 ÷ 2 = 18 ÷ 8 = 2 1/4 inches or 91.5 ÷ 2 = 45.75 ÷ 8 = 5.7 cm).

For the front eighth line, square out (away from you) from the width-of-back line the same amount (one half the chest divided by 8). Square up and down from this point as shown in Figure 14.2.

These lengths and widths are the perimeters within which you will design your bodice back. You should now check your work, making certain that your calculations are correct and that your lines are drawn precisely. All the lengths and widths should be accurately labeled on your draft; the instructions will refer to these lines by name as you continue the bodice.

Shaping the Bodice Back

9. Shoulder neck point. This point is placed on the top horizontal. Square out half the chest measurement divided by 6 and mark this point. Calculating on the basis of a 36-inch (91.5 cm) chest, the distance from the center back to the shoulder neck point would be 3 inches or 7.6 cm (36 ÷ 2 = 18 ÷ 6 = 3 inches or 91.5 ÷ 2 = 45.75 ÷ 6 = 7.6 cm). Using a curved ruler, shape in the neckline from the center back on the neck run to the shoulder neck point on the top horizontal (Figure 14.2).

10. Shoulder seam. Place the short arm of the L square at the shoulder neck point established in Step 9, and position the arm of the L square so that a line can be drawn from this point to the point where the *front* eighth line (established in Step 8) meets the shoulder height line. Dot in a temporary shoulder seamline. Raise the shoulder seamline line 2/16 to 3/16 of an inch (3–5 mm) for ease on the *back* eighth line. Extend the new shoulder seamline approximately 1 1/4 inches (3.2 cm) beyond the *back* eighth line. The length of the shoulder seamline should correspond to your measurements, but a shoulder dart must be included in the bodice back for good fit over the shoulder area.

11. Back shoulder dart. This dart is placed approximately at the midpoint of the shoulder seam unless some body curve indicates that a different placement would contribute to better fit and appearance. A depth of 1/2 inch (1.3 cm) is typical, depending on the prominence of the shoulder blade. The dart should be directed toward the center of this body bulge and should extend slightly below the shoulder height line. Draft in the dart stitching lines and a fold line down the center of the dart. Fold the dart as it will be stitched, with the dart tuck turned toward the center back, and correct the shoulder seam. This step gives the dart the shape needed for a straight edge at the shoulder seamline. Compare your shoulder seam measurement to that of your draft with the dart folded. You may need to lengthen or shorten the seamline at this time.

12. Armscye. Use the armscye sloper provided in the Appendix of this book for shaping this seamline. The armscye is shaped in from the shoulder seam to the scye line. Before drafting the permanent armscye seamline, check the width of the back draft halfway between the shoulder height line and the scye line to be sure your draft and your personal measurements correspond. The armscye seamline can be moved toward the width-of-back line if additional width is needed across the back. If the draft is too wide in this area, move the armscye seamline toward the back eighth line.

13. Back notch. This notch will be placed on the armscye seamline. Determine its location by squaring up from the scye line on the back eighth line half the chest measurement divided by 4.

Place the notch at this level on the back armscye seamline. For the 36-inch (91.5 cm) chest, the notch would be placed 4 1/2 inches (11.5 cm) up from the scye line (36 ÷ 2 = 18 ÷ 4 = 4 1/2 inches or 91.5 ÷ 2 = 45.75 ÷ 4 = 11.5 cm).

14. Side seam and waistline. The back waistline measurement will be one half of the waistline measurement minus 1/2 inch (1.3 cm). The 1/2 inch (1.3 cm) is subtracted from the back to allow for the front waistline's being 1 inch (2.5 cm) larger than the back. For example, for a 26-inch (66 cm) waist, the back waistline measurement equals 12 1/2 inches, (31.7 cm) and the front waistline measurement equals 13 1/2 inches (34.3 cm). As the pattern draft is for one half of the back bodice, divide the back measure by 2. For example, the back 12 1/2 inches (31.7 cm) divided by 2 equals 6 1/4 inches (15.8 cm).

Measuring the distance from the center back to the width-of-back line, you find that the distance exceeds this back waistline measurement. Take out the extra by removing one third of the extra from the side seam and by placing two thirds of it in the waistline dart. In the example above, the draft measured 9 1/2 inches (24 cm) from the center back to the width-of-back line. When 6 1/4 inches or 15.8 cm (the back waistline measure) is subtracted from this amount, a total of 3 1/4 inches (8.2 cm) remain. One inch (2.5 cm) may be removed from the side seam, and the remaining amount may be placed in the dart.

Draw the side seamline from the end point of the armscye seamline on the width-of-back line to the point established for the waistline measure. The side seamline will slant toward the center back and the back eighth line.

15. Back waistline dart. The depth of this dart was determined in Step 14. The dart usually ends 1/2 to 1 inch (1.3–2.5 cm) below the fullest part of the body bulge. This termination point is placed one half the distance between the center back and the back eighth line. On the waistline, it may be located at the midpoint between the center back and the side seam. The starting point for the stitching line of the dart is placed 1/2 inch (1.3 cm) closer to the center back than the termination point, giving the dart a slight slant toward the center back. For example, if the termination point of the dart is 3 1/2 inches (8.8 cm) from the center back, the starting point for the dart's stitching line at the waistline will be 3 inches (7.5 cm) from the center back. Draft in the dart's stitching lines and a fold line down the center of the dart.

16. Back waistline shape. Extend the center back 1/2 inch (1.3 cm) in length (below the waistline) for ease, and then extend the side seam 3/8 inch (1 cm) below the waistline for ease. This step provides a slight downward slope of the waistline from the center back to the side seam. Fold in the back waistline dart as it will be stitched, and reshape the waistline using a curved ruler.

17. Grainline. The bodice is to be placed on the lengthwise grain of the fabric. Indicate this placement on your draft by drawing an arrow parallel to the center back.

PROCEDURE FOR DRAFTING BODICE FRONT

Establishing Lengths and Widths for Bodice Front

18. Width of front. The bodice front is drafted beside the bodice back by means of the same lengths established for the bodice back. It is therefore necessary to extend each of these lines (top horizontal, neck run, shoulder height, scye line, and waistline) to provide for the width of the bodice front. Extend these lines established for the bodice back so that the total width equals one half of the *bust measurement* plus 1 inch (2.5 cm) of ease. For a 38-inch (96.5 cm) bust, the total measurement would be 20 inches or 51 cm (38 ÷ 2 = 19 + 1 = 20 inches or 96.5 ÷ 2 = 48.25 + 2.5 = 50.75 cm). Square up and down through this point. This line becomes the center front of the bodice (Figure 14.3).

Shaping the Bodice Front

19. Shoulder neck points. These points will be used in shaping the front neckline. On the top horizontal, square toward you from the center

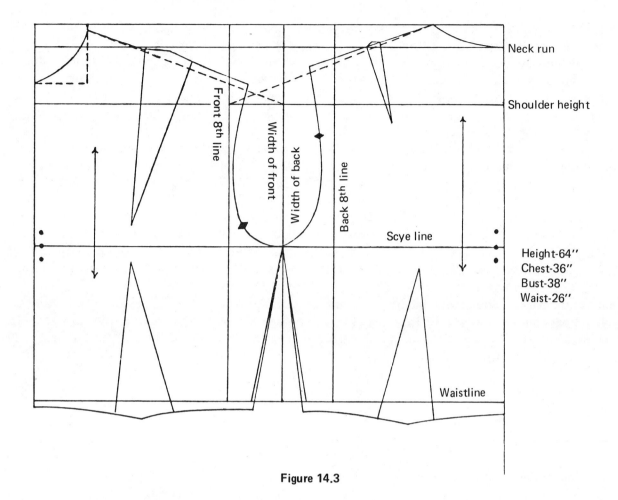

Figure 14.3

front one half the *chest* divided by 8; square down from the top horizontal on the center front line one half the *chest* divided by 8. Thus, for a 36-inch (91.5 cm) chest, your two points would be placed 2 1/4 inches (5.7 cm) out from the corner (36 ÷ 2 = 18 ÷ 8 = 2 1/4 inches or 91.5 ÷ 2 = 45.75 ÷ 8 = 5.7 cm). Next, lower each of these points 1/4 inch (6 mm) and dot in a box between the points. See Figure 14.3 for these procedures. Using a Vary Form curve, shape the neckline within the box.

20. Shoulder seam. Establish a temporary shoulder seamline by placing the short arm of the L square at the shoulder neck point (see Step 19) and dotting in a line to the width-of-front line. The shoulder seamline stops at the point where the shoulder height line and the width-of-front line (also the width-of-back line) meet. The back and front shoulder-seam lines must cross in the space between the front eighth line and the width-of-front/back lines (side seamlines). The length of the front shoulder seam depends on the length of the back shoulder seam and will be adjusted after the front shoulder dart has been drafted.

21. Front shoulder dart. This dart is usually 2 to 2 1/2 inches (5 to 6.3 cm) deep, depending on the fullness of the bust. It should be placed so that it will match the back shoulder dart when it is stitched and placed in the shoulder seam. The dart is slanted toward the fullest part of the bust, which is the midpoint between the center front and the front eighth line. The termination point of the dart is about 1 inch (2.5 cm) above the fullest part of the bust. Draft the dart stitching and fold lines. Fold the dart as it will be stitched, and turn it toward center front. Correct the shoulder seamline with the dart folded. Establish the shoulder seam length to correspond to the back shoulder seamline excluding the darts.

22. Armscye. Using the armscye sloper provided in the Appendix, shape the front armscye by drawing a line from the shoulder seam to the width-of-front/back line (side seamlines).

23. Front notch. The front notch is placed on the armscye seamline level with a point that you locate by squaring up on the front eighth line from the scye line one half of the chest divided by 16. Thus, for the 36-inch (91.5 cm) chest, the notch would be placed 1 1/8 inches (2.8 cm) above the scye line (36 ÷ 2 = 18 ÷ 16 = 1 1/8 inch or 91.5 ÷ 2 = 45.75 ÷ 16 = 2.8 cm).

24. Side seam and waistline. As discussed earlier, the front waistline is 1 inch (2.5 cm) larger than the back waistline. To proportion the bodice, take one half of the waistline measure plus 1/2 inch (1.3 cm). If we use a 26-inch (66 cm) waistline as an example, the front would be 13 1/2 inches (34.3 cm), whereas the back was drafted to 12 1/2 inches (31.7 cm). Because the front pattern draft is for one half of the front, the waistline measure is 6 3/4 inches (17 cm). The distance between the center front and the width-of-front/back line exceeds this amount (see Figure 14.3 and note that the measurement is 10 1/2 inches or 26.8 cm).

Remove the extra amount by taking one third of the amount from the side seam and placing the remaining two thirds in the waistline dart. If we refer again to the 26-inch (66 cm) waistline, the calculations for dividing the extra amount are 10 1/2 − 6 3/4 = 3 3/4 ÷ 3 = 1 1/4 inch or 26.8 − 17 = 9.8 ÷ 3 = 3.2 cm. Therefore 1 1/4 inch (3.2 cm) would be removed from the side seamline and 2 1/2 inches (6.3 cm) would be placed in the waistline dart.

The side seamline is now drawn from the end point of the armscye on the width-of-front line to the point established for the waistline measure.

25. Front waistline dart. This dart's depth was determined above as being two thirds of the extra amount on the waistline. The position of the dart is a design feature and may be changed in the fabric fitting shell for a more attractive appearance. It is directed toward the fullest part of the bust. The dart point is usually the midpoint between the center front and the front eighth line. Position the inside stitching line of the dart 1/2 inch (1.3 cm) closer to the center front than the dart point. Check to see that the stitching lines next to center front for the shoulder dart and the waistline dart are in line with each other. These darts should terminate above and below the scye line, creating fullness for the bust.

26. Shaping the front waistline. Extend the center front below the waistline 1/4 to 1/2 inch (6 to 13 mm) for ease. Extend the side seam below the waistline 3/8 inch (1 cm) in length for ease. The measurements should be checked with your measurements so that adequate bodice length is provided. Be sure that the front and back side seamlines correspond in length. Fold in the waistline dart, and turn the dart toward center front. Reshape the waistline seam by placing the curved ruler so that the new waistline curves from the side seamline toward center front.

27. Grainline. Indicate that the center front is to be placed on the lengthwise grainline of the fabric by placing an arrow parallel to the center front. The center front may be placed on the lengthwise fold of the fabric.

The basic bodice draft is now complete. Add seam allowances to the draft, and make the pattern in fabric. It is helpful to machine-baste the fitting shell so that changes can be easily made. Have someone check the fit with you, applying the principles of good fit described in Chapter 4. When a satisfactory fit has been achieved, transfer your alterations to your original drafts. Make a cardboard copy of your drafts including all changes. These will serve as your block patterns to be used in designing. Mark the darts on the cardboard by either cutting away the darts or by notching the edges and punching holes on the dart stitching lines.

DESIGNING BODICES

In using your basic bodice draft, you must retain the pattern outline, size, and ease at all times, thus ensuring personalized fit in the garments you design. The basic bodice has many design possibilities, and you will be pleased with the patterns you design as long as the relationships determined in the draft are maintained.

148 • DRAFTING YOUR OWN BASIC PATTERN

The techniques for designing with your basic drafts are referred to as *flat pattern methods*. Flat pattern differs from draping a pattern in several ways. In draping a pattern, the designer creates the garment in fabric on a form. The designs are applicable only to the fabric in which they are created and are difficult to reproduce. In contrast, the flat pattern designer works from drafts using accurate measurements that are readily reproducible. Draping is also a very time-consuming method requiring numerous fitting operations. The speed of flat pattern techniques appeals to most persons.

To design with your bodice, trace around the blocks on the pattern paper. Be sure to mark all the darts in your blocks. Remember that the blocks have no seam allowances. These are to be added after your designs are finished.

The suggestions given here provide only a taste of the many variations you can create with your blocks. References giving additional ideas are listed in the Bibliography. However, you are limited only by your own imagination and the thought and time you give to designing once the basic techniques are understood.

Darts

The darts drafted into your blocks are there essentially for fit. They can serve design purposes but are usually varied from the type in the draft to enhance appearance. Darts may be moved or changed to dart equivalents such as seams, gathers, tucks, or yokes. You must *not eliminate* these darts, or your personalized fit will be lost. You can, however, convert them or move them, depending on the effect you wish to create.

1. Stitching line variations. The stitching lines of the draft darts are straight lines. You may

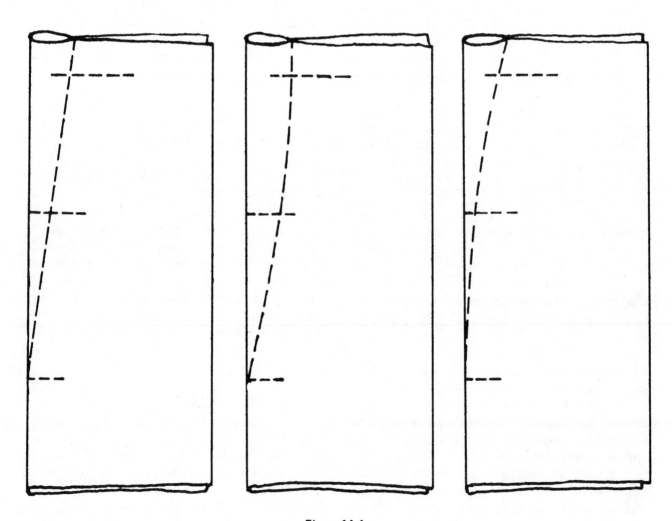

Figure 14.4

wish to use curved stitching lines so that the design conforms more to body curves. Dart stitching lines that curve outward (concave) create a more snug fit. Those that curve inward (convex) allow more ease in the garment and may be more appropriate for the full figure. See Figure 14.4 for examples of these variations.

2. Dart location variations. Darts may be moved to new locations on the pattern outline. You can achieve this on a paper copy of the bodice draft by first determining the pivot point of your dart. The pivot point is the fullest part, sometimes called the *crown*, of the body curve. Fullness taken up by darts can be moved around this point without changing the fit of the garment. Establish the pivot point of the dart you wish to move. Dart stitching lines terminate short of the pivot points. Rule in the line indicating the new position of the dart from the outside seamline to the pivot point. A typical design change would be to move the front shoulder dart from the shoulder seamline to the underarm position (Figure 14.5).

To move the dart, fold in the existing dart in the paper pattern. Secure it with tape or pins. Slash the pattern along the line you have ruled for the new location to the pivot point. The pattern will spread, creating a new dart opening. The pattern should lie flat when slashed. Place pattern paper under the opening and pin or tape it in place. You will now draft the new stitching lines for the dart using a termination point that falls short of the pivot point, thereby creating the fullness needed for the body curve. When the dart has been redrawn, fold in the dart and correct the seamline.

Darts may be moved to any part of any seamline. However, you will achieve better fit by retaining shoulder darts in the upper part of the bodice and waistline darts in the lower part of the bodice. In moving darts, consider other design features of the bodice, such as the location of the zipper or buttons. Too many design lines result in a cluttered appearance, and spacing can be critical to good design.

3. Number of darts. Both the shoulder and the waistline darts in the basic bodice draft are deep (two thirds of the extra amount between the center and the side seamline on the waistline).

You may prefer to divide deep darts, placing the same measurement in two or three darts rather than in one large dart. The darts should be shorter when this change is made. Follow the same procedure as for moving the darts. Begin by drawing the lines for the new dart locations. Close the existing dart and slash along the new lines until the pattern is flat. Underlay the new darts with pattern paper, secure it, and draw the new dart stitching lines. Fold in the new darts and correct the seamline.

4. Gathers. When darts are converted to gathers, the effect is one of added softness in the design. Gathers that replace darts are called dart equivalents because the fullness they create is located where the original darts were placed. Trace around your block and include all pattern markings on your paper. For a dart to be converted to gathers, mark out the existing dart stitching lines. Using a curved ruler, correct the seamline where the dart had been by drawing a smooth curve. Mark all notches needed for joining the

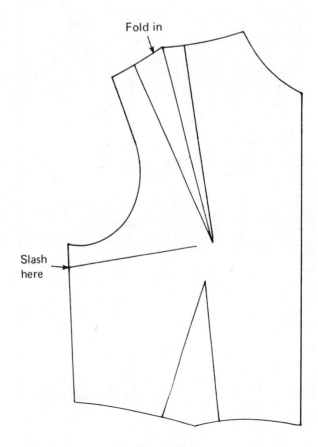

Figure 14.5

pattern pieces, and indicate on your pattern that the former dart will now be gathered. Allowing the gathers to spread over a wider area than the dart contributes greater softness to the design (Figure 14.6).

If the design needs additional fullness, you may wish to slash and spread the pattern. The amount of fullness to be added depends on the fabric to be used, the formality of the garment, and the fullness of the figure. With experience, one can estimate closely the needed amount of fullness, but this may be a trial-and-error task for the beginning designer.

5. Tucks or pleats. When darts are not stitched to the termination point, they are often called *tucks* or *pleats*. These dart equivalents may be stitched partially or not at all. If no stitching is done, the dart is simply folded in and stitched in the seamline stitching. It may be desirable first to move the darts to different positions along the seamlines when you are using tucks or pleats for decorative effects.

6. Yokes. A yoke may be used to replace part of a dart. The wide end of the dart is closed, and the yoke is designed for the area. The remainder of the dart may then be gathered, tucked, or pleated, or it may remain as a shortened dart (Figure 14.7). The design line of the yoke may be straight, curved, or pointed. Experiment with the design lines by marking the proposed lines with pins. These can be moved until you have achieved the effect you desire. Once the yoke line has been determined, place notches on the yoke cutting line and separate the pattern along this line. The wide end of the dart remains closed, but the remainder of the dart is released to form gathers or ease (Figure 14.7).

Although shoulder area yokes are used more frequently, yokes may also be used at the waistline to create midriff effects. The procedure is the same in either instance, except that you are working with the waistline dart rather than the shoulder dart for a midriff yoke. Shoulder and waistline yokes are shown in Figure 14.7.

Bodice back yokes often cross the shoulders below the termination point of the shoulder dart. When this occurs, you may move the shoulder dart to the armscye and let it become part of the seamline. When the yoke line crosses the dart, the remaining part of the dart is eased into the seam, or it can be gathered if there is enough fullness. Figure 14.7 shows the procedure.

Facings

The purposes of facings are twofold: to provide a durable finish to the garment's edges and to support the garment openings, giving them shape and stability. Facings may also be decorative and add design features to garments.

1. Fitted facings. To draft a fitted facing, duplicate the outer edges of your block where the facing is to be used. The facing will be cut on the same grainline as the bodice piece to which it will be attached. Seam allowances are added

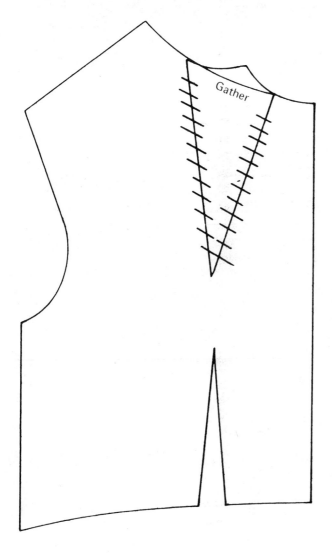

Figure 14.6

GENERAL DRAFTING TECHNIQUES • 151

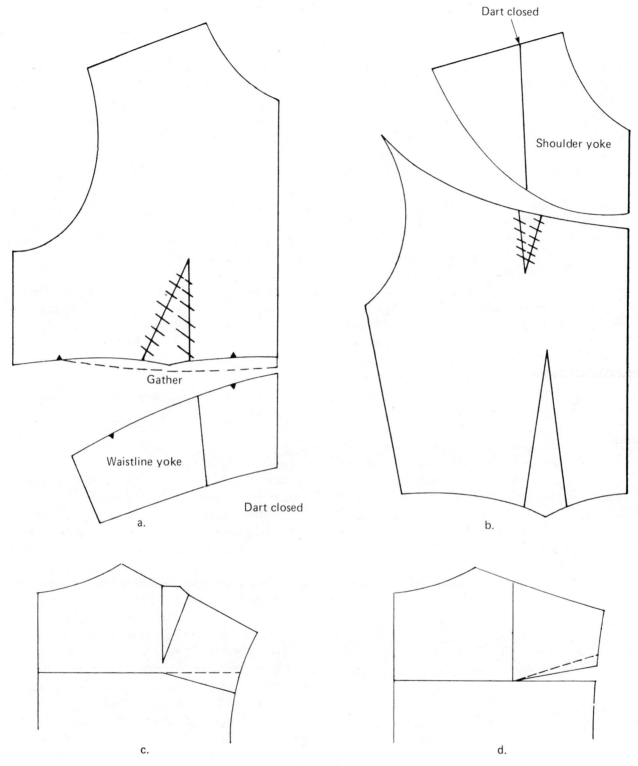

Figure 14.7

to the facing where it will be joined to the garment. The width of facings varies from 2 to 3 inches (5 to 7.5 cm) for most garments. Generally facings are narrower at the shoulder seam and slightly wider at the waistline seam on the center front of bodices. Using a gentle curve to design the outer edge of the facing makes it easier to finish the edge.

Facings are often wider when they contribute to design features in the garment (e.g., in double-breasted jackets, full sleeves, or collars). The facing may be visible in these cases, and extra width ensures that the facing edges will not be exposed.

Interfacing pattern pieces are cut as are facing pieces. It is extremely important that these pieces duplicate the garment's shape in order for the interfacing to support and stabilize the garment's edges.

When the bodice opening must be overlapped (e.g., for buttons and buttonholes), it is necessary to add an extension to both the bodice piece and the facing. The extension must enable the edges to overlap, and its total width is usually 3/4 to 1 1/2 inches (2 to 3.8 cm). The diameter of the buttons selected for the design can be used to determine the width of the extension. The distance from the center front line to the garments edge should be equal to the button's diameter. As the pattern is half of the bodice, add the same amount of extension to each side of the garment for the overlap. When the facing is cut as a separate piece, the extension must be included in your facing pattern.

Fitted facings are often joined to other facings (e.g., the front and back neck facings are joined). When this occurs, it is necessary for all facings to be the same width so that when they are joined, the edges match.

2. Cut-on facings. It is desirable to cut the facing in one piece with the bodice whenever possible. This procedure eliminates the seam, and matching problems are minimized. To design this type of closure, first add the overlap extension described above. Fold under (do not cut) your pattern paper on the outer edge of the extension. Now trace the remaining garment edges (e.g., the neckline) onto the pattern paper, and cut along these lines. Shape the inside edge of the facing with a curved ruler. Figure 14.8 details this type of a facing.

3. Bias strips. Edges may also be finished with bias strips. *Bias* refers to the point of greatest stretch in a woven fabric, where warp and filling yarns meet. To cut a true bias, cut straight strips on the diagonal of the fabric, thereby crossing the yarn intersections. These strips are usually narrow because they must be shaped to the garment's edges.

Collars

Collars are often the focal point of the bodice, and many variations are possible. Changing the width, the length, the grainline, or the shape of the outer edge of the collar leads to unlimited possibilities. The length of the neckline of the bodice determines the length of the collar neckline. You can create different collar shapes by increasing or decreasing the length of the outer edge of the collar pattern. Decreasing the outer edge results in a collar that stands above the neckline for part of its width (called the *stand*) and then folds over, covering the neckline seam (called the *roll*). Increasing the outer edges results in a collar with flare or ruffles.

Collars may be divided into two pattern pieces with the stand and the roll being separate pieces as in the shirt pattern (see Chapter 16). The stand may be used independently, giving a narrow band collar with no roll. Such a stand collar will have a neck edge that curves in the opposite direction to that of the neckline.

Collars are most often designed as separate pattern pieces and sewn to the neckline of the garment. However, collars may be cut in one

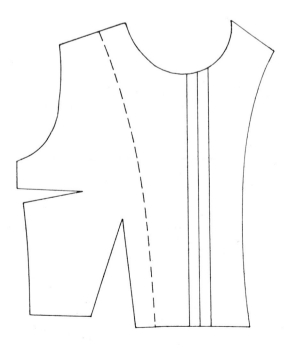

Figure 14.8

piece with the front bodice. These collars are called "shawl" collars.

To decide on the design of your collar, consider the design in the remainder of the garment, the shape of your face, and your hairstyle. Basic collar shapes are described below.

1. Flat collar. This collar lies flat to the bodice and is a duplicate of the bodice area it covers. It may be any width or shape. To create this collar, close the shoulder darts on the bodice front and back. Next join your bodice front and back blocks at the shoulder seam. These seamlines should meet exactly at the neckline but should overlap 1/4 to 3/4 of an inch (6 to 20 mm) at the armscye. These patterns must meet at the neckline. Trace the neckline (front and back) onto your pattern paper. Decide on the collar width and extend the pattern out from the neckline. Shape the outer edge of your collar. The center back will be the grainline of this collar. Usually the collar is cut on the lengthwise grain to match the bodice, but crosswise grain may be used to create special effects. Mark these reference points on your collar: center back, shoulder seam, and center front (Figure 14.9).

2. Roll collar. Collars vary in the amount of roll established in the design. You can create an easy pattern for a rolled collar by measuring the combined lengths of the necklines of your front and back bodice blocks. Draw a rectangle using this neckline measurement as your rectangle's length, and the width will be the desired depth of the collar at the center front. The rectangle could be used as the pattern, but the stand at the center back would be very high. It would be a full roll equal to the half of the collar's center back width. Therefore extend the center-back collar width so that the finished collar will cover the neckline seam. This amount can be determined after the collar has been shaped. To reduce this stand, you may lengthen the collar's outer edge by cutting the pattern toward the neckline and spreading. There will be two or three slashes toward the neckline, and each opening should be 1/2 to 3/4 of an inch (1.3 to 2 cm) in width. Secure the redesigned collar to paper to maintain its shape. Mark the center back, the shoulder seamline, and the center front on the collar pattern. See Figure 14.10 for the diagram of spead-

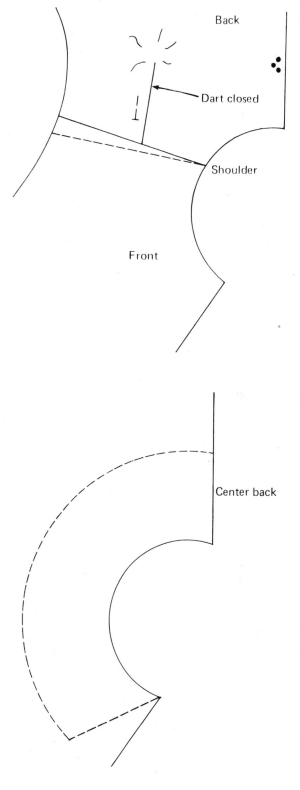

Figure 14.9

ing the rectangle to achieve the collar pattern. Correct the curve of the outer edge of the collar with a curved ruler. The collar corners at the

154 • DRAFTING YOUR OWN BASIC PATTERN

center front may be rounded or pointed, depending on your design preferences.

You may convert this basic collar to a ruffled collar by increasing the number of slashes and speading the collar's outer edge until the neckline edge becomes a half circle. There should be enough space at the center front for a seam allowance (Figure 14.11).

For rolled collars, it is desirable to design upper and under collar pieces. If both layers of the collar are the same size, the seam around the collar's outer edge will show or even roll to the outside. The upper collar must be larger than the under collar to prevent this unattractive curl. The amount to be added varies with the weight of the fabric to be used. No addition is made to the neckline edge, and usually 1/4 to 1/2 of an inch (6 to 13 mm) of additional width is sufficient around the outer edge. The grainline of the upper collar corresponds to that of the bodice, but under collars may be cut on the bias to ensure a soft roll, especially in heavy fabrics. The interfacing pattern is the same as the undercollar. It can be bias-cut or cut in the direction of stretch of the interfacing fabric.

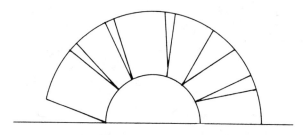

Figure 14.11

3. Stand-up collar. A stand-up collar is a modification of the roll collar that does not fold or roll. Sometimes called *Chinese, Mandarin, military,* and *Nehru collars,* the collar has a variety of applications. These collars may be continuous around the neckline, but they are often open at the center front. For the top edge to fit closely to the neck, it must be 1 to 1 1/2 inches (2.5 to 3.8 cm) shorter than the neck edge of the collar.

To design a stand-up collar, first measure the necklines of the front and back bodices. Use this measurement as the length of your rectangle; the width will be determined by your personal preference. On the rectangle, mark the center back, the shoulder seamline, and the center front. Cut the rectangle out of pattern paper. Divide the distance from the shoulder seamline to the center front into three equal divisions and mark these points. Fold in darts at these points about 1/4 inch (6 mm) deep at the top edge of the collar. Measure the top edge to be sure that it is now 1 to 1 1/2 inches (2.5 to 3.8 cm) shorter than the neckline edge. A close fit at the side of the neck is desirable, and this measure-

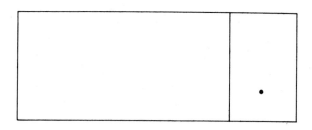

Figure 14.10a

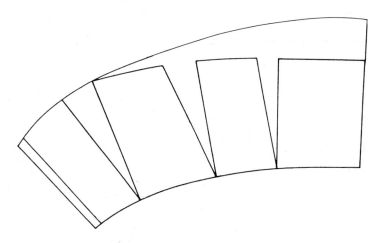

Figure 14.10b

GENERAL DRAFTING TECHNIQUES • 155

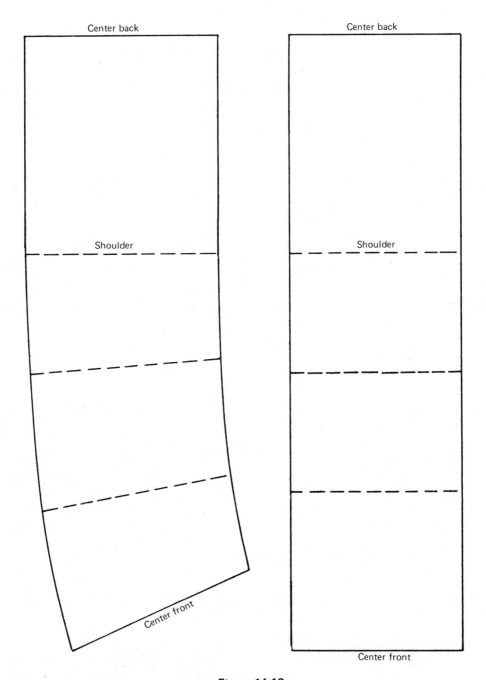

Figure 14.12

ment should achieve this effect. The grainline for stand-collars may be placed parallel to the center back or the center front, or at right angles to the center front or back. The design of the garment and the choice of fabric will influence your decision on grainline (Figure 14.12).

4. Cut-on collars. Many names are used for these collars: *shawl, rever,* and *all-in-one-piece,* among others. Generally these terms refer to collars that have these distinguishing characteristics:

a. The undercollar and the bodice front are cut in one piece. The draft is made by joining the collar to the neckline of the front bodice and eliminating the neckline seam.
b. The upper collar is cut in one piece with the front facing.
c. The collar has a seam at the center back neckline.

You may create design variations by varying the shape of the collar's outer edge and by vary-

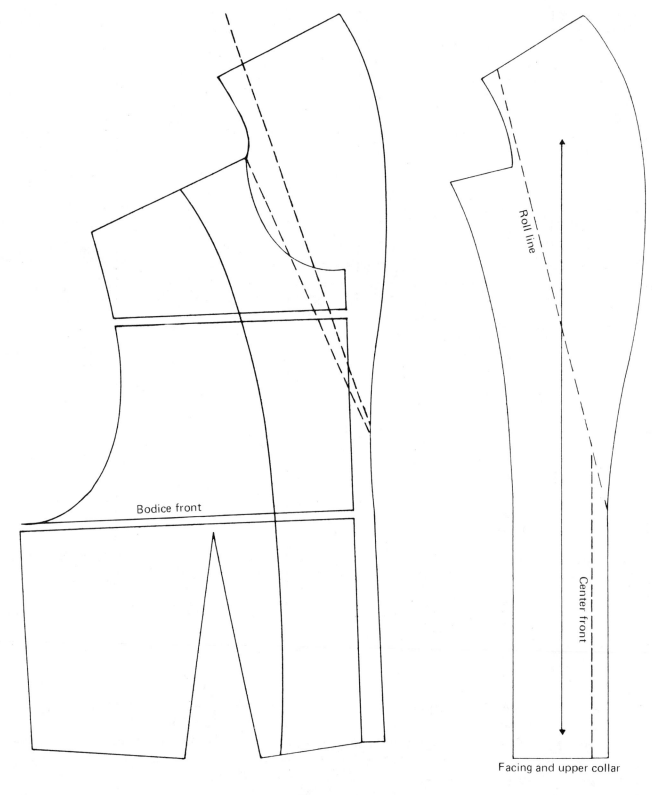

Figure 14.13

ing the height of the collar's stand. These collars may lie flat on the bodice or stand 1/4 inch to 2 inches (6 to 50 mm) depending on the look to be achieved. The height of the stand is determined by the length of the collar's outer edge. The longer the outer edge, the lower the stand compared with the length of the neck edge. The shorter the collar's outer edge, the higher the stand.

To draft this collar variation, trace the bodice front on your drafting paper. Be sure to allow at least 6 inches (15 cm) above the bodice for drafting the collar. Include the extension to the center front needed for the overlap as explained earlier in this chapter.

The roll line is related to the placement of the buttons on the bodice. The roll line begins at the top button and extends through the shoulder neckpoint and beyond 4 inches (10 cm). To draft this line, extend the shoulder seamline into the neckline 1 inch (2.5 cm), and mark this point. Draft a line from the start of the roll at the top of the buttons through this point, and extend the line 4 inches (10 cm) above it.

Turn your bodice back sloper upside down so that the neckline curve is reversed. Position this sloper so that the shoulder neck points (back and front) meet and the center back overlaps the roll line by 1 inch (2.5 cm). Trace the back neckline along the sloper. Decide on the depth of the collar you want at the center back. Remember that the collar will stand 1 to 1 1/2 inches (2.5 to 3.8 cm) before rolling. Draft the line for the center back seam to the desired length with the L square positioned at the center back of the neck.

Design the curved outer edge of the collar from the center back to the front edge where the roll line began. The curve stick will be helpful in designing this edge. To get an idea of the finished shape, fold the collar back along the roll line and check this appearance.

Dot in a line from the start of the roll line at the top button to the original shoulder neck point. Note the space between the neck edge of the bodice and this line. This space may be incorporated into a two-ended dart, which will make the cut-on collar drape more smoothly around the neck. The width of the dart at the middle should be about 1/2 inch (1.3 cm), and it should taper sharply to a point at each end. The stitching line of the dart will follow the bodice neckline.

Draft the facing and the upper collar by duplicating the bodice front as drafted earlier. The width of the facing from the shoulder neck point to the facing's edge should be approximately 2 inches (5 cm). The width of the facing at the waistline should be 3 to 4 inches (7.5 to 10 cm). Shape the facing's edge with the curve stick.

Increase the outer edge of the upper collar-facing piece by 1/8 inch (3 mm) all around. This step makes the undercollar slightly smaller which helps to hide the seam and prevents the outer edge of the collar from rolling.

The upper collar facing does not have the two-ended dart stitched in as does the under collar.

Figure 14.13 shows the bodice with a cut-on collar and facing pattern pieces.

Many collar variations are possible with your basic bodice as well as variations in the necklines of the bodice. The ideas presented here are meant to stimulate your imagination and to encourage further research and experimentation. Informative references containing additional designs are listed in the Bibliography.

15
Drafting Sleeves

Properly fitted sleeves contribute greatly to the style and the appearance of a garment. The set-in sleeve lends itself to many design variations, and when drafted to the individual's measurements, it offers comfort to the wearer. The sleeve should hang in a smooth, rounded column with no diagonal wrinkles. The lengthwise grainline should fall directly from the center of the shoulder to the center of the second finger, creating a center line perpendicular to the floor. The crosswise grainline should form a straight line at the base of the sleeve cap parallel to the floor.

Setting the sleeve into the armscye can be difficult if the shape of the sleeve cap has not been carefully drafted. The length of the sleeve cap seamline must be equal to the combined front and back bodice armscyes' lengths plus ease of 1 or 2 inches (2.5 to 5 cm). The ease allows freedom of movement. Good construction techniques allow this amount of ease to be shifted into the sleeve seamline without the formation of gathers or pleats at the seamline. Shirt sleeves may have less than 1 inch (2.5) of ease, giving a flat appearance at the seamline. In contrast, puffed or gathered sleeves have more than 2 inches (5 cm) of fullness over the top of the sleeve cap. Between these two extremes, the natural sleeve seam with 1 to 2 inches (2.5 to 5 cm) of ease presents a smooth, rounded appearance over the cap.

The width of the sleeve cap must be adequate to cover the bicep of the arm. The circumference of the arm at the muscle plus 2 to 3 inches (5 to 7.5 cm) of ease is usually adequate for the sleeve cap width. The sleeve cap width is determined by the line of pitch described later in the drafting procedures.

The shape of the sleeve cap is drafted differently for the front and the back armscyes. The armscye of the bodice front is shorter and curved more deeply than the bodice back armscye (see Figure 15.1). You may observe these differences by folding a commercial sleeve pattern in half lengthwise. The curve of the front sleeve cap is deeper than the back. The ease of the sleeve cap must be distributed along these curves when the sleeve is set into the armscye.

To maintain the straight grain across the top of the sleeve, no attempt should be made to ease the top curve of the sleeve for at least 1/2 inch (1.3 cm) on either side of the shoulder seam. This is consistent with the flat contour of the arm at the shoulder. There should be slightly more ease in the front than in the back to provide for forward arm movement. Notches are included in the basic sleeve draft to aid in the distribution of ease and the shaping of the sleeve cap.

Long sleeves generally extend about 1 inch (2.5 cm) beyond the wristbone. Extra length should be added if the sleeve is to be gathered to a wristband. Long, fitted sleeves have a short dart or soft gathers at the elbow to provide for the bending of the arm. The elbow dart or fullness is placed in the back of the sleeve. The length of short sleeves is a matter of personal preferences and fashion. Use the proportions of your arm as a guide in selecting a smart-looking length for a short sleeve.

PROCEDURE FOR DRAFTING SLEEVES

Establishing sleeve lengths

1. Top horizontal. Use a sheet of drafting paper the length of your arm plus 12 inches (30.5 cm).

Fold under 6 inches (15 cm) of your drafting paper lengthwise (Figure 15.2), and place your L square at the fold line. Folded paper is used so that it will be possible to trace the back of the sleeve after the front has been drafted. Work from right to left on this draft, except where noted. Square out from the fold line. Label all lines, once established.

2. Base of sleeve cap line. Square *down* (right to left) from the top horizontal along the fold line one half of the chest measurement divided by 3 (for example, when the chest measures 36 inches [91.5 cm], 18 ÷ 3 = 6 inches or 45.75 ÷ 3 = 15.25 cm). Square out from this point. This base-of-sleeve-cap line corresponds to the scye line of the bodice. The crosswise grainline of the fabric must follow this line for fit and proper hang of the sleeve. Label the base-of-sleeve-cap line.

3. Front notch line. Square *up* (left to right) 1 inch (2.5 cm) from the base-of-sleeve-cap line. Square out from this point. Label this line.

4. Back notch line. Square up from the base-of-sleeve-cap line one half the chest measurement divided by 4 (e.g., when chest is 36 [91.5 cm], 18 ÷ 4 = 4 1/2 inches or 45.75 ÷ 4 = 11.4 cm. Label this line.

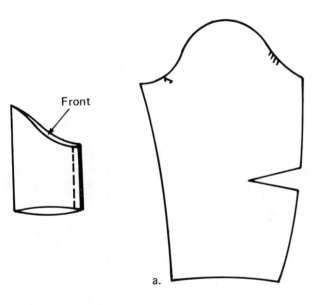

a.

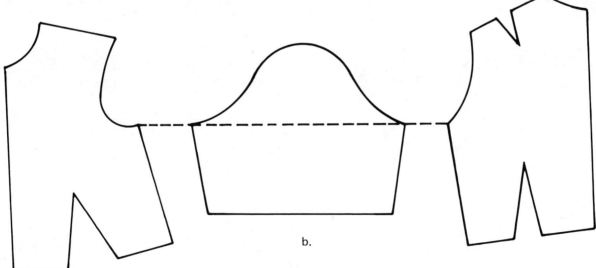

b.

Figure 15.1

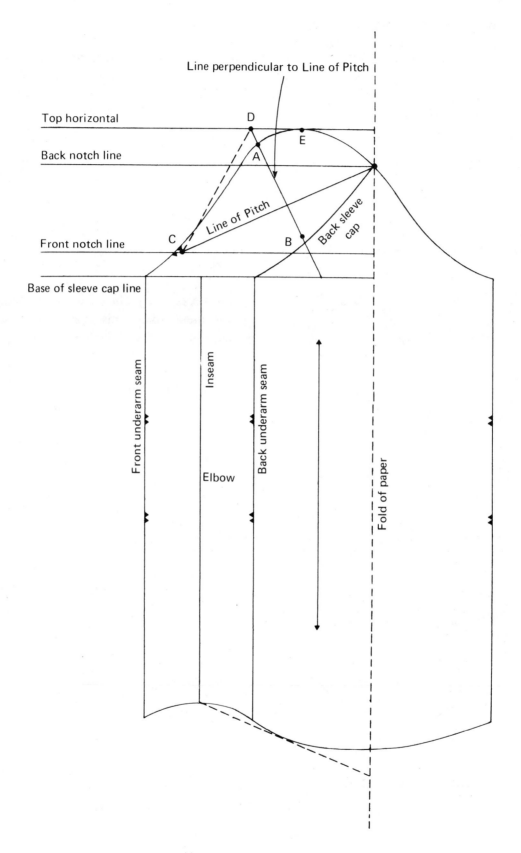

Figure 15.2

Establishing Sleeve Reference Lines

1. **Line of pitch.** This line determines the width of the sleeve cap. Establish it by pivoting the short arm of the L square between the front and the back notch lines. The length of this line is one half the chest divided by 2 minus 1 inch (2.5 cm) (when the chest is 36 inches [91.5 cm] the line of pitch equals 18 ÷ 2 - 1 inch or 8 inches; in metric, 45.75 ÷ 2 - 2.5 cm = 20.4 cm).

2. **Line perpendicular to the line of pitch.** Find the midpoint of the line of pitch, and square up and down through this point from the top horizontal to the base-of-sleeve-cap line.

3. **Inseam.** Starting at the base-of-sleeve-cap line, square down even with the termination point of the line of pitch. The length of the inseam is one fourth the height plus 1 inch (2.5 cm). When the height is 64 inches (162.5 cm), the inseam equals 64 ÷ 4 + 1 inch = 17 inches (162.5 ÷ 4 + 2.5 cm = 43 cm).

4. **Underarm seams.** Establish the front underarm seam by squaring *forward* from the inseam line one half the chest (36 inches or 91.5 cm) divided by 8 (18 ÷ 8 = 2 1/4 or 45.75 ÷ 8 = 5.7 cm). For the back underarm seam, square *backward* from the inseam line, one half the chest divided by 8 (2 1/4 inches or 5.7 cm). The underarm seams are equal distances from the inseam when drafted.

Shaping the Sleeve Cap

Establish the following guide points on your draft to assist you in shaping the sleeve cap.

1. *Point A.* Square up from the base of the sleeve cap line one half the chest (36 inches or 91.5 cm) divided by 3 (18 ÷ 3 = 6 inches or 45.75 ÷ 3 = 15.25 cm) *on* the line perpendicular to the line of pitch. Place a guide mark here and label it *A*.
2. *Point B.* Place a guide point *about* 3/8 of an inch (1 cm) up from the front notch line *on* the line perpendicular to the line of pitch. Mark this point *B*.
3. *Point C-D.* Starting at the front notch line where the line of pitch terminates, dot in a guide line to the top horizontal where the line perpendicular to the line of pitch ends. Label the starting point *C* and the end point *D*.
4. *Point E.* Find the midpoint between the fold of the paper and the line perpendicular to the line of pitch on the top horizontal. Place a guide mark here and label it *E*. You may choose to lengthen the sleeve cap for ease and for a more rounded seam appearance by raising point E above the top horizontal. Remember that the length of the sleeve cap must correspond to the armscye of the bodice plus ease. Extra length may also be needed if shoulder pads or a sleeve header are to be used in the garment's construction. Using guidepoints A, C, and E, shape in the front of the sleeve cap with the Vary Form curve ruler. This is a design feature and may require some experimentation. Next shape in the back sleeve cap line, starting at the back underarm seamline and proceeding through point B to the back notch line at the fold line of the paper. Remember the shaping of the sleeve cap described earlier (see Figure 15.1).

Shaping the Lower Edge of the Sleeve

1. Position the L Square so that the angle is at the lower end of the inseam line, with the short arm of the L square extending to the fold of the paper and the long arm of the L square extending through the point where the line of pitch and the back notch line meet. Dot in a temporary line along the lower edge of the short arm of the L square. Raise this line 1/2 inch (1.3 cm) at the fold of the paper. Correct the line from the fold of the paper to the back underarm seam with the curve stick.
2. Adjust the front underarm seam length to correspond with the back underarm seam. Using the Vary Form curve ruler, restyle the lower edge of the sleeve to give gentle, curved lines (see Figure 15.1).

Placement of the Notches

1. *Underarm seam notches.* In order to determine where the elbow will be, find the midpoint on the inseam line and raise this point 1 inch (2.5 cm). Square over to both the front and the back underarm seams from this point and place notches 2 inches (5 cm) above and below the point on both the front and the back underarm seams.
2. *Front notch on sleeve cap.* Two notches should be placed at the front notch line where the line of pitch terminates.
3. *Back notch on sleeve cap.* Place one notch at the back notch line where the line of pitch originates.
4. *Shoulder seam notch.* One notch should be placed at the center and top of the sleeve where the sleeve will be matched to the shoulder seam of the bodice. Indicate that no ease will be placed on either side of this point for 1/2 inch (1.3 cm).

Grainline

The arrow indicating that the sleeve is to be placed on the lengthwise grainline of the fabric is drafted perpendicular to the base-of-the-sleeve-cap line and even with the shoulder seam notch.

Completing the Sleeve Back

Using carbon paper and/or a tracing wheel, trace the back section of the sleeve onto the folded part of the paper. Unfold the paper, and the draft is complete.

Matching the Sleeve to the Bodice

Check first to see that the length of the seamline of the sleeve cap is equal to that of the bodice armscye plus 1 to 2 inches (2.5 to 5 cm) of ease. You can make this comparison most accurately by matching the front underarm curve of the sleeve draft with the front underarm curve of the bodice armscye. Continue matching the sleeve to the bodice by pivoting the sleeve draft to the shoulder seam of the bodice. Note the point on the sleeve draft where the shoulder seam and sleeve cap meet. Repeat the matching on the back of the sleeve and the bodice, starting at the underarm curve and continuing to the shoulder. The space left over between the front and the back marks on the sleeve draft is the ease. The ease is to be divided equally between the front and the back, so check to see that your shoulder seam notch is placed at the center of the space.

Once your sleeve draft is completed, add seam allowances and make the sleeve in fabric. Set the sleeve into your basic bodice and check the fit, the grainline, and the style. When you are pleased with the results, transfer all changes to your draft. You are now ready to reproduce your corrected sleeve draft on cardboard. This sloper, along with your bodice slopers will be used as the basis for further designs.

DESIGNING SLEEVES

Many design variations are now possible with your basic sleeve draft. As with the bodice, flat pattern methods may be used to create different designs. The important factor is retaining the individualized fit by observing the pattern outline, size, and ease that you have perfected. Begin by tracing around the sleeve block on the pattern paper. Seam allowances will be added after you have finished the designs.

Variations in Sleeve Length

1. Short sleeves. You can change sleeve length easily by tracing around the sloper, being careful to retain the sleeve cap seamline and then measuring down the underarm seam to the desired length. The length of short sleeves varies with fashion, but attractive proportions of the wearer's arm should be the first consideration. Using the length you have established on the underarm seamlines, draft in a cutting line parallel to the base-of-sleeve-cap line. This line may be straight, requiring only an extension for the hem of the desired width, usually 1 1/2 to 2 inches (3.8 to 5 cm). Or you may choose to curve the lower edge of the sleeves. A fitted facing pattern will be needed to finish a curved edge. Design this by duplicating the lower edge of the sleeve and

DRAFTING SLEEVES • 163

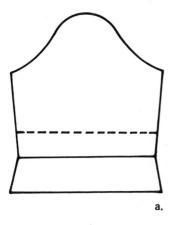
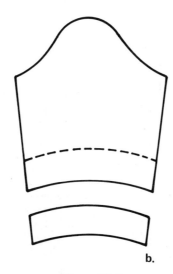
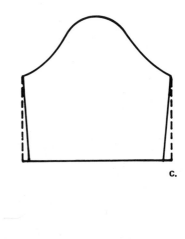

Figure 15.3

coming up the underarm seamline the width desired for the facing, usually 2 inches (5 cm). Draft in a cutting line between the underarm seam markings parallel to the lower edge of the facing. Seam allowances must be added at the lower edge of the facing and the sleeve (see Figure 15.3).

The sleeve width or circumference may feel too bulky made from the sloper, as 2 to 3 inches (5 to 7.5 cm) of ease was built into the long-sleeved sloper. To remove this extra width from your pattern, take equal amounts from each side of the short sleeve at the hemline. Redraft the underarm seamline, terminating it at the base-of-sleeve-cap line (see Figure 15.3). Again, a shaped facing is preferable for finishing the lower edge. Care should be taken to have enough ease remaining for the sleeve to be comfortable. No changes should be made in the sleeve cap seamline.

2. Roll-up shirt sleeves. Popular for sportswear, these sleeves are designed to have enough length so that a cuff of self-fabric can be rolled up from the elbow. Select an appropriate finished length for the sleeve. This would be the position where you want the sleeve to rest with the cuff rolled. Trace your basic draft, and come down along the underarm seam the length you have selected and mark this point. Add to this length twice the width of the cuff plus a hem allowance. When the sleeve is hemmed, it will be folded back on itself.

3. Long sleeves. The basic sleeve draft has sufficient room to allow finishing the lower edge with a casing and inserting elastic. An additional 1 inch (2.5 cm) added to the sleeve length will make this variation more comfortable. If a blousy appearance is desired, see the fullness variation below. The lower edge of the sleeve may be finished with a bias strip of the same fabric or a commercial bias tape. In constructing the sleeve, leave an opening in the casing at the seam for the insertion of the elastic. The elastic will be comfortable if its length is the wrist measurement plus 1 inch (2.5 cm).

Another variation of the long sleeve is the addition of a cuff. Two drafting procedures are needed to complete this sleeve: drafting an opening on the basic long sleeve and designing a cuff. Sleeve openings are of two types: the pleat style and the slashed opening (see Figure 15.4). The pleat-style opening involves placing two circles on the lower sleeve seamline at the place where the opeining will be. The circles are placed 1 inch (2.5 cm) apart, and the center point between the circles should be in line with the elbow and the little finger. Thus the cuff will close at that point on the outside of the arm. To construct this opening, place small reinforcing machine stitches on the seamline between the

164 • COMPARATIVE ANALYSIS OF PATTERN TECHNIQUES

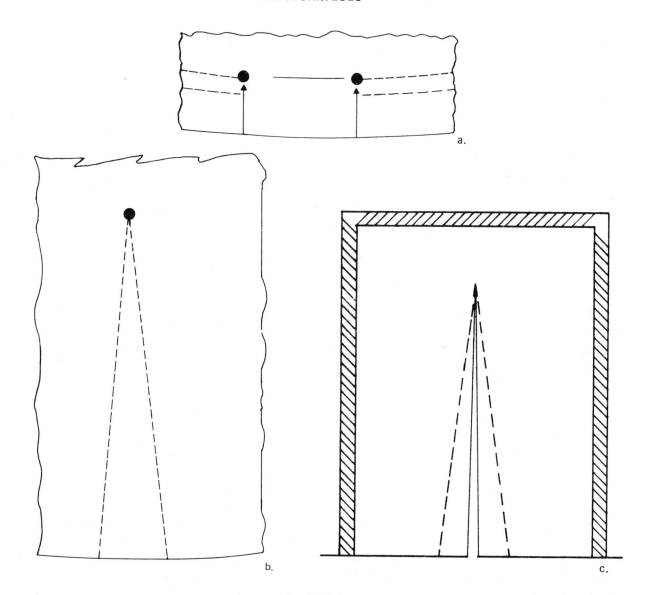

Figure 15.4

circles. The seam allowances are then clipped to the circles. The seam allowance between the circles is finished with a rolled hem. The ends of the cuff are matched to the seam allowances at the circles. The slashed opening requires the drafting of a triangle at the lower edge of the sleeve. The triangle should be 1/2 inch (1.3 cm) wide at the base and about 3 inches (7.5 cm) long. The triangle is placed so that the center is on a line from the elbow to the little finger. The opening must be parallel to the straight grain of the fabric. This opening may be faced with self-fabric about 4 by 3 1/2 inches (10 by 9 cm), or it may be bound and treated as a continuous lapped opening.

Cuffs vary both in width and in design. The length of the cuff should be equal to your wrist measurement plus 2 to 3 inches (5 to 7.5 cm) for overlap when finished. The cuff may be designed so that the cuff and the facing are one piece folded in the center. Or the cuff and facing may be separate pieces joined by a seam. If trim is to be inserted, this second design should be chosen. The finished cuff width is usually between 1 and 2 inches (2.5 to 5 cm). The French cuff is designed so that it folds back on itself

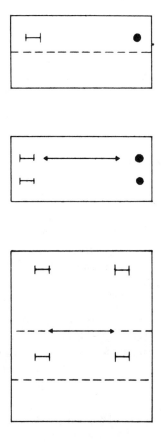

Figure 15.5

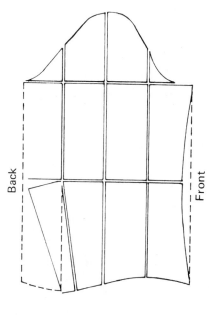

Figure 15.6

and is worn with cuff links. The finished width is about 3 inches (7.5 cm) for this style of cuff (see Figure 15.5).

It will be necessary to gather the lower edge of the basic sleeve to fit the cuff. More fullness at the lower edge of the sleeve may improve the appearance. This variation is described later in the chapter under "Variations in Sleeve Width."

In contrast, an adaptation that makes the sleeve more fitted may be desired. Because the basic sleeve draft is straight at the sides, the drafting of an elbow dart would improve the shape and fit. It would be inappropriate simply to remove width from the side seams for a close-fitting long sleeve, as poor shape would result and there would be insufficient room to bend the elbow. The following procedure gives a shaped but not a tight sleeve.

Trace around the basic sleeve sloper. Mark the base-of-the-sleeve-cap line on your pattern. At the elbow, draw a horizontal line parallel to the base-of-the-sleeve-cap line. From the front sleeve seamline, measure in 1 inch (2.5 cm) on the elbow line just drawn, and mark this point. With the curve stick, shape a new front sleeve seamline starting at the base-of-the-sleeve-cap line through the elbow point to the wrist. From the back sleeve seamline, measure in 3/4 inch (2 cm) on the elbow line, and mark this point. Connect the base-of-sleeve-cap line and the elbow point with a straight line (see Figure 15.6).

To shape the sleeve from the elbow to the wrist, slash the pattern along the elbow line, starting at the back seamline and slashing about one fourth of the sleeve width. Fold a vertical dart at the lower sleeve edge perpendicular to the slash. A dart will now open at the elbow. It should be 1 inch (2.5 cm) deep. Reshape the lower sleeve edge with the dart closed. Check the wrist measurement to be sure its width is adequate. Sleeves to be made of knitted fabrics may be fitted more closely than those to be made in woven fabrics. Making this sleeve in fabric to check its fit before using the pattern is recommended. You may wish to have a cardboard sloper of this sleeve also.

The lower edge of fitted sleeves may be finished with shaped facings, cuffs, ruffles, lace, and other trims.

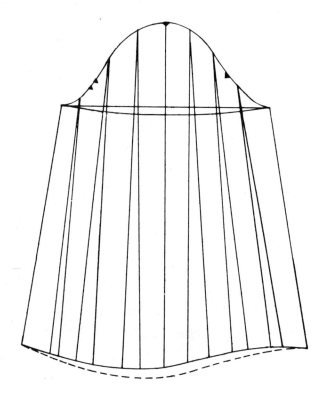

Figure 15.7

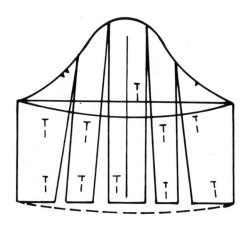

Figure 15.8

Variations in Sleeve Width

1. Fullness at the lower edge. When fullness is added at the lower edge of a long sleeve, the sleeve is called a *bishop sleeve*. Create this fullness by slashing the pattern parallel to the center of the sleeve (straight grain) and spreading to the desired width. The slashes are spaced evenly across the sleeve width and extend *to but not through* the sleeve cap seamline. The bishop sleeve has a smooth sleeve cap seamline (see Figure 15.7). The lower sleeve-edge seamline must be reshaped to include the added fullness and curve of the lower edge. Additional length may be added if desired. The lower edge may be finished with a casing and elastic, or the added fullness may be gathered or pleated to a band or cuff.

This same procedure may be used with a short sleeve to create a puffed sleeve with the fullness at the lower edge gathered to a band or cuff. A sleeve with added fullness at the lower edge that is not gathered but is allowed to drape freely is called a *bell sleeve*. The lower edge of a bell sleeve is finished with a shaped facing (see Figure 15.8).

2. Increased fullness at the sleeve cap. Parallel slashes starting at the sleeve cap and extending to but not through the lower seamline are used to create fullness at the sleeve cap. The pattern is spread at the slashes for the desired width, and the sleeve cap seamline is reshaped from notch to notch. This involves adding length at the top of the sleeve (see Figure 15.9), which adds more puff to the sleeve. The extra fullness may be gathered, pleated, or darted so that the sleeve cap fits the armscye of the bodice.

Puffed sleeves with fullness at both cap and hem are often found in children's garments. Create this design by slashing the sleeve from cap to hem and spreading the desired amount. Slashes should be an equal distance from the sleeve's center, and the added amount should be the same on either side of the center. Both the cap and the hem must be reshaped, with additional length being added at cap and hem (see Figure 15.10).

Another variation of sleeve cap fullness is the leg-o'-mutton sleeve, so named because it is close-fitting from elbow to wrist but very full at the sleeve cap. This design appears in theatrical costumes and wedding gowns and frequently reappears in women's fashions. Start with the close-fitting pattern developed earlier (see "Long Sleeves" above), and from elbow to wrist, fit it even more snugly than in the previous draft. This will require that you include a zipper or a button and button loop closing at the lower sleeve seamline. On

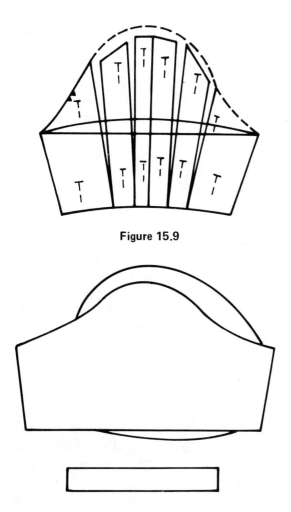

Figure 15.9

Figure 15.10

Figure 15.11

your draft, center this opening on a line from the elbow to the little finger. Draw a horizontal line from seamline to seamline at the elbow. Draw vertical slash lines from the sleeve cap to the elbow line. Slash the pattern on both the horizontal and the vertical lines, and spread the sleeve cap to achieve the desired fullness. Reshape the sleeve cap to include the fullness, which will add some length, but you may wish to raise the cap more for greater puffiness (see Figure 15.11). In constructing this sleeve, it may be necessary to include both underlining and interfacing to maintain the shape.

3. Decreased fullness in the sleeve cap. A smooth, flat sleeve cap is needed in shirts, uniforms, and many designs for knitted fabrics. To achieve this effect, reduce the ease in the sleeve cap. After tracing the basic sleeve, mark the base-of-the-sleeve-cap line from seam to seam. Draw a line perpendicular to this line, starting at the shoulder seam point. Slash the pattern from the shoulder seam to the base-of-the-sleeve-cap line, and then slash on the base-of-the-sleeve-cap line to each side seam. Overlap the pattern until you have removed sufficient ease from the cap so that it will set into the armscye of the shirt smoothly. Reshape the sleeve cap curve. Measure the sleeve cap and the armscye to be certain that the seamlines match. This type of sleeve is often sewn into the armscye before the closing of the side seam. The body of the shirt and the sleeve seams are sewn in the same stitching. This technique is necessary when you are using flat-felled seams.

Sleeves cut on the bodice. Attractive designs are achieved by a combining of the bodice and sleeve slopers to produce a bodice and sleeve all in one piece. These garments are easy to cut, sew, and wear but may compromise the fit offered by a set-in sleeve. Wrinkling under the arm and at the shoulder is often visible when the arms rest at the sides. Improving the fit, which reduces wrinkling, also restricts arm movement. This difficulty is minimized by use of a gusset to restore freedom of movement. Sleeves included in this design group are kimono, raglan, and dolman sleeves. Students may wish to experiment with the fullness, depth, and angle of these before completing a sloper. These sleeves are often very satisfactory for growing children and persons with body irregularities, as the arm position is not precisely defined, allowing flexibility.

Kimono pattern. The procedure for drafting the kimono pattern begins with tracing the close-fitting sleeve sloper on paper. Mark the shoulder seam (center of the sleeve cap). Measure 1/2 inch (1.3 cm) toward the front of the sleeve from the shoulder seam and mark point A (see Figure 15.12). Measure the wrist width, and mark the center point B. Draw a line from the center of the sleeve cap (A) to the center of the wrist line (B). Next measure down from point A 1/2 inch (1.3 cm) along the center line (A to B), and re-establish A at this point. Separate the sleeve pieces along the line A to B. The back pattern section of the sleeve will be wider than the front (see Figure 15.12).

After tracing your bodice back pattern, move the shoulder dart to the armscye. This will

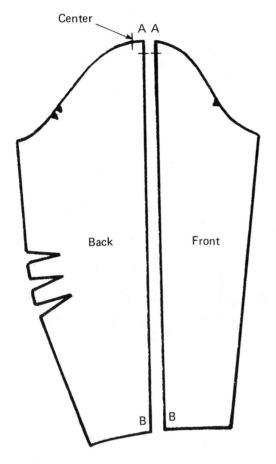

Figure 15.12 Kimono sleeve

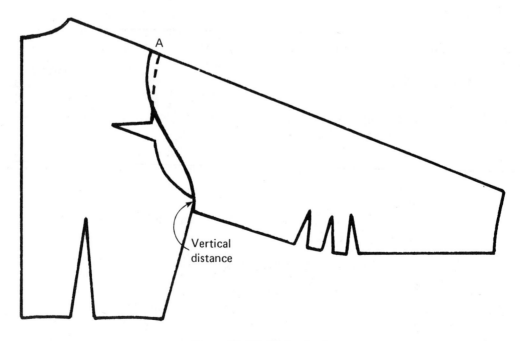

Figure 15. 13 Bodice back

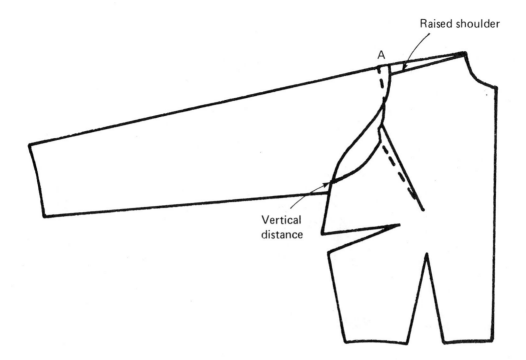

Figure 15.14 Bodice front

help compensate for the loss of the fitting curve of the original armscye seam. Join the bodice back and sleeve back by placing point A of the sleeve to the end of the bodice-back shoulder seam. Note that this laps the sleeve 1/2 inch (1.3 cm) over the end of the shoulder (see Figure 15.13). Move the sleeve downward until it meets the bodice underarm seam. Note the vertical distance along the underarm seam from the bodice underarm to the sleeve seam (see Figure 15.13). Measure and mark the same distance at the same point on the bodice front underarm seam. Reshape the underarm seamline so that the bodice and the sleeve meet and form a gentle curve.

Trace around your bodice front. Raise the shoulder seam 1/2 inch or 1.3 cm (1/4 inch or 3 mm on small sizes or children's clothes). Move the shoulder dart to the front armscye by drawing a straight line from the notch, slanting toward the bust. Slash along this line, but do not secure the pattern (see Figure 15.14).

Join the bodice front and the front sleeve at the new shoulder seamline. Pivot the sleeve downward, and spread the bodice front along the dart slash until the sleeve meets the underarm seam at the point you marked to correspond to the back. Secure the pattern to paper, filling in the armscye area. You will need to correct the shoulder sleeve seamline, giving both front and back a slightly curved line. Reshape the front underarm seam to correspond to the back underarm seam.

Place the bodice front and back together, and check the length of your seamlines.

Kimono sleeve with gusset. A gusset allows greater freedom of movement in a fitted kimono sleeve. Draft a line on the kimono front and back patterns from the underarm to the shoulder neck point (see Figure 15.15). This defines the position of the underarm gusset. Mark a point 3 to 4 inches (7.5 to 10 cm) up this line from the underarm. This will be the length of one side of the gusset. The pattern will be slashed to this point for inserting the gusset in constructing the garment. The basic gusset shape is a diamond. On this diamond-shaped gusset, each side should be equal to the length of the gusset slash line. The gusset may be divided into two pieces for

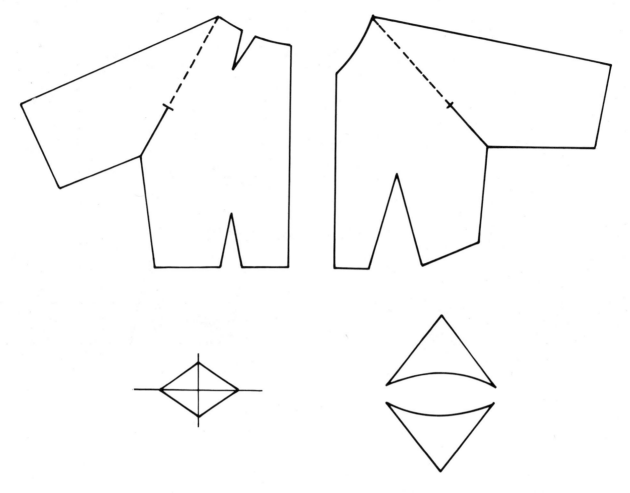

Figure 15.15

more precise underarm shaping. The gusset is then stitched with the underarm seam.

Raglan sleeve. Using the bodice front and back developed for the kimono sleeve, design a slightly curved seamline extending from the neckline to the underarm. Fashion may help determine the placement of this line, but the line originates in the neckline 1 to 2 inches (2.5 to 5 cm) below the neck point, curving toward the underarm seam. It can terminate as much as 2 inches (5 cm) below the underarm point. This line should curve up slightly near the neckline (see Figure 15.16).

Separate the pattern pieces on the seamlines you have designed for the bodice front and back.

You now have a two-piece raglan sleeve. When the sleeve sections are joined, a dart forms at the top of the sleeve. This shoulder dart gives a tailored effect and provides fit over the arm at the shoulder. To make the dart deeper, slash horizontally toward the curved arm seam, and spread. This is especially helpful for broad shoulders and padded designs. You may also prefer to have a one-piece raglan sleeve and need only to omit the shoulder seam by joining the front and back sleeve sections. For a more comprehensive discussion of raglan sleeves, see Hollen (1981).

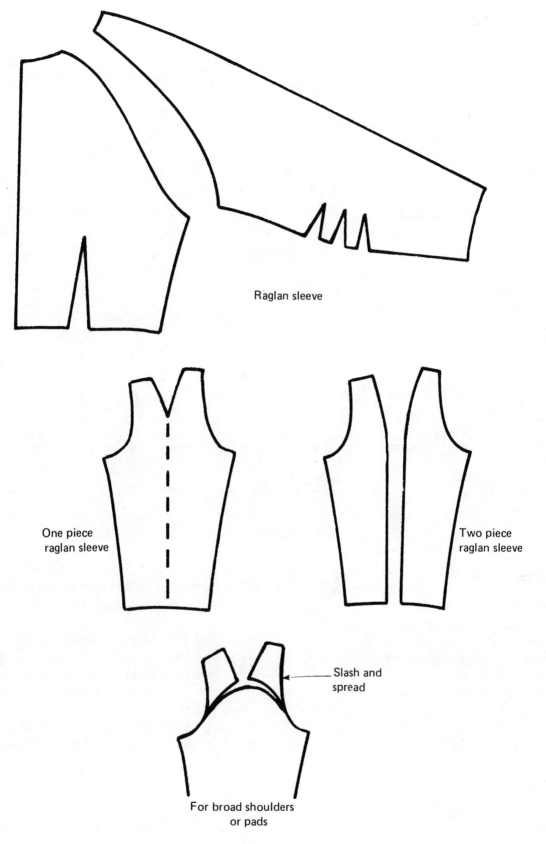

Figure 15.16

172 • COMPARATIVE ANALYSIS OF PATTERN TECHNIQUES

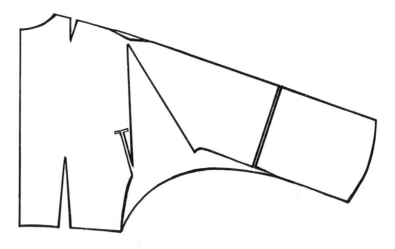

Figure 15.17

Figure 15.18

Dolman sleeve (Bat-wing sleeve). This sleeve variation is very loose as the underarm seam curves deeply from the waist to the wrist. Make the pattern by slashing the kimono draft from the slash line designed for the gusset at the underarm to the shoulder point. Spread the pattern until the length of the underarm seam is equal to the length of the side seam of the bodice block plus the length of the side seam of the sleeve block. Curve the underarm seam from the waist to the wrist (see Figure 15.17).

Cap sleeve. This sleeve variation is a very short cut-on sleeve with no underarm seam. The design is used in warm weather clothing and in dropped-sleeve seam designs. It can be drafted from the bodice block or the kimono block. Using the bodice slopers, extend the shoulder seam enough to cover the shoulders. Lower the armscye 1 to 2 inches (2.5 to 5 cm). Design a connecting line between the extended shoulder and the lowered armscye (see Figure 15.18). Check to see that the bodice front and back match at the seamlines.

16
Drafting Shirts

This shirt draft fits close to the body, and the sleeves are cut high under the arms. It is adaptable for several flat pattern variations, some of which are included in the chapter. Be sure to read Chapter 13, "General Drafting Techniques," before beginning. Follow the sequence given in the instructions, and be accurate.

PROCEDURE FOR DRAFTING SHIRT BACK

Establishing Back Lengths

Unroll approximately 3 feet (91.5 cm) of drafting paper, and lay it on the table so that the length is parallel to the edge of the table. Work from right to left.

1. Top horizontal. Place your L square at the edge of the paper, with the long arm of the L square extending the length of the paper and the short arm extending away from you. Square out and down along the L square. This vertical line will be the center back of the shirt.

2. Neck run. Square down 1 inch (2.5 cm) from the top horizontal and out from this point.

3. Shoulder height. Establish the shoulder height line by squaring down from the *neck run* three sixty-fourths of the *height* minus 1/2 inch (1.3 cm). For a person 5 feet 11 inches (71 inches, or 180.5 cm), the shoulder height would be placed 2 13/16 inches (7.2 cm) from the neck run (71 × 3/64 = 3 5/16 - 1/2 = 2 13/16 inches, or 180.5 × 3/64 = 8.5 - 1.3 = 7.2 cm). Square out from this point.

4. Scye line. Square down from the shoulder height line one half of the chest measurement divided by 3. A person with a 38-inch (96.5-cm) chest would square down 6 3/8-inches (16 cm) and square out from this point (38 ÷ 2 = 19 ÷ 3 = 6 3/8 inches, or 96.5 ÷ 2 = 48.25 ÷ 3 = 16 cm). Note that this measurement corresponds to a woman's high chest measurement. The scye line goes around the body from underarm to underarm and is a critical line for achieving good fit.

5. Waistline. This line is established from the *neck run* and is equal to the back waist-length measurement (Appendix) plus 1/2 inch (1.3 cm) of ease. Measure this amount down from the neck run, and square out at this point.

6. Hipline. From the waistline, square down one eighth of the height minus 1 inch (2.5 cm) and out from this point. For a person 71 inches (180.5 cm) tall, the hipline would be placed 7 7/8 inches (20.1 cm) from the waistline (71 ÷ 8 = 8 7/8 - 1 = 7 7/8 inches, or 180.5 ÷ 8 = 22.6 - 2.5 = 20.1 cm).

7. Hemline. From the waistline, square down approximately 10 inches (25.5 cm) or the desired shirt hemline. Square out from this point.

Once these lines are established (see Figure 16.1), you have determined the length lines necessary for drafting a shirt. Proceed to establish the widths.

Establishing Back Widths

8. Width of back. The width of the back is established on the scye line. Square out on the scye line one fourth of the chest measurement plus 1 inch (2.5 cm) ease. Square up and down from this point (Figure 16.2). A person with a 38-inch (96.5-cm) chest would square out 10 1/2 inches (27 cm) calculated as follows: 38 ÷ 4 = 9 1/2 + 1 = 10 1/2 inches (96.5 ÷ 4 = 24.12 + 2.5 = 27 cm). This formula gives the shirt a snug to moderately snug fit, but additional ease can be included for various styles.

9. Eighth lines. Both the back and the front eighth lines are placed in reference to the width-of-back line established in Step 8. For the back eighth line, square in (toward you) from the width-of-back line one half of the chest measurement divided by 8. Square up and down from this point. For a 38-inch (96.5-cm) chest, the back eighth line would be placed 2 3/8 inches (6 cm) from the width of back line (38 ÷ 2 = 19 ÷ 8 = 2 3/8 inches, or 96.5 ÷ 2 = 48.25 ÷ 8 = 6 cm).

For the front eighth line, square out (away from you) from the width-of-back line the same amount. Square up and down from this point, shown in Figure 16.2.

Now you are ready to design the shirt back within these perimeters. Before proceeding, check your work to make certain that your calculations are correct and that the lines are precisely drawn. All the lengths and widths should be accurately labeled on your draft, as further instructions will refer to these lines by name.

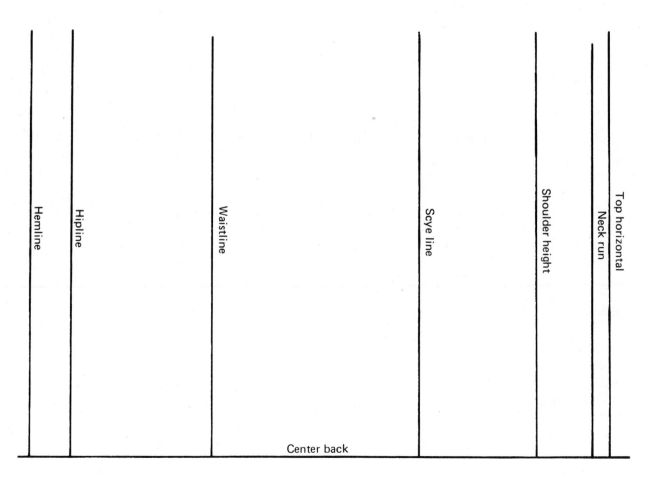

Figure 16.1

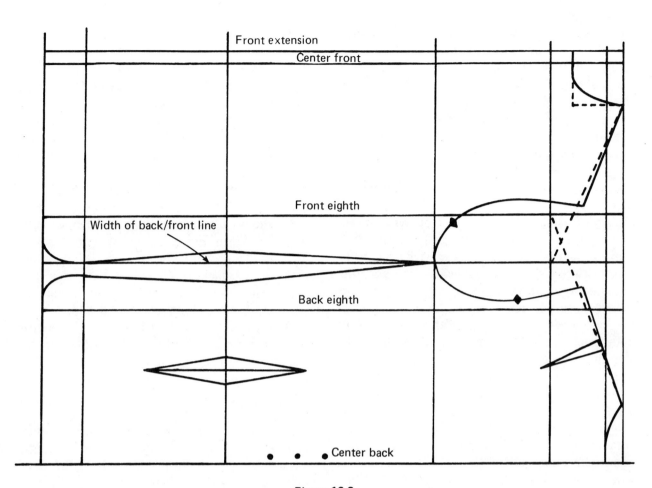

Figure 16.2

Shaping the Shirt Back

10. Shoulder neck point. This point is placed on the top horizontal. Square out from the center back line one half of the chest measurement divided by 6, and mark this point. For example, square out 3 1/8 inches, or 8 cm (38 ÷ 2 - 19 ÷ 6 = 3 1/8 inches or 96.5 ÷ 2 = 48.25 ÷ 6 = 8 cm). Using the vary form curve, shape the neckline from the center back on the neck run to the shoulder neck point on the top horizontal (Figure 16.2).

11. Shoulder seam. Place the short arm of the L square at the shoulder neck point established in Step 10, and position the arm of the L square so that a line can be drawn from this point to the point where the *front* eighth line (established in Step 9) meets the shoulder height line. Dot in a temporary shoulder seamline. Raise the shoulder height line 3/16 inch (5 mm) for ease on the back eighth line. For square shoulders, you may raise the shoulder height line as much as 1/2 inch (1.3 cm). Extend the new shoulder seamline approximately 1 1/4 inches (3.2 cm) beyond the back eighth line. The length of the shoulder seamline should correspond to your shoulder length measurement plus 1/2 inch (1.3 cm). A shoulder dart is included in the back shirt for good fit over the shoulder area, but for most styles, this back shoulder dart is converted to a yoke and moved to the armscye. Draft in the shoulder length needed.

12. Back shoulder dart. This dart is placed approximately at the midpoint of the shoulder seam unless some body characteristic or disability indicates that a different placement would contribute to better fit and appearance. A dart depth of 1/2 inch (1.3 cm) is typical, depending on the prominence of the shoulder blade. Direct the dart toward the center of the body bulge, and extend it slightly below the shoulder height line.

Fold the dart as it will be stitched, with the dart tuck turned toward the center back, and correct the shoulder seam. This step will give the dart the shape needed for a straight edge at the shoulder seamline. Compare your shoulder seam measurement to that of your draft with the dart folded in. You may need to lengthen or shorten the seamline at this time.

13. Armscye. Use the armscye sloper provided in the Appendix for shaping this seamline. The armscye is shaped in from the shoulder seam to the scye line. Before drafting the permanent armscye, check the width of the back draft halfway between the shoulder height line and the scye line to be sure your draft is wider than your personal measurement. The armscye seamline can be moved toward the width-of-back line if additional width is needed across the back. If the draft is too wide in this area, move the armscye seamline toward the back eighth line.

14. Back notch. This notch is placed on the armscye seamline. Determine its location by squaring up from the scye line on the back eighth line one half of the chest measurement divided by 4. Place the notch at this level on the back armscye seamline. For a chest of 38 inches (96.5 cm), the notch would be placed 4 3/4 inches (10 cm) up from the scye line (38 ÷ 2 = 19 ÷ 4 = 4 3/4 inches, or 96.5 ÷ 2 = 48.25 ÷ 4 = 12.06 cm).

15. Waistline width. The back waistline measurement should be one half of the waistline measurement minus 1/2 inch (1.3 cm). The 1/2 inch (1.3 cm) is subtracted from the back so that the front waistline will be 1 inch (2.5 cm) larger. For example, for a 32-inch (81.5 cm) waist, the back waistline measurement equals 15 1/2 inches (39 cm), and the front waistline measurement equals 16 1/2 inches (42 cm). As the pattern draft is for one half of the shirt back, divide the back measurement by 2.

The side seamline is not tapered to the waistline width mark. Instead the difference between the width-of-back line and the waistline width is divided by 3, and this amount is removed from the side seam at the waistline. In the example above, the width-of-back line measures 10 1/2 inches (27 cm), and the back waistline width is 7 3/4 inches (19 cm). Thus 1 inch, or 2.7 cm (10 1/2 − 7 3/4 = 2 3/4 ÷ 3 = 1 inch, or 27 − 19 = 8 ÷ 3 = 2.7 cm), is removed from the side seam, and the remaining 1 3/4 inches (5.3 cm) is placed in a waistline dart. This dart is seldom stitched into the shirt back except in designer or European shirts. Subtract the amount (1 inch, or 2.7 cm) from the width-of-back line at the waistline.

16. Hipline width. The back measurement is 1 inch (2.5 cm) smaller than the front hip measurement and is calculated in the same manner as the waistline width. For example if the hip measurement is 39 inches (99 cm), the back hip measurement is 19 inches (48.5 cm), and the front measurement is 20 inches (51 cm). Divide the back hip measurement by 2, and add 1/2 inch (1.3 cm) ease (19 ÷ 2 = 9 1/2 + 1/2 = 10 inches, or 48.5 ÷ 2 = 24.25 + 1.3 = 26 cm). Measure this distance out from the center back along the hipline, and square down to the hemline, using a dotted line.

17. Side seam. Draft the side seamline from the end point of the armscye on the width of the back line to the point established for the waistline and on to the hipline width mark. Create a gentle curve at the waistline and a round side-hem corner (Figure 16.2).

18. Back waistline dart (optional). The depth of this dart was determined in Step 15. The dart usually ends 1/2 to 1 inch (1.3 to 2.5 cm) below the fullest part of each body bulge. The termination points are placed one half the distance between the center back and the back eighth line. It is usually easier to draw the fold line of the dart from termination point to termination point. Then locate the stitching lines at the waistline equally on each side of the foldline. Draft in the dart stitching lines.

19. Grainline. Indicate that the shirt back is to be placed on the lengthwise fold of the fabric.

PROCEDURE FOR DRAFTING SHIRT FRONT

20. Establishing lengths and width of front. Draft the shirt front beside the back, using the same lengths as established for the back. It is necessary to extend each of these lines (top horizontal, neck run, shoulder height, scye line, waistline, hipline, and hemline) to provide for the width of the front. Extend these lines so that the total width equals one half of the chest measurement plus 2 inches (5 cm) of ease. For a 38-inch (96.5 cm) chest, the total measurement would be 21 inches, or 53.25 cm (38 ÷ 2 = 19 + 2 = 21 inches or 96.5 ÷ 2 = 48.25 + 5 = 53.25). Square up and down through this point. This line becomes the center front of the shirt.

Shaping the Shirt Front

21. Shoulder neck points. These points will be used in shaping the front neckline. On the top horizontal, use a dotted line and square toward you from the center front one half the chest measurement divided by 8. Thus, for a 38 inch (96.5 cm) chest, you would square in 2 3/8 inches, or 6.5 cm (38 ÷ 2 = 19 ÷ 8 = 2 3/8 inches, or 96.5 ÷ 2 = 48.25 ÷ 8 = 6.5 cm). Square down from the top horizontal on the center front the same amount plus 1/2 inch (1.3 cm) of ease. Use a vary form curve to shape the neckline within the box. Check this neck measurement with your neckband size measurement plus ease (Appendix). If it needs to be made larger, lower the neckline at the center front.

22. Shoulder seam. Establish a temporary shoulder seamline by placing the short arm of the L square at the shoulder neck point (see Step 10) and dotting in a line to the width of front line. The shoulder seamline stops at the point where the shoulder height line and width-of-front line (also the width-of-back line) meet. The back and front shoulder seamlines must cross in the space between the front eighth line and the width-of-front/back lines (side seamlines). Raise the shoulder height line the same amount as for the back shoulder height line on the front eighth line. Draft in the shoulder seam length, which corresponds to your body's shoulder length measurement. This length measurement should correspond to the back shoulder length measurement minus the dart.

23. Armscye. Use the armscye sloper (Appendix), and shape the front armscye by drawing a line from the shoulder seam to the width-of-front/back line (side seamlines). Check the width across the chest at a midpoint between the scye and the shoulder height lines with your body measurement.

24. Front notch. The front notch is placed on the armscye seamline level. Locate the point by squaring up on the front eighth line from the scye line one half of the chest measurement divided by 16. Thus, for a 38 inch (96.5 cm) chest, the notch would be placed 1 1/8 inches (3 cm) above the scye line (38 ÷ 2 = 19 ÷ 16 = 1 1/8 inches, or 96.5 ÷ 2 = 48.25 ÷ 16 = 3 cm).

25. Waistline width. As discussed earlier the front waistline is 1 inch (2.5 cm) larger than the back waistline. Use the front waistline measurement, which you determined in Step 15, and divide the amount by 2 (16 1/2 ÷ 2 = 8 1/4 inches, or 42 ÷ 2 = 21 cm). To determine the amount of tapering needed at the side waistline, subtract the waistline width from the width-of-front measurement, and divide by 3. In our example, the width of the front is 10 1/2 inches (27 cm), and the waistline width is 8 1/4 inches (21 cm). Thus the calculation is 10 1/2 − 8 1/4 = 2 1/4 ÷ 3 = 3/4 inch (27 − 21 = 6 ÷ 3 = 2 cm). Measure this amount out (away from you) from the width-of-front/back line on the waistline to determine the side seam location.

26. Hipline width. The front hip width was determined in Step 16. Divide this front hip width by 2, and add 1/2 inch (1.3 cm) of ease (20 ÷ 2 = 10 + 1/2 = 10 1/2 inches, or 51 ÷ 2 = 25.5 + 1.3 = 27 cm). Measure this distance in from the center front along the hipline, and square down to the hemline, using a dotted line.

27. Side seam. Draft the side seamline from the end point of the armscye on the width of the front line to the point established for the waistline and on to the hipline width mark. Create a gentle curve at the waistline and a round side-hem corner (Figure 16.2).

28. Grainline. The shirt front is to be placed on the lengthwise grain of the fabric. Indicate this on your draft by placing an arrow parallel to the center front.

The back and front shirt drafts are now complete. Add seam allowances to the drafts, and test them in fabric. Machine-baste the fabric fitting shell so that changes can be easily made. Have someone check the fit of the shell while applying the principles of good fit described in Chapter 4. Remember that the fitting shell should fit moderately close to the body and high under the arms. When satisfactory fit has been achieved, transfer all changes to your initial drafts. Reproduce your corrected drafts on cardboard. These will serve as the block patterns you will use in designing.

After you have the fit corrected on the shirt front and back blocks, draft a sleeve pattern (Chapter 15). Use flat pattern methods to create a shirt-sleeve pattern. Check the sleeve length measurement by measuring the shirt back and the sleeve patterns from the center back neckline to the sleeve hem and by comparing the length with your body measurement (measurement worksheet in Appendix). Correct the sleeve draft if necessary, before testing the sleeve draft in fabric.

DESIGNING SHIRTS

When using your shirt draft, you must retain the pattern outline, size, and ease at all times, thus maintaining your personalized fit. The shirt draft has several possibilities, and you will be pleased with the patterns you design as long as the relationships established in the draft are maintained.

To design with your shirt drafts, using flat pattern methods, trace around the block on pattern paper. Remember that the blocks have no seam allowances. These are added after your designs are finished. The suggestions given here provide only a taste of the many variations you can create with your blocks. Observe ready-made shirts for other design possibilities.

Back Yokes

To create a back yoke, draw a line across the back where the lower yoke seam is desired, usually 1 1/2 to 3 1/2 inches (3.8 to 9 cm) below the shoulder–armscye corner. Place notches on the yoke cutting line. Fold in the existing shoulder dart, and secure with tape or pins. Slash along the yoke line to the center back, separating the pattern. The yoke pattern should lie flat, and the seam will curve close to the armscye, moving the dart to the seamline. Correct the shoulder seamline, if necessary. Straighten the lower yoke seamline by squaring across the pattern at the upper edge of the dart spread (Figure 16.3). Redraw the upper edge of the shirt back, removing the dart width and creating a smooth curve. If the yoke line crosses the dart, the lower part of the dart is eased into the seam.

Shoulder seams on menswear are never at the

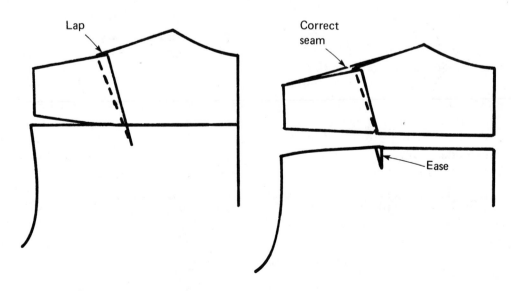

Figure 16.3

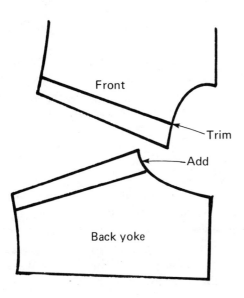

Figure 16.4

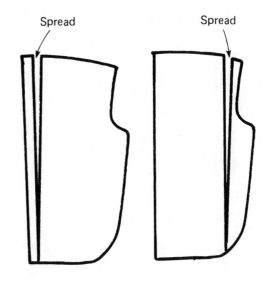

Figure 16.5

true shoulder line; they are moved forward to give a square-shouldered appearance. Move the shoulder seams by drafting a line across the front pattern that is located 7/8 inch (2.2 cm) from the armscye corner and 1 inch (2.5 cm) from the neck corner. Cut the pattern apart on this line, and tape the section to the back yoke pattern (Figure 16.4).

Back Pleats

Some styles have a center box pleat or side pleats stitched into the back yoke seam. Determine the location of the pleat on the back pattern, and draw a vertical line to the hem. Cut on this line from the upper yoke seam almost to the hemline. Spread the yoke seam the desired width of the pleat (Figure 16.5). The spread is usually 1 inch (2.5 cm) for a side pleat and up to 2 inches (5 cm) for a center box pleat.

Front Openings

An extension must be added to the shirt front so that there is an overlap for buttons and buttonholes. Because shirts use small buttons, the extension width is generally 3/4 inch (2 cm). Add this amount to the center front of the shirt draft (Figure 16.2). After the extension has been added, the shirt front opening may be finished with either a facing or a front band.

Front facings. Because the front extension is straight, a cut-on facing is always used on shirts. To determine the width of the facing, double the extension width, and add this total amount to the pattern (Figure 16.6). Fold (do not cut) the pattern along the extension line, and trace the remaining edges (e.g., the neckline) onto the pattern. Label the center front and the fold lines.

Front bands. The extension width also determines the width of the front band because it must be drafted with the buttonholes placed on the center front line. If the extension width was 3/4 inch (2 cm), draft a line that is 1 1/2 inches (4 cm) from the extension line, or 3/4 inch

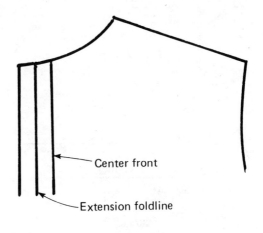

Figure 16.6

180 • COMPARATIVE ANALYSIS OF PATTERN TECHNIQUES

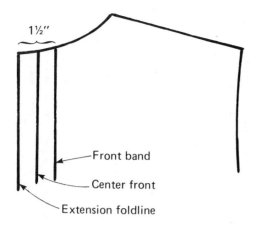

Figure 16.7

(2 cm) from the center front line (Figure 16.7). Locate notches along this line and cut, separating the front band from the shirt front. The front band is usually designed for both shirt fronts; however, you could design a front band for the outer overlap and a fitted facing for the underlap. Men's shirts lap left over right, and women's shirts are usually lapped right over left.

Front Yokes

Front yokes are designed after the back yoke has been created and the shoulder seams have been relocated. Front yokes are usually found on Western-style shirts, and the yoke seamline may be placed at any location. As there are no darts in the shirt front, the yoke seam is drafted where desired. Locate notches along the yoke seam and cut the pattern apart on the line. The only limiting factor in a yoke design may be your sewing ability, especially if you design intricate curves along the yoke seam.

Collars

Collars are the focal point of many shirts because they often frame a tie. Shirt collars may not offer as many design possibilities as those used on women's wear; however, the width, the points, and the spread of the collar can be varied. Shirts are generally designed with separate collar and neck band pattern pieces.

Neck band. Measure the complete neckline seam of the shirt, including the extension, or front band. Draw a rectangle that is one half of this length and 1 1/4 to 1 5/8 inches (3.2 to 4 cm) wide. Draft a line the width of the front extension at one end of the rectangle, and label the center front line. Label the other end of the rectangle "center back foldline." Measure the back neckline, and indicate the location of the shoulder seam along the neck edge of the rectangle (Figure 16.8). Draft a line parallel to and 1 1/2 inches (3.8 cm) from the center front line. Slash on this and the center front line from the collar of the band almost to the neck seamline. Lap each cut 3/16 inch (.5 cm) at the collar edge, and secure with tape. Correct the shirt seamline, and square the collar seamline from the center back to about 1/2 inch (1.3 cm) from the center front. From this point, curve the collar seamline to the neck seamline (Figure 16.9). Draw the grainline arrow parallel with the center back fold.

Collar. Working from right to left, square out and down along the L square. Square out (away from you) 3/8 inch (1 cm), and draft a second line. Label the first line "base line" and the second line "neck band seam." Lay the neck band along this neck band seamline, and locate a notch on both drafts at a midpoint between the center back and the center front. Because the collar seam needs to curve more than the one on the neck band, match the two seamlines

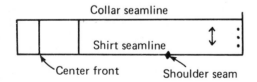

Figure 16.8

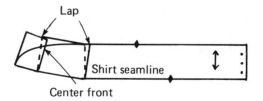

Figure 16.9

at the notch, and slide the end of the band in (toward you) so that the center front line meets the base line on the collar draft (Figure 16.10). Trace the seamline of the collar band from the notch to the center front, creating a curved neckband seam on the collar pattern.

On the center back fold line (Figure 16.10), square out the width of the neck band plus 5/8 inch (1.5 cm), and square down from this point. This line may be used as the outer edge of the collar, or the edge can be curved outward from the center of this line (Figure 16.11).

Before designing the collar points (or the curves, if a rounded collar is to be designed), square out from the center front mark on the base line. The points are extended beyond this as desired. See Figure 16.11 for possible collar shapes.

Finishing the Shirt Pattern

Refer to Chapter 15 for creating cuffs with your sleeve draft. Add seam allowances to all patterns, and sew the garment in fabric. If you are not satisfied with the design or the fit of the pattern, check your pattern draft and design methods. Observe ready made shirts for current shapes and widths of collars, cuffs, and yokes.

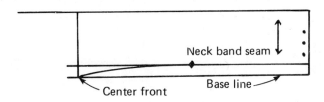

Figure 16.10

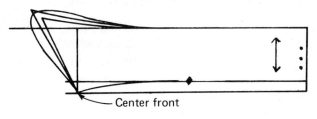

Figure 16.11

ADAPTING THE SHIRT DRAFTS FOR CHILDREN

The men's shirt draft can be used for drafting children's clothing. Thus the methods in this chapter are usable for boys' shirts and for girls' (up to the age of puberty) blouses, jumpers, and all-in-one dresses. After puberty, girls should use the bodice drafts (Chapter 14) for shirts as well as blouses, as darts will be needed for fit.

For a child, unroll enough drafting paper for the length of the intended garment plus 3 inches (7.5 cm). Proceed as directed for the shirt draft with the following exceptions:

1. When establishing the neck run (Step 2), square down 1/2 inch (1.3 cm) for children with chest measurements of 25 inches (63.5 cm) or less. Square down 3/4 inch (2 cm) for children measuring 26 to 32 inches (66 to 81.5 cm). For children measuring over 32 inches, square down 1 inch (2.5 cm).
2. Deduct only 1/4 inch (6 mm) when establishing the shoulder height line (Step 3) for children under 5 feet (1.5 m) tall.
3. Establish the hip length (step 6) by squaring down 5 inches (12.5 cm) from the waistline for children under 48 inches (122 cm) tall, and square down 6 inches for children from 4 to 5 feet (1.22 to 1.5 m) tall.
4. The back shoulder dart needs to be only 1/4 inch (6 mm) deep (Step 12). This increases the back-shoulder seam length by 1/4 inch (6 mm) in Step 11.
5. Unless the child has a large stomach, make the front and back waistlines equal (Steps 15 and 25). The same is true for the hipline widths (Steps 16 and 26).

After creating a draft for your child, test it in fabric. Apply the principles of good fit that are found in Chapter 4 as you would for any adult garment. Study all of the chapters on pattern drafting for ideas of various styles that can be used on children's garments. Enjoy creating garments for your child. The design possibilities are limitless, and both you and your child will enjoy your creations.

17
Drafting Skirts

The basic skirt draft is a straight skirt with front and back panels. For fitting purposes, the center front is placed on the lengthwise fold of the fabric, and the center back is a straight seam placed on the lengthwise fabric grain. The fit of the skirt is achieved above the hipline with darts and curved side seams. These darts are essential to the skirt's fit and may be moved but never omitted in design variations. In the front, two short darts (2 1/2 to 3 1/2 inches or 6.3 to 9 cm) are used on each side for fitting. These are often converted to gathers or pleats in design variations but should be stitched darts in the fitting shell. There is one dart on each side of the skirt back. These are longer than the front darts, usually extending down to within 2 inches (5 cm) of the hipline, and should be stitched for fitting. The placement, length, and shape of the darts are related to the person's body curves and may be determined only by fitting the skirt on the person. Convex darts (those that curve inward) provide more ease in the skirt and may be more appropriate for the full figure.

Flare of 1 1/2 inches (3.8 cm) is added at the hemline of the basic draft. This additional width added to the side seam prevents the skirt from cupping under at the hipline, thus displacing the side seam. Side seam placement, fabric grainline, and wrinkles are the points to check in fitting the basic skirt.

The skirt patterns you derive from the basic draft may include additional seams. The panels created by the addition of seams are called *gores*.

A gored skirt is described by the number of gores and seams (e.g., a four-gored skirt has four gores and four seams). Gores can provide fullness, help in achieving fit, and give the illusion of height because of the vertical lines. The width of the panels and the position of the seamlines on the body determine whether the illusion created is one of height or width. Many other design possibilities exist with pleats and gathers in the basic skirt draft.

The figure used for illustration in this draft has a 26 inch (66 cm) waist and a 38 inch (96.5 cm) hip measurement. You must substitute your personal measurements in each step of the procedure.

PROCEDURE FOR DRAFTING THE SKIRT FRONT

Skirt Front: Establishing the Skirt Lengths

You will need a piece of drafting paper one half of your hip measurement plus 6 inches (15 cm) in width and long enough to allow your appropriate skirt length (without hem allowance) to be drafted. Unroll the paper lengthwise in front of you, and work from right to left (Figure 17.1).

1. Hip length. Establish a top horizontal by squaring out along the short arm of the L square

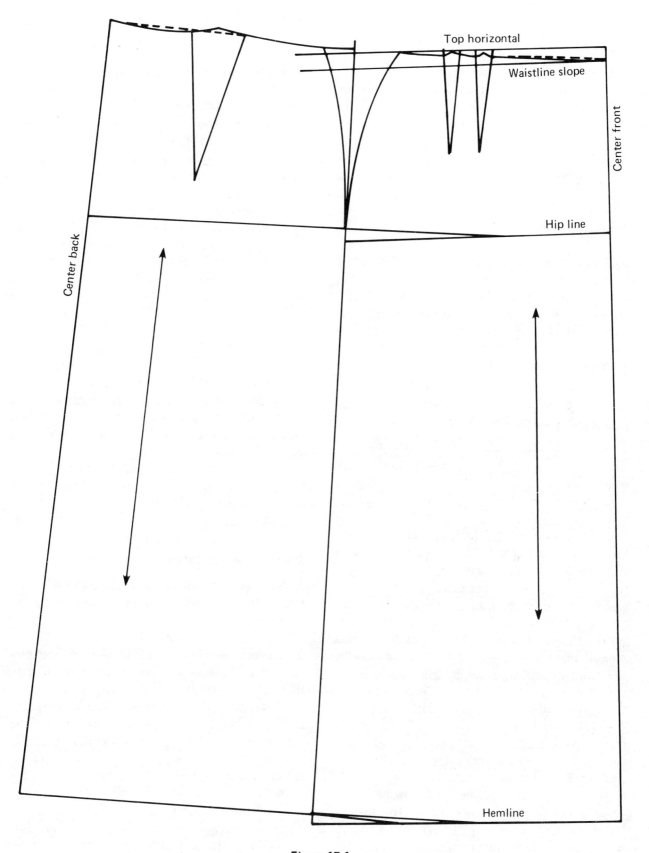

Figure 17.1

on your paper. Square down from the top horizontal one eighth of your height minus 1 inch or 2.5 cm (e.g., height = 64 inches or 162.5 cm; 64 ÷ 8 = 8 – 1 = 7 inches or 162.5 ÷ 8 = 20.3 – 2.5 = 17.8 cm). Square cut out from this point. Label this horizontal line the "hipline." Label the vertical line "center front."

2. **Hemline.** Determine a fashionable and appropriate hem length for you. Square down from the top horizontal the amount you have selected. Square out from this point and label this horizontal line "hemline."

3. **Waistline slope.** Because the natural waistline slopes downward from the center back to the center front, square down 1/2 inch (1.3 cm) from the top horizontal, and square out from this point. This line will be the guide for the slope toward the center front. Label this horizontal line "waistline slope."

Establishing the Skirt Widths

1. **Front waistline widths.** The front waist measurement is 1 inch (2.5 cm) larger than the back waist measurement. Calculate the front waist measurement by dividing the total waist measurement by 2; add 1/2 inch (1.3 cm) to the front, and subtract 1/2 inch (1.3 cm) from the back. The front is now 1 inch (2.5 cm) larger than the back. For example, for a 26 inch (66 cm) waist, the front equals 13 1/2 inches (34.3 cm) and the back 12 1/2 inches (31.7 cm).

To establish the front waistline, square out on the top horizontal one half of the front waist measurement plus ease and 1 inch (2.5 cm) for the front darts. For example, for a 26 inch (66 cm) waist, with 13 1/2 inches (34.3 cm) in the front as calculated above, the width of the front waistline draft would be 13 1/2 ÷ 2 = 6 3/4 inches (34.3 ÷ 2 = 17.1 cm) plus 1 inch (2.5 cm) for darts plus ease. A total of 1 to 1 1/2 inches (2.5 to 3.8 cm) ease is usually allowed at the skirt waistline, whether the skirt is to be joined to a skirtband or to a bodice. To the front waistline measurement, add 1/4 to 3/8 inch (6 to 10 mm) of ease. This amount will be adequate for the body curve at the waistline. Therefore the total front waistline measurement is 6 3/4 + 1 + 3/8 = 8 1/8 inches (17 + 2.5 + 1 = 20.5 cm).

2. **Hipline width.** The front hip measurement is 1 inch (2.5 cm) larger than the back hip measurement and is calculated in the same number as the waistline above. For the 38 inch (96.5 cm) hip measurement, the front would equal 19 1/2 inches (49.5 cm) and the back 18 1/2 inches (47 cm).

The average amount of ease added to a straight skirt is 2 inches (5 cm), which is distributed equally between front and back. Therefore the width of the hip draft equals one half of the front hip measurment plus 1/2 inch (1.3 cm) of ease. In example above, 19 1/2 ÷ 2 = 9 3/4 + 1/2 = 10 1/4 inches (49.5 ÷ 2 = 24.75 + 1.3 = 26 cm).

3. **Hem width.** Flare is the difference between the hipline and the hemline width measurements, and it is needed in a straight skirt to prevent cupping at the hipline. The total amount of flare added to a straight skirt is 6 inches (15 cm) which is distributed 1 1/2 inches (3.8 cm) on each side seam.

To establish the hem width, square out the width of the hip plus flare of 1 1/2 inches (3.8 cm) on the hemline length.

Shaping the Side Seam

1. **Side seam.** Connect the hipline and the hemline with a ruled line. Extend this line to the top horizontal.

2. **Corrections.** Find the midpoint on the hipline. Place the L square, with the long arm on the side seamline and the short arm extending to the midpoint of the hipline. Draft a corrected hipline between the hipline midpoint and the side seam. Turn the L square so that the long arm is on the side seam and the short arm extends to the midpoint of the hemline. Draft a corrected hemline between the midpoint on the hemline and the side seam.

Raise the waistline side seam (front waistline width) from the hipline correction to correspond to the hip length (e.g., 7 inches or 18 cm). Using the curve stick, shape the side seam from the hipline to the waistline point.

Placement of the Front Darts

The skirt front usually has two short darts. These slant away from the center front toward the hipbone. The depth of the darts depends on the difference between the hip and the waist measurements. Two darts of 1/2 inch (1.3 cm) depth were provided in the original waistline width. However, if the difference between hip and waistline measurements is greater than a total of 10 inches (25.5 cm) or if the abdomen is prominent, you may prefer deeper darts. Gathers or pleats are often used in place of these darts in skirt designs.

To shape the waistline seam, fold the darts as they will be stitched, and turn them toward the center front. Using the curve stick, draft a seamline starting at center front on the waistline slope line and ending at the corrected waistline width line.

PROCEDURE FOR DRAFTING THE SKIRT BACK

Skirt Back

Draft the skirt back at the side of the skirt front (see Figure 17.1), using the lengths established for the skirt front. The skirt widths must be extended as follows.

1. **Extended hipline.** Square out on the corrected hipline, one half of the back hip measurement plus 1/2 inch (1.3 cm) of ease. In the example, the back hip width would be extended 9 3/4 inches or 25 cm (18 1/2 ÷ 2 = 9 1/4 + 1/2 = 9 3/4 inches or 47 ÷ 2 = 23.5 + 1.3 = 25 cm).

2. **Extended hemline.** Square out the width of the hip plus 1 1/2 inches (3.8 cm) for flare (9 3/4 + 1 1/2 = 11 1/4 inches or 25 + 3.8 = 28.8 cm).

3. **Center back.** Connect the extended hiplines and hemlines with a straight line. Correct the hiplines and hemlines as on the front draft. Find the midpoints of each line. Place the L square so that the short arm extends through these points and the long arm is placed on the seamline.

Extend the center back seamline above the corrected hipline the amount calculated for the hip length for the skirt front (height = 64 ÷ 8 = 8 − 1 = 7 inches or 162.5 ÷ 8 = 20.3 − 2.5 = 17.8 cm). Label this line "center back."

4. **Waistline seam.** Pivot the L square so that the long arm extends down the center back seam and the short arm extends to the side seam (the vertical line established from the hipline to the top horizontal, not the curved side seam on the skirt front).

Measure the length of this line from the center back to the side seam, and subtract one half of the back waist measurement plus 1/4 to 3/8 inch (6 to 10 mm) of ease. Distribute this difference by placing two thirds of the extra amount in the back waistline dart and removing the remaining one third from the side seam.

Shape the side seam from the hipline to the back-waistline width point with a curved ruler. The curve should be comparable to the curve on the skirt-front side seam.

Draft in the back waistline dart, slanting the dart away from the center back toward the fullest part of the hip. Fold the dart as it will be stitched, and turn it toward the center back. Correct the waistline seam with a curved ruler.

5. **Grainlines.** Draft the grainlines parallel to the center front and the center back of the skirt.

Skirt Waistband

You may wish to include a standard waistband with your skirt draft. However, the initial fitting of the skirt should be done before the waistband is attached. The length of the waistband should be your waist measurement plus 1 to 1 1/2 inches (2.5 to 3.8 cm) for an overlap plus seam allowances at the ends. The lengthwise direction of the band should follow the lengthwise grain of the fabric. The width of the waistband is 2 to 3 inches (5 to 7.5 cm) plus two seam allowances. A straight waistband with a finished width of 1

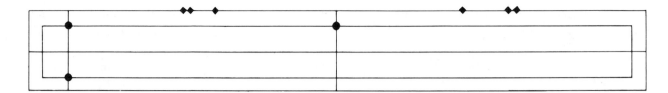

Figure 17.2 Folded waistband

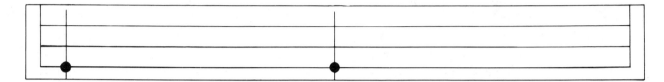

Figure 17.3 Self interfaced waistband

to 1 1/2 inches (2.5 to 3.8 cm) hugs the waist well. Shaping of the waistband is necessary when the width exceeds this amount. This waistband is folded at the top (see Figure 17.2) and interfaced. Another waistband possibility is the self-interfaced band. The width of the band is 3 times the desired finished width plus one seam allowance (e.g., 3 × 1 + 5/8 inches or 3 × 2.5 + 1.6 cm). In constructing this waistband, fold the fabric one third of the finished width; stitch it and fold it one third again to form the waistband. The self-fabric thus becomes the interfacing (see Figure 17.3). Mark the center front, the side seams, the center back, and the overlap on the waistband. In positioning these markings, remember that your waist measurement in the front is 1 inch (2.5 cm) larger than the back waist measurement. The opening for the skirt should be at the center back for fitting the basic skirt.

DESIGNING SKIRTS

The basic skirt has many design possibilities, and the fit will be maintained if you carefully retain the pattern outline, size, and ease at all times. Flat pattern techniques are used to vary the basic skirt draft. Start with a paper copy of your skirt draft, with the darts marked. Seam allowances are added to the patterns after the designs are completed. The following variations may be used independently or in combination to produce distinctive skirt patterns.

Darts

Skirt darts are used to produce different designs with the same techniques as are described in Chapter 14. The pivot points of the darts are established, and the darts are lengthened to these points. The pivot points of skirt darts are more difficult to define than bodice darts, as the body curves are less pronounced. To find the pivot point, divide the distance between the termination point of the darts and the hipline, and mark this point. Mark a pivot point for each dart, or establish a pivot point at the midpoint between two darts if both are to be moved. Draw a line indicating the new position of the darts on the pattern; close the original darts; and slash the pattern along the new dart line until the pattern lies flat.

1. Flare. The A-line skirt is a popular design created by conversion of the fitting darts to flare. Using the pivot point established at the midpoint between the two darts, draw a slash line from the pivot point to the hemline. Close the darts, and cut along the slash line from the hem to the pivot point. The pattern will spread, giving flare, and the A-line shape has been achieved. Secure the slashed pattern to paper with tape. You may prefer to convert only one

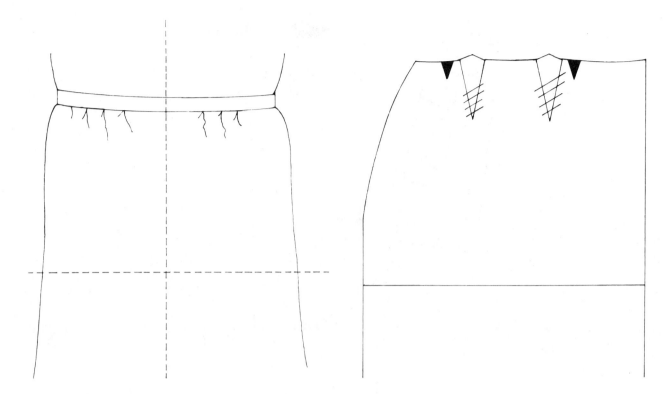

Figure 17.4

of the darts to flare, retaining one dart at the waistline for fit.

2. **Gathers.** You can add softness to the skirt pattern by converting the fitting darts to gathers. Gathers may be used in the front, with the back retaining stitched darts, or in both front and back. Simply remove the dart stitching lines from the pattern, and indicate that the fabric is to be gathered between the appropriate points. More fullness may be desired; it can be added above the hipline or from the waist to the hemline (see Figure 17.4).

To add fullness above the hipline, draw slash lines from the pivot point of the darts diagonally toward the side seam (see Figure 17.5). Slash the pattern along the fold line of the darts and across the diagonal slash line to the side seam. Spread the pattern at the waistline the desired amount. Reshape the waistline seam.

To add fullness from waist to hemline, extend slash lines from the dart pivot points to the hemline. Slash along the dart fold lines to the hem, and spread the pattern. Use diagonal slashes to the side seam above the hipline to correct the

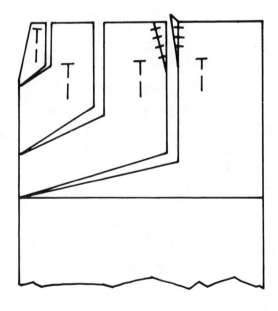

Figure 17.5

side seam. This design is called a *hobble skirt* when the skirt is long and extremely narrow at the hemline. The short version is called a *Dutchboy skirt*. A narrow hemline may require a shaped facing because the edge is now curved (Figure 17.6).

188 • COMPARATIVE ANALYSIS OF PATTERN TECHNIQUES

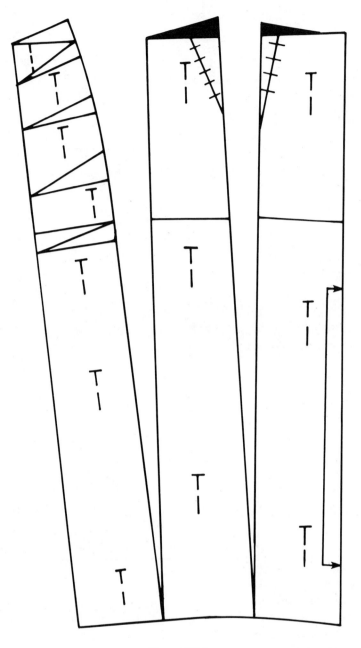

Figure 17.6

3. **Yokes.** Darts may be moved to the seamlines of yokes. Design the yoke line on the skirt pattern. Yoke lines are generally placed above and close to the hipline. Place notches on the yoke line so that you can match the adjoining edges after they are separated. Close the darts, and separate the pattern pieces at the yoke line. If the yoke line crosses darts above their termination points, the remaining dart in the lower skirt section must be eased to the yoke when you are constructing the skirt.

4. **Gores.** In gored skirts, the basic fitting darts are converted to vertical seamlines. When you are using the skirt draft for a four-gored skirt, substitute a seamline at the center front in place of the fold. Before making any changes, draw a grainline in the center of the front pat-

DRAFTING SKIRTS • 189

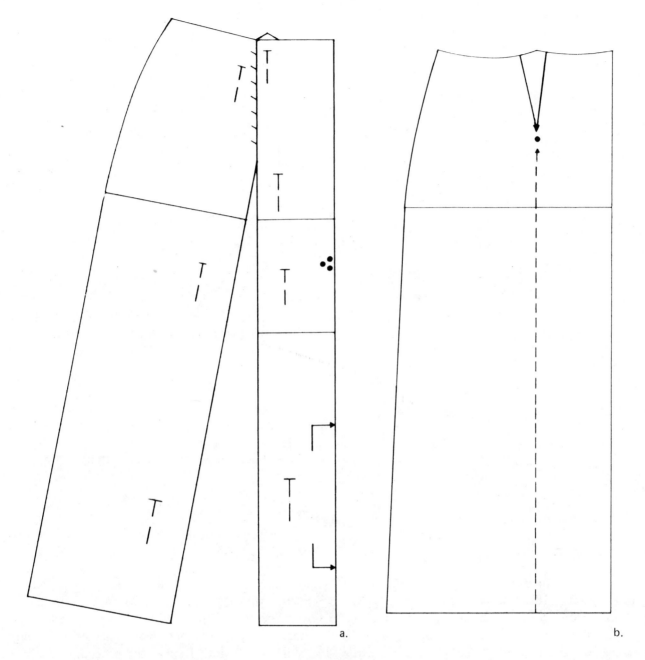

Figure 17.7

tern section parallel to the center front. The fitting dart closest to the center front will be moved to the center front seamline. The other dart will be repositioned in the center of the front pattern piece. Draw a slash line about 3 inches (7.5 cm) from the center front, starting above the hipline and extending to the hemline. Connect this line and the center front seam with a diagonal line. Close the fitting dart, redraw it along the center front, then slash and spread the pattern until the center front seamline is a straight line. This variation adds flare at the hemline. Converting the remaining dart to flare (see Figure 17.7) will give an A-line four-gored skirt with no waistline darts. The same procedure should be followed on the skirt back.

Another versatile design is the six-gored skirt.

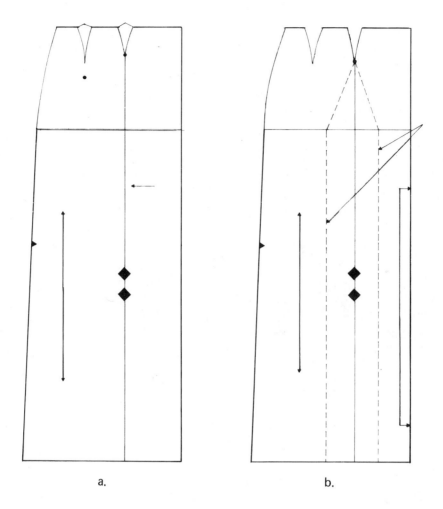

Figure 17.8

Used in combination with a princess-line bodice (see Chapter 18), this skirt is flattering to the short person. Draw a slash line parallel to the center front from the termination point of the fitting dart closest to the center front to the hemline. This will be the new seamline. Before separating the pattern, mark the grainline in the center of the side section, and place notches on the seamline. Draw slash lines on both sides of the new seamline, extending from the hipline to the hemline. Connect these lines to the dart pivot point with diagonal lines (see Figure 17.8). These slashes will be used to add flare at the hemline, which will give the illusion of narrowing the hipline. You will cut the dart along the stitching lines as you separate the pattern pieces along the new seamline, thereby converting the dart to a seamline. Slash and spread each gore for flare (1/2 to 2 1/2 inches or 1.3 to 6.3 cm). Secure the slashed pattern to paper with tape. Reshape the hemline with the curve stick, and label the pattern sections: "skirt front" and "skirt side front." Repeat the procedure on the skirt back.

Yet another variation of this design involves eliminating the side seams and converting the darts to gathers (see Figure 17.9). Inseam pockets can be placed in the front gore seams, or the zipper can be placed under one side and the other seam topstitched to simulate a zipper. Using two zippers is helpful to the person with limited movement below the waist (Figure 17.10).

5. Pockets. Pockets vary in shape, size, and placement on the basic skirt. Study current

DRAFTING SKIRTS • 191

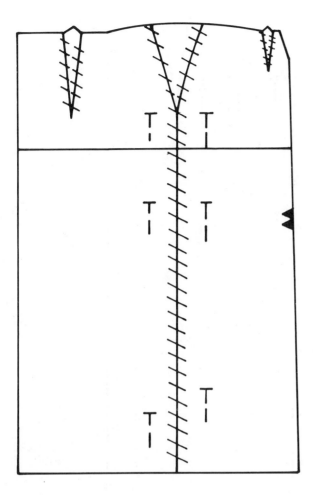

Figure 17.9

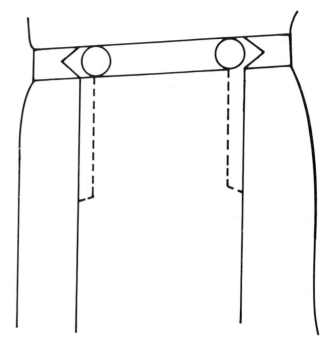

Figure 17.10

fashion designs for ideas, but consider the function of the pockets also. Patch pockets are sewn to the right side of the skirt, whereas inseam pockets are concealed in seams (e.g. side and yoke seams). Welt pockets are used in sport skirt designs, often on the back hip.

An inseam pocket with a cutaway top placed in the (front) side seams is an attractive variation for both skirts and pants. Design a pocket line starting at the dart closest to the side, curving downward toward the hip at the side seam. Determine the shape of the pocket at the lower edge, and dot in this line on the skirt pattern. Mark the pocket grainlines parallel to the center front. Underlay the pocket area with two layers of paper, and trace the design lines of the pocket on both layers. Trim the underlays even with the draft at the waistline and the side seams. Cut away the skirt pattern, and first underlay at the top pocket design line. Cut the lower pocket edge of both underlays, making sure that the pieces are identical in length. You now have the skirt front cut away for the pocket, a pocket facing pattern, and the pocket pattern, which extends into the side seam and the waistline (see Figure 17.11). This pocket design will fit snugly to the body and prevent the hand from slipping into the pocket easily. Therefore opening the pocket facing and the skirt front for extra width is desirable. Slash the skirt front in two places: from the pocket line close to the dart to the hemline, and slightly lower on the pocket line straight for about 3 inches (7.5 cm) and then diagonally to the side seam at the hipline (see Figure 17.11). Slash the pocket facing to correspond to the skirt. Spread the skirt and pocket facing a total of 1/2 to 3/4 of an inch, (1.3 to 2 cm) and secure the patterns to paper with tape.

6. **Hem lengths.** Controversy over the length of skirts is always present in fashion news. The basic skirt draft can be modified for various fashion lengths. The concern about fit and appearance has to do with the circumference of the hem width. The skirt must always be wider at the hemline than at the hipline and therefore

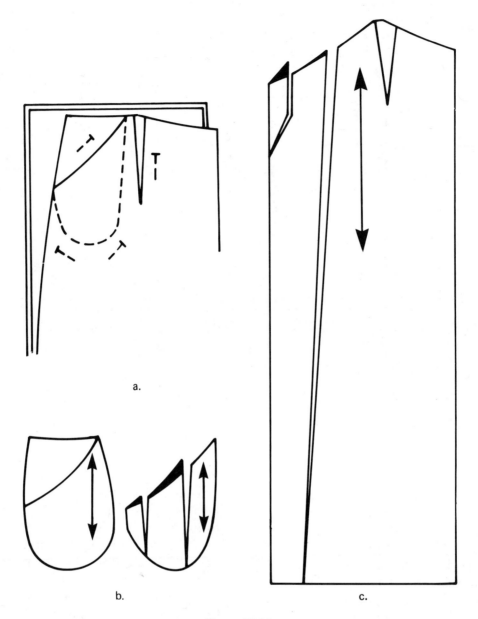

Figure 17.11

requires adding flare. Follow the procedure for converting darts to flare outlined above for floor length skirts. The same amount of flare should be added to each skirt gore to maintain the grainline. Additional slashes from hem to waist may be placed to the side of the dart slashes in a full-flared skirt design. If the skirt is to hang evenly and have an even hemline, the straight lengthwise grain should be placed in the center of the gores on flared skirts.

7. Waistline treatments. In addition to the standard waistband discussed earlier, the waistline may be faced. Draft the facing pattern by closing the darts at the skirt waistline and reproducing the waistline and side seam edges on pattern paper. The facing pattern should be about 2 to 3 inches (5 to 7 cm) wide and placed on the fold at the center front. If the skirt opening is on the side, the center back facing may be placed on the fold. If the skirt opens at center back, remember to add seam allowances to the facing pattern at the center back. In lieu of a facing, grosgrain ribbon is often used to finish the skirt waistline.

A contour or shaped waistband may be designed to complete the skirt. Such a band may be either a "hip-hugger" or a midriff style. Design the hip-hugger band by the procedure outlined for a skirt yoke, as this band is essentially a narrow hip yoke. A midriff band is a combination of the lower bodice edge and skirt waistline. Join the waistline edges of the bodice and the skirt slopers with darts closed. Decide on an attractive width for your height. This style tends to accentuate the waistline and to divide the body in half. Be sure to add extra length to these bands for the overlap.

8. Circular skirt. You can make this skirt from the basic draft by folding in the darts and slashing from the hemline to the pivot point midway between the darts. Slash several times from hem to waist, and spread the pattern until the side seams are at right angles to the center front and the center back (see Figure 17.12). Reshape the waistline and the hemline with the curve stick, and straighten the side seam.

9. Pleats. The comfort and wearability of the basic skirt is often improved by the addition of a kick pleat to the center back seam. The pleat is opened 6 to 8 inches (15 to 20.5 cm) above the hemline. Add the pleat extension of 1 1/2 to 2 1/2 inches (3.8 to 6.3 cm) to the center back seamline. The preferred construction is to carry both or at least one side of the pleat extension all the way to the waistline for support. The thickness of the fabric may restrict the use of this method. The pleat extension may then be only the length of the pleat plus seam allowances, stitched, turned to the left, and topstitched to hold it in place. This is called a *knife kick pleat*. An alternative to this method is an inverted kick pleat. The extensions are added to both sides of the seam. The seam is stitched to the point where the pleat is to open and then pressed opened. An underlay is designed to cover the center back opening. This piece is equal in width to the two extensions and equal in length to the skirt opening plus seam allowances. It is centered over the center back opening and stitched in place. The pleat is topstitched from the seamline diagonally to the edge of the extension on both sides (see Figure 17.13).

Pleats add variety to the basic skirt and may

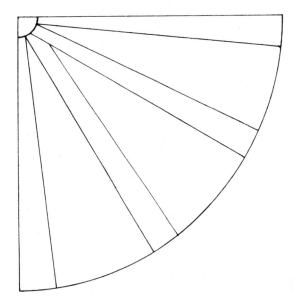

Figure 17.12

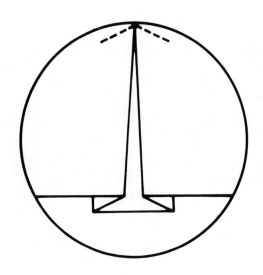

Figure 17.13

be used in different widths and styles. Basically the procedure for adding pleats involves opening the pattern from the waist or hipline to the hemline and spreading the amount needed for the pleat. The amount of spread should be the desired pleat depth times 2. Place the pleats on the lengthwise fabric grain to hold their shape and press. The construction involves bringing the original pattern lines together and stitching. Pleats may begin at yoke lines, may be placed at seamlines, or may start at the waistline and extend the entire skirt length. Some are top-

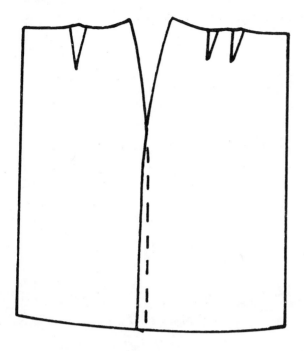

Figure 17.14

stitched, some are only pressed, and still others are unpressed.

10. One-piece skirt. When you are using a fabric that is wider than the total hip measurement, a quick pattern is the one-piece skirt. To draft this pattern, outline the sloper back. Join the front side seam to the back side seam. To maintain a straight side seam, you may need to overlap the patterns at the hemline, thereby reducing flare. Outline the skirt front and note that the center front is to be placed on the fold. The fitting curve from waist to hipline at the side seam becomes a fitting dart. The skirt opening is in the center back seam (Figure 17.14).

Skirts are easily designed and constructed. They add variety and versatility to a wardrobe when combined with blouses and sweaters. The basic skirt draft can be made in fabrics of different colors, textures, and fiber content, providing the distinctive and functional garments needed in today's wardrobes.

18
Combining Drafts for All-in-One Dresses

The basic bodice, skirt, and sleeve drafts can be combined to create designs for an all-in-one dress. You can apply all the procedures you have learned and experiment with darts, seam placement, flare, and different sleeves to develop a variety of patterns. An all-in-one dress omits the waistline seam and relies on vertical seams and darts for design effects. Many terms are applied to these designs including *sheath, shift, and skimmer*. The fit of these dresses is less close, as the fitting darts of the basic drafts are often partially or fully released. For a person with large bust and hips but a small waist, the design is particularly difficult to fit, and the pattern should be tested in fabric. Converting the shoulder dart and the waistline dart to a diagonal dart originating at the side seam may resolve the fitting difficulties.

PROCEDURE FOR THE ALL-IN-ONE DRESSES

This dress design is created by a joining of the basic bodice including the sleeve, and skirt drafts. Initially the bodice and the skirt drafts are combined; then the sleeve is added.

1. Preparation of the bodice draft. Move the shoulder dart to the underarm position on the bodice front. Remove the lengthwise ease that was added to the bodice length in the basic back and front drafts. For most persons, these amounts were 3/8 inch (1 cm) at the side seams and 1/2 inch (1.3 cm) at center front and the center back.

2. Preparation of skirt draft. Combine the skirt darts into one dart on the skirt front and back drafts. Slash the fold line of the dart closest to center, and close the other dart, shifting the dart depth to the open dart.

3. Joining the drafts. Unroll sufficient paper for a dress length. Square down along the paper's edge. Align the center front of the bodice and skirt drafts on this line. Check the waistline width of the two drafts. You will need to widen whichever pattern piece has the more narrow waistline. The bodice and the skirt must meet at the side seams. If the bodice is more narrow, slash from the pivot point of the waistline dart to the armscye, and spread the pattern until the width is the same as that of the skirt. If the skirt is more narrow, slash from the pivot point of the waistline dart to the side seam at the hipline, and spread until the width is the same as that of the bodice.

Join the waistlines at the center front. Depending on the fit of the drafts, these waistlines may or may not meet at the center front. Overlap the drafts at the center front until the drafts meet at the side seams. Trace the drafts as joined.

Follow the same procedure in drafting the dress back. Remember that the waistlines must meet at the side seams. When the front and back dress drafts are completed, check the side seams, and reshape the curves if necessary (see Figure 18.1).

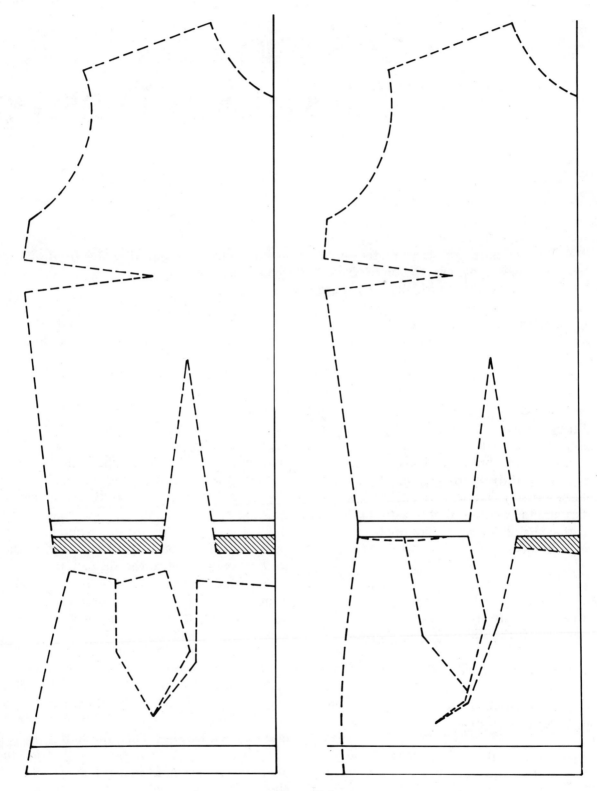

Figure 18.1a

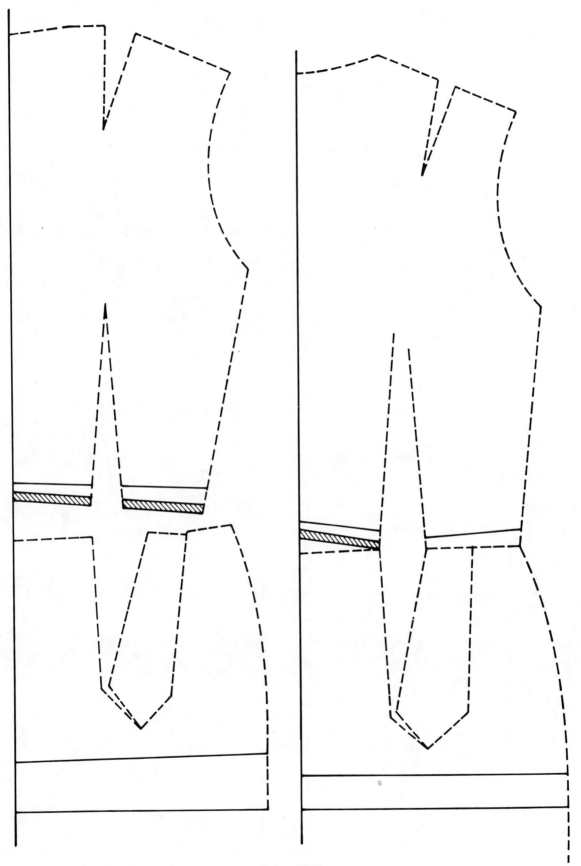

Figure 18.1b

198 • COMPARATIVE ANALYSIS OF PATTERN TECHNIQUES

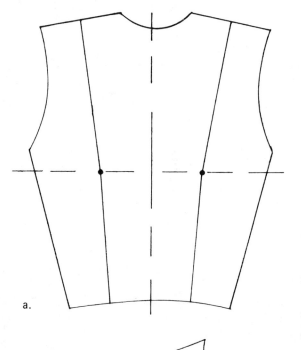

DESIGNING ALL-IN-ONE DRESSES

4. Darts. The all-in-one dress requires double taper waistline darts. The dart stitching lines may be curved or straight. Curved dart lines often help fit the full figure. The dart depth may be less than in the basic drafts. When you are releasing the dart's fit, it will be necessary to straighten the side seams to balance the design. The position and the length of the darts should be similar to those in the original drafts. If it is necessary to reposition the darts, remember that the bodice dart should terminate just below the fullest part of the bust or back and just above the hipline in the skirt. If the fit is to be divided into two darts for design effects, position the second dart between the original dart and the side seam. Maintain the same width between the original dart and the center front.

Design variations using the underarm dart in-

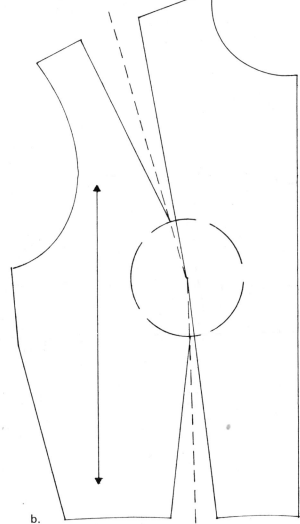
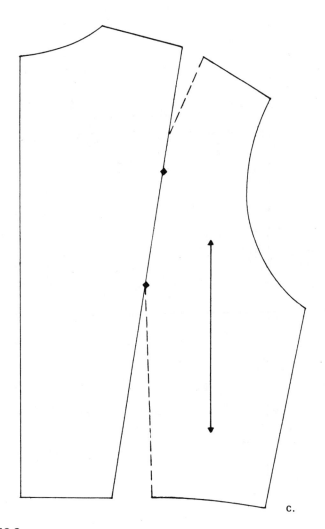

Figure 18.2

clude moving it to the neckline or to the armscye; combining it with the waistline dart and placing it at the side seam, creating a diagonal line to the bust; and converting it to dart equivalents or yokes.

5. Princess line dress. The princess-line dress (also called a *French-dart-line* dress) is a combination of a princess bodice and the six-gore skirt. In the princess bodice, the darts are converted to seamlines. Connect the termination points of the shoulder and waistline darts with a curved line. Draw a grainline between this line and the side seam parallel to the center. Cut along the stitching lines of the shoulder darts, follow the curved line connecting the darts, and cut along the stitching line of the waistline darts. You have separated the front and back drafts into two pieces (e.g., bodice front and side front, bodice back and side back; see Figure 18.2). These pattern pieces should match the sections of the six-gore skirt designed in Chapter 17. If they do not, reposition the skirt seamlines.

Draw a center front line on your paper, and position the front bodice and skirt sections along the line. Again remove the lengthwise ease added to the basic bodice (1/2 inch or 1.3 cm at the center front and back, and 3/8 inch or 1 cm at each side seam). There may be a slight gap at the princess seam. Align the side sections of the patterns, matching the waistlines at the side seams. Correct the princess-line seam with a smooth curved line. Flare added to the princess skirt often enhances the design. Repeat the procedure for the back dress pattern.

An interesting variation of this design includes shifting the shoulder dart to the underarm position and connecting it with the waistline dart for a more curved princess line. Equally attractive is a design in which the shoulder dart is shifted to the armscye and then converted to a princess-line seam.

Precautions in drafting the princess-line patterns include always marking grainlines before separating the pattern sections and placing notches on the seamlines so that adjoining edges can be matched when you are constructing the garment. Easing is essential for smoothness on the curved princess-line seams.

6. Sleeves. Once the bodice and the skirt sections have been properly joined to create the all-in-one dress, the sleeve is added to complete the garment. You may use the basic set-in sleeve, with its many variations, or one of the cut-on sleeves, with no changes in the drafting procedures.

The all-in-one dress is often used in sleeveless styles. The sleeveless dress needs a slightly higher, closer-fitting armscye. Raise the armscye seamline at the side seam 1/2 inch (1.3 cm). Using the armscye sloper, reshape the armscye seamline. A further modification may be needed for smooth fit, especially for a person with a full bust. Draw a dart line from the front armscye notch to the bust pivot point (see Figure 18.3).

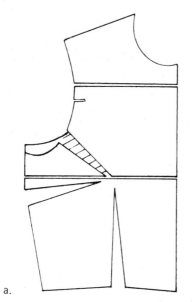

a.

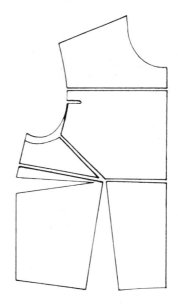

b.

Figure 18.3

A dart 3/4 to 1 1/4 inches (2 to 3.2 cm) may be needed, but the exact size can be determined only by testing in fabric. You will probably prefer not to have this dart stitched in the garment and therefore should shift it to the shoulder, the underarm, or the waistline darts in the paper pattern. With the dart closed, correct the armscye seamline. Repeat the procedure on the back. Raise the underarm 1/2 inch (1.3 cm), and reshape the armscye seam. Draw the dart line from the armscye to the waistline-dart pivot point. The dart depth on the back will be about half the front dart depth. Shift the dart to another dart position, and correct the armscye seam.

The sleeveless all-in-one dress pattern may be used for jumpers or yoke styles such as smocks and can be cut off at the hipline for a overblouse pattern.

19

Drafting Pants

Pants are essential garments in the wardrobes of men, women, and children. Fit is often difficult to achieve, but it is necessary if the pants are to look and feel right to the wearer. Persons differ in the closeness of the fit and the amount of ease they prefer. Fashion trends also influence preferences. The key points to check in the fit of pants are the waistband, the hip area, the crotch length, and the leg length. As you observe pants, you will find the designs to be very similar, but fit distinguishes the attractive from the unattractive.

PROCEDURE FOR DRAFTING PANTS

The procedure starts with the draft of the pants front, which is then used as a basis for drafting the pants back. Accurate measurements are essential to the fit of the pants. Refer to the measurement chart you completed earlier for the specific pants measurements.

Establishing the Pants Lengths

Unroll sufficient paper for the total pants length plus 6 inches (15 cm). Place your L square in at least 3 inches (7.5 cm) from the right-hand edge of your paper.

1. Top horizontal. Select either the *hip* or the *thigh* measurement, whichever is larger, in establishing this length. Square out one fourth of this measurement plus 3/4 inch (2 cm) of ease (Figure 19.1).

2. Pants length. Square down from the top horizontal the length desired for the pants. Label this line "center front." Do not include a hem allowance at this time. Complete a rectangle, using the width and length measurements for the remaining two sides. This rectangle establishes the perimeters for your draft. The vertical outside line is the side seam.

3. Hip line. Square down from the top horizontal your hipline measurement, determined earlier as one eighth your height less 1 inch (2.5 cm). Thus, a person 64 inches (162.5 cm) tall would place the hip line at 7 inches or 17.8 cm (64 ÷ 8 = 8 − 1 = 7 inches or 162.5 ÷ 8 = 20.3 − 2.5 = 17.8 cm). Square out from this point to the other side of the rectangle. Label this line.

4. Crotch depth line. Square down from the top horizontal your crotch depth measurement plus 1 inch (2.5 cm) of ease. This measurement is so critical that you may wish to compare your calculations with those used in commercial patterns. In a misses' size 12, the draft allows 12 1/2 inches (31.75 cm) for crotch depth. The draft is then graded upward for each size by the addition of 1/4 inch (6 mm) to the crotch depth, (e.g., size 14 = 12 3/4 inches or 32.4 cm; size 16 = 13 inches or 33 cm; up to size 44 = 14 1/4 inches or 36 cm). These measurements include the 1 inch (2.5 cm) ease. Label this line on your draft.

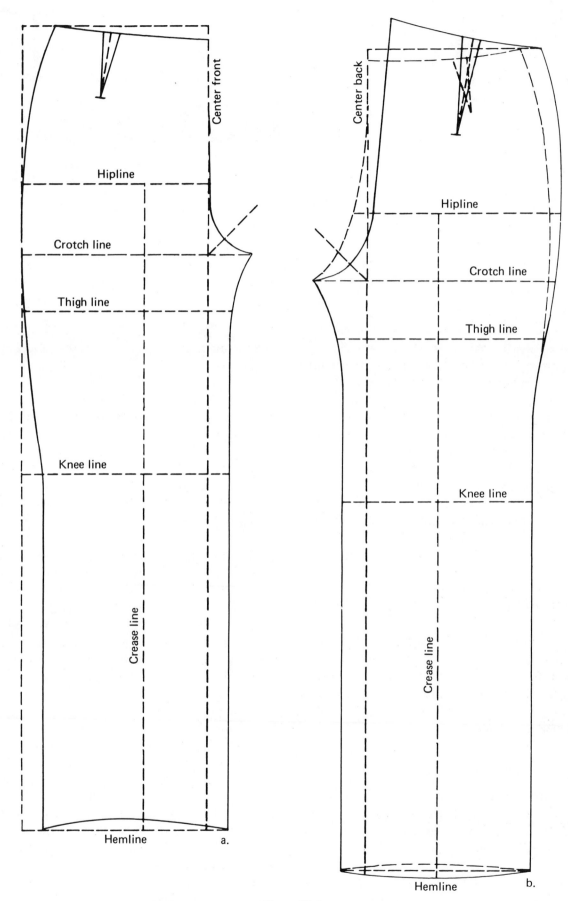

Figure 19.1

5. Thigh line. Square down 3 inches (7.5 cm) from the crotch depth line. Square out on this line. If the thigh placement differs from this amount, the line may be repositioned to correspond to your measurement. Label this line.

6. Kneeline. Square down from the top horizontal the measurement determined for your knee position. Square out on this line.

Shaping the Pants Front

1. Waistline. Square down 1/2 inch (1.3 cm) from the top horizontal on the center front line, and mark the center front waistline point. Square out along the top horizontal one fourth the total waist measurement plus 1 inch (2.5 cm) for the dart. Mark this point as the waistline side seam. Shape the waistline seam from the side seam point to the center front point with the curved stick.

2. Front waistline dart. The front dart is needed for fitting purposes. It may be converted to dart equivalents or divided into two darts in later designs. The dart's depth will be 3/4 inch (2 cm) and its length about 3 inches (7.5 cm), and it should be placed closer to the side than to the center front. It should slant away from the center front toward the side seam and toward the fullest part of the body curve (hipbone).

3. Center front seam. Find the point where the center front line and the crotch depth line meet. Square back (toward you) on the crotch depth line one twelfth of your hip measurement less 3/4 inch (2 cm), and mark this point. Extend the crotch depth line to the crotch point. The center front seam and the inseam of the pants leg meet at the crotch point. The line is called the *crotchline extension.*

Using the Vary Form curve, dot in a temporary center front seamline from the hipline to the crotch point. The seam will be deep and rounded (see Figure 19.1). To check the curve's position, measure from the point where the center front line and the crotch depth line meet at a 45-degree angle to the center front seamline. This distance will be half of the crotchline extension plus 1/2 inch (1.3 cm). In most drafts, the total will be approximately 1 1/2 inches (3.8 cm).

The center front seam from the hipline to the waistline follows the vertical center front line established initially.

4. Inseam. Find the point where the center front line and the knee line meet. Square back (toward you) half of the crotch line extension (one twelfth of your hip measurement less 3/4 inch or 2 cm) on the knee line. Connect the crotch point and this knee point with a curved line. The inseam should curve inward at the thigh line and straighten as it nears the knee point (see Figure 19.1).

Find the point where the center front line and the hemline meet. Square back (toward you) one half of the crotch line extension (one twelfth of your hip measurement less 3/4 inch or 2 cm) on the pants hemline. Connect the knee point and the hemline point with a straight line.

5. Side seam of pant leg. Starting at the waistline side-seam point, curve the seam line to the point where the hipline and the side of the rectangle (side seam) meet (see Figure 19.1). Calculate the width of the pant leg at the knee line by dividing one half of the hip measurement plus 1 inch (2.5 cm) by 2 (e.g., 38 ÷ 2 = 19 + 1 = 20 ÷ 2 = 10 inches or 96.5 ÷ 2 = 48.25 + 2.5 = 50.75 ÷ 2 = 25.5 cm). Measure this length (e.g. 10 inches or 25.5 cm) from the inseam at the knee line to the side seam of the leg. Mark this point. Repeat this measurement at the hemline, and mark this point. Connect the kneeline point and the hemline point with a straight line.

Complete the side seam by shaping from the hipline to the knee line as follows. Curve the seam in slightly at the crotch depth line, further in as the line approaches the thigh line, and then straighten the line as it nears the knee line point. Figure 19.1 illustrates the shaping of this seam. The seamline must curve smoothly and allow adequate room for movement. Check the width of the pant leg against your thigh, crotch, and hip width measurements.

6. Crease line. Crease lines give balance to the pants and must be carefully drafted. Find the center point of the knee line and the hemline. Connect these two midpoints with a straight line. Extend this straight line to the hipline. The crease line should be placed on the lengthwise grain of the fabric.

7. Shaping the hemline. A slightly curved hemline enhances the appearance of the pants. Mark a point 1/4 inch (6 mm) up from the hemline on the crease line. Curve the hemline from side seam to inseam through this point on the crease line.

Shaping the Pants Back

The pants front is the basis for the draft of the pants back. When the front draft is complete, cut it out along the seamlines. Place the front draft face down on your drafting paper, and draw around it. You will need at least 3 inches (7.5 cm) of paper all around the pattern. Reproduce *all* of your markings on the new pattern piece except for the center front line, which now is labeled "center back line." The back pants draft is identical to the front except for the hemline curve.

1. Center back seam. The crotch line extension for the back is 1/2 inch (1.3 cm) longer than the front. Extend the crotch depth line to this point. The center back seam and the inseam of the pants leg meet at this point.

Extend the crease line to the waistline. From the crease line, measure 2 inches (5 cm) toward the center back line, and mark this point. Square up 1 1/2 inches (3.8 cm) from this point, and establish a new waistline point (where the center back and the waistline meet). Dot in a guideline between the new waistline point and the point where the center back line and the crotch depth line meet. The center back seam follows this guideline from the waistline point to the hipline and then curves to meet the crotch point (see Figure 19.1). The curve is deep and round and is best shaped with a Vary Form curve.

2. Waistline. The length of the back waistline seam is one fourth the total waist measurement plus 1 inch (2.5 cm). Starting at the center back waistline point, draft a waistline with a downward slant above the point where the front waistline and the side seam meet. The termination point of this line is the point where the back waistline and the side seam meet (see Figure 19.1).

3. Back waistline dart. This dart is needed for fitting purposes and may be varied in later designs. The dart's depth is 3/4 inch (2 cm) and its length about 5 inches (12.5 cm). It should be placed about midway between the center back and the side seam. The dart should slant toward the fullest part of the hip. The placement and the depth of this dart vary greatly with the individual, and a fitting shell will best illustrate where the dart should be placed.

4. Side seam of pants leg. Starting at the waistline side-seam point, curve the seam line to the point where the thigh line and the side seamline meet. Use the curve stick for this shaping. The side seam is straight from the thigh line to the knee line and down to the hemline. Check your leg measurements to be certain there is sufficient width in the pants leg.

Place the front draft on the back draft to be sure the side seams match.

5. Inseam. Draft in a curved seam from the crotch point to the knee line. The inseam from the knee line to the hemline is the same as on the front draft. Place the front draft on the back draft to check the inseams.

6. Shaping the hemline. The back draft should have a slight downward curve at the hemline. Mark a point 1/2 inch (1.3 cm) below the hemline on the crease line. Curve the hemline from the inseam to the side seam through this point on the crease line.

The basic pant draft is now complete and should be constructed in fabric so that you can check the fit. In observing the fit, note that the crease lines hang perpendicular to the floor. There should be no diagonal wrinkles and no cupping under at the hipline. The design of this draft provides a close fit over the hips and the thighs, and the legs fall straight from thigh to hemline. This basic draft is easily adapted for a variety of designs.

DESIGNING PANTS

1. Closures. Zippers are most frequently used for closures in pants. For women's pants, the zippers can be installed in the side seam or at the center back. Zippers 9 inches in length rather than the standard 7 inches provide more room for bringing the pants over the hips. For men's pants and for certain styles in women's pants, the fly-front closure is needed. To the center front seam, add an extension 1 1/2 inches (3.8 cm) wide from the waistline to about 1/2 to 3/4 of an inch or 1.3 to 2 cm below the end of the zipper. Curve the outer edge of the extension in to the seam allowance (see Figure 19.2).

For knitted and other stretch fabrics, an elastic casing may be preferred. Extend the draft 1 1/2 inches (3.8 cm) above the top of the waistline. This extension can be folded at the waistline and stitched to form a tube; then the elastic is inserted to complete the waistline. The darts are not stitched when the casing is used, as the elastic provides gathers for fit. If elastic wider than 1 inch (2.5 cm) is used, the casing extension should be widened accordingly.

Waistbands used with the pants are the same designs as are described in Chapter 17, "Drafting Skirts."

2. Variations in length. You can use the basic pant draft to design pants ranging in length from shorts to full-length pants. You can create different styles by positioning the hemline at different points on the leg. For regular shorts, draft the hemline half the distance from the crotch depth line to the knee line, that is approximately 4 inches or 10 cm (depending on the individual) below the crotch depth line. Increase the width of the hemline by adding 3/4 inch (2 cm) at the inseam and 1/2 inch (1.3 cm) at the side seam. Draft new inseams and side seams from the crotch depth line to the new hemline-width points. Add 1 inch (2.5 cm) to the lower edge for the hem.

The term *short shorts* refers to a modification of the basic draft in which the hemline is curved and reduced in width. Measure down 2 1/2 inches (6.3 cm) from the crotch depth line on the inseam. From this point, curve the hemline to the side seam at the crotch depth line. For

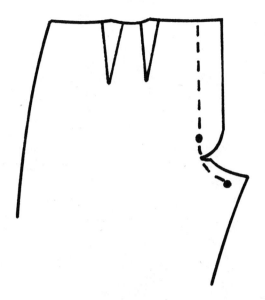

Figure 19.2

a close fit around the leg, reduce the width of the lower edge of each leg by 1 inch (2.5 cm). Fold a 1/2-inch (1.3 cm) dart in the leg that terminates about 4 inches (10 cm) from the inseam on both the center front and the center back seams. This curved lower edge of the shorts leg will need a shaped facing 1 1/2 inches (3.8 cm) wide (see Figure 19.3).

Another popular shorts style ends just above the knee and is called *Bermuda-length shorts.* The hemline is three fourths of the distance from the crotch depth line to the knee line (about 8 inches or 20.5 cm). Increase the hemline width by 1 inch (2.5 cm) on the inseam of both front and back and 1/2 inch (1.3 cm) on the side seams. Draft new inseams and side seams from the crotch depth line to the new hemline-width points. This design gives a straight, full shorts leg to which a 1 inch (2.5 cm) hem extension is added. These shorts often have cuffs and soft pleats rather than stitched darts in front; there are often stitched darts in the back.

Pants that end below the knee take their name from the sport for which they were originally designed: bicycling. Thus pedal pushers reduce the chance of the pants legs being caught in the bicycle chain. Design these pants with your basic draft by placing the hemline one third of the distance between the knee line and the hemline (about 14 inches or 35.5 cm below

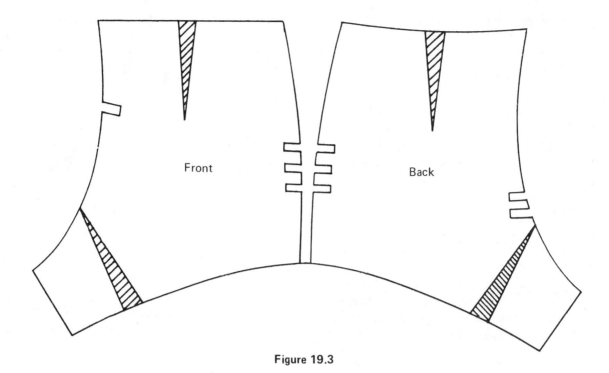

Figure 19.3

the crotch depth line). Add 1 inch (2.5 cm) for the hem.

In a slightly longer pants design, the hemline is placed about 18 inches (46 cm) from the crotch depth line or slightly below the calf of the leg. The hemline is approximately two thirds of the distance between the knee line and the hemline. Fashion names for these pants include *Capris* and *clam diggers*.

Fashion trends in pants length change often, as do fashions in skirt lengths. The proportions of your body, especially the leg, determine what lengths are attractive for you.

3. Variations in width of pants legs. Pants may be flared from the knee down or at the hemline only or may hang loosely from the waist. It is essential that the crease line remain on the lengthwise grain of the fabric. Therefore one usually adds flare to the seams rather than slashing and spreading for flare. The flare is added from the waist or the knee or at the hem, depending on your design needs. Add one fourth of the desired amount of flare to each seamline, making sure the seams match in shape and length.

For active sports (e.g., skiing, horseback riding, and running, you may prefer close-fitting pants. Fabrics that offer stretch properties are needed for these designs—either knits or woven stretch fabrics. Trace your front and back pants slopers. On *both* the inseams and the side seams, decrease the leg width by the following amounts: crotch depth line—1/2 inch (1.3 cm); knee line—1 inch (2.5 cm); and hemline—1 1/2 inches (3.8 cm), see Figure 19.4. Raise the point where the inseams and the center front and back seams meet 1/4 to 1/2 inch (6 to 13 mm). Using the curve stick, redraft the inseam from this new crotch point through the new width points to the hemline. Reshape the center front and back seams to the raised crotch point. Redraft the side seams, using the curved stick. The shaping of the side seams should begin slightly below the waistline and should connect the new width points. Identical changes are made on the back and the front drafts. Because of the close fit of the pants and the stretch fabric, you may find that these pants tend to ride up the leg. Using stirrups under your foot will help with this problem. This stirrup should be the width of your foot's arch and may be either straight or shaped from seam to seam. You may use self-fabric if it is firm enough, or cover a firm elastic with self-fabric. The waistlines of these pants are often finished with shaped facings rather than waistbands. Zippers that extend the entire length of the side seam and open from either end are very helpful in getting the pants on and off. Another interesting variation is to design a bib front for the pants, using suspenders over the shoulders and a long zipper down the center front seam. This overall design provides greater warmth for winter sports clothing.

4. Pockets and yokes. Variety in pants designs is most often achieved through combinations of pockets and yokes. Western jeans have a curved yoke in the back and occasionally in the front. Back yokes are combined with patch pockets of different sizes and shapes. You can create yokes by drafting a yoke design line on the pattern, folding in the waistline darts, and slashing along the yoke line. The darts are thus placed in the yoke seamline. This procedure was illustrated in Chapters 14 and 16. Welt pockets are often used in the back of pants without the yoke. Both one-piece welt pockets and double-welt pockets are used in pants, often combined with a button and buttonhole to protect the pocket's contents. Consult a clothing-construction text for details regarding the construction of pockets (e.g., Vogue Sewing Book, 1980, p. 294–303).

Seam pockets stitched into the waistline and the side seams may be added to the pants front. These pockets require a pocket pattern and a pocket facing pattern. The pants front is often cut away, exposing the pocket section. To draft this style of pocket, place two layers of paper under the pocket area of the pants front. Design the upper edge of the pocket by curving a line from the stitching line of the waistline dart closest to the side seam to the side seam above the hipline. The lower edge of the pocket starts at the same dart stitching line and extends downward, shaping the bottom of the pocket, and then curves upward to meet the upper edge of the pocket on the side seam. Another option is to have the pocket stitched into the side seam, but this method adds bulk to the seam, which interfers with the fitting curve. Cut away the pants front and the pocket facing (first and second layers of paper) on the design line of the upper pocket edge. Cut the pocket facing and the pocket (second and third layers of paper) along the lower pocket edge (see Figure 19.5). To provide space for putting your hands into the pockets and for having the pocket stand away

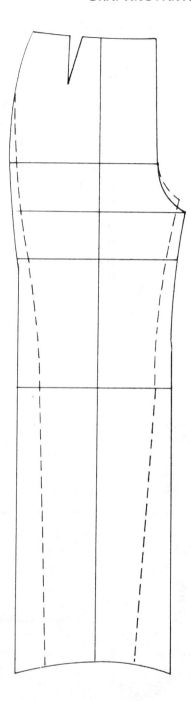

Figure 19.4

from the pants, slash and spread the pants front and the pocket facing a total of 1/2 inch or 1.3 cm (1/4 inch or 6 mm in two places; see Figure 19.5). The slashes should divide the upper edge of the pocket into thirds, extend straight down, and then angle toward the side seam. The pocket facing must be slashed and spread in exactly the same place as the pants front. On pants that are

208 • COMPARATIVE ANALYSIS OF PATTERN TECHNIQUES

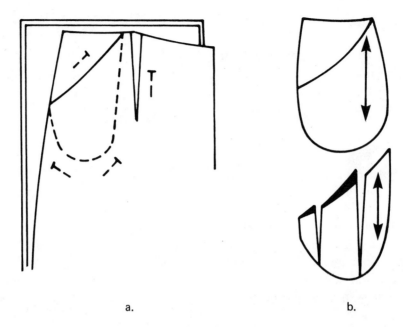

a.   b.

Figure 19.5

to fit snugly and flat against the body, no slashing is done.

Converting Darts to Trouser Pleats

You may convert the darts on the front pants draft to pleats by folding them in and stitching across the top of the dart at the seamline. Another variation is to topstitch the pleat for 1 to 1 1/2 inches (2.5 to 3.8 cm) below the waistline seam and then to release the dart below this point. When fullness is fashionable or needed for fit, additional width can be achieved with slashing and spreading. Add the fullness above the hipline but retain the fit of the pants below the hips. Slash along the foldline of the waistline darts and then diagonally toward the hipline at the side seam. Spread the waistline to provide for the depth of the pleats (see Figure 19.6).

Culottes

Pants with sufficient flare in the legs to give the appearance of a skirt are called *culottes*. These may be drafted from the basic pant or skirt slopers. Those from the pant draft have better fit and appearance, and the modifications are easier. Cut the basic pant at the knee line. Convert the waistline darts to flare at the hemline, as described in Chapter 17, "Drafting Skirts" Extend the center back seam beyond the crotch point 2 1/4 inches, (5.7 cm) and extend the center front seam beyond the crotch point 1 inch (2.5 cm). Redraft the inseam as a straight line from the extended crotch point to the hemline. Be sure the inseams—front and back—are the same length. Correct the curve of the knee line (now the hemline) from inseam to side seam. Add 2 inches (5 cm) to the corrected curve for the hem.

Culottes can be varied with yokes, pockets, and pleats that extend from the waistline to the hemline. The techniques used for these variations are the same as those described earlier. Culottes give a sporty appearance, are comfortable, and often represent a good compromise between skirts and pants in your wardrobe.

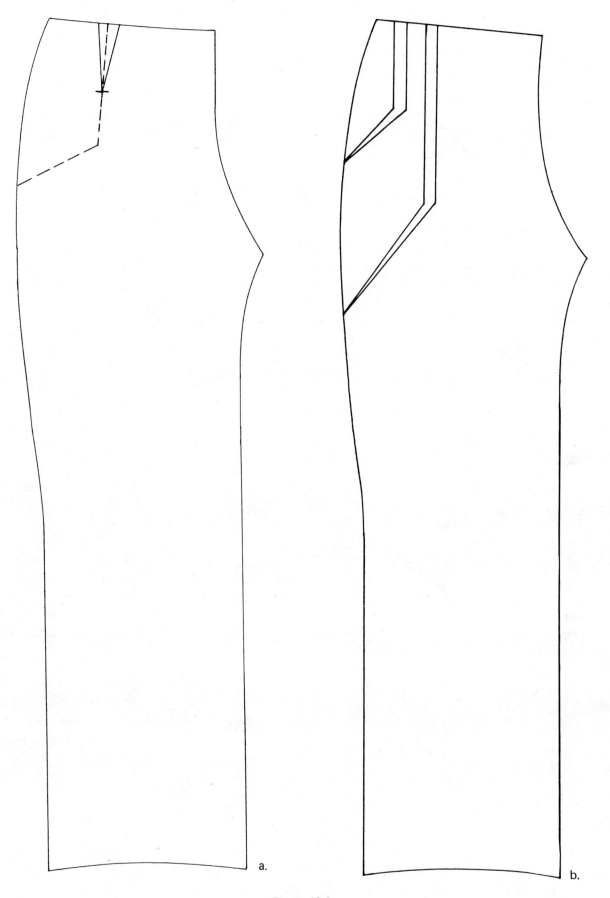

Figure 19.6

209

Part Four
Designing Skills in Use

20 Adapting Clothing Designs for the Handicapped

ASSESSING THE NEEDS OF THE INDIVIDUAL

Designing clothing for the handicapped must take into consideration the type of clothing each person needs for social, professional, and business activities and his or her special body build, figure characteristics or problems, and clothing preferrences. For a handicapped person, this list of needs includes clothing that does not limit motion or restrict participation in activities. Thus you must consider the movements and activities of each handicapped person before selecting clothing designs.

If movement is limited in the arms and the upper torso, select styles with front or shoulder openings and large armscyes. Long sleeves need to fit close to the arm; however, moderately full sleeves can be gathered with an elastic casing or onto a cuff. If leg and lower torso movements are limited, select styles that permit dressing while seated. For women, skirts may be easier to don than pants. For either type of limited movement, clothing may still need to be adapted with longer-than-average openings and designed for larger buttons.

If figure irregularities—lordosis, kyphosis, or scoliosis—are slight, styles that do not fit the body closely or outline the silhouette may be selected. If the irregularity is more severe, all-in-one dresses will be more difficult to alter or design than those with a waistline seam. Skirts with moderate fullness and pants with straight legs are less figure-revealing. Because the figure is apt to have one higher and more rounded hip, skirts and pants without yokes and decorative pockets are easier to alter or design, and they are more becoming. Styles with back bodice fullness soften shoulder irregularities and are easier to adapt than princess or very fitted styles. Because vertical and horizontal lines are difficult to maintain, stripes and plaids may be difficult to match and less becoming than plain or all-over designs.

If the person uses crutches, clothing must be cut high under the arms. Thus high, set-in sleeves or close-fitting kimono styles designed with gussets will be more durable and comfortable. Chapter 15, "Drafting Sleeves," describes techniques for achieving these design variations. As walking with crutches pulls garments up from the waistline, design blouses and shirts with long tails or as overblouses. Moderately flared or dirndl skirts are becoming, but very full skirts are apt to wrap around crutches. Avoid designs with very full or draped sleeves, which can impede crutch walking.

Garments for people using wheelchairs need large openings so that they will easily slip over the head. Long sleeves need to be close-fitting so that they will not catch in the wheels or become soiled when the person is operating the chair. Two-piece garments or dresses and jumpsuits with waistline seams can be more readily adapted for prolonged sitting. Crutch and wheelchair users who have enlarged shoulder and arm muscles need garments designed with back fullness, such as tucks or gathers released from a shoulder yoke. Raglan and kimono sleeves also provide this needed back width.

Many of the drafting techniques described

earlier are applicable to clothing for handicapped persons. Often an increase in fullness or flare is sufficient to provide freedom of movement, while retaining a fashionable appearance. You can achieve both by slashing and spreading the pattern the amount needed to correspond to the body measurements. Converting stitched darts to gathers or pleats may also provide more flexibility in the design. Personalized fit for a handicapped person often requires that patterns be altered or drafted separately for the left and the right sides. Comprehensive body measurements will help you detect the body inconsistencies that you must consider in altering or drafting for good fit.

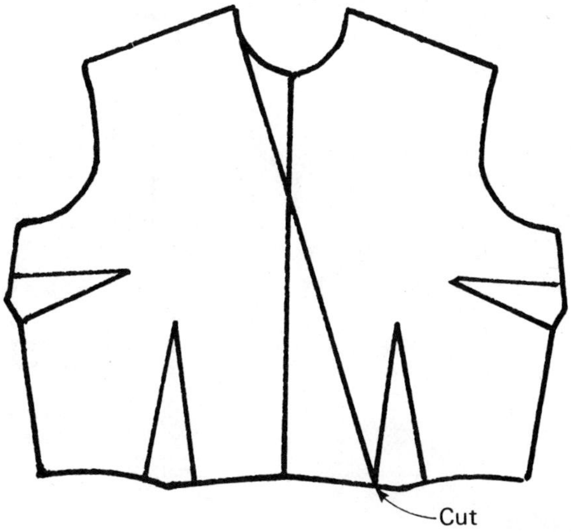

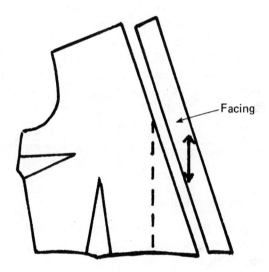

Figure 20.1

DESIGN ADAPTATIONS

The following suggestions offer specific design possibilities for handicapped persons.

Crossover V Design (Surplice Front)

This design provides convenience in dressing and adjusts to minor waistline changes without major alterations. Begin by tracing the bodice front sloper, flip the sloper over at the center front, and trace so that you have a full bodice. Mark the center front line. Design the opening by drawing a straight line from the shoulder neck point on the right side to the stitching line of the waistline dart on the left side (Figure 20.1). Slash the pattern along the line you designed. Both sides of the pattern will be the same, so save only the right side of the pattern (see Figure 20.2). Draft a facing to duplicate the edge it will finish. This bodice can be combined with the wraparound skirt, creating a wrap dress (see the instructions for the wrap skirt below).

Action Back Pleats

Action pleats may be added to the backs of dresses, blouses, and skirts to give more width and freedom for a person using crutches, a walker, or a wheelchair. For women, use the back bodice draft and draw a line close to the armscye that is parallel with the center back (Figure 20.3). Cut the pattern apart on this line, and spread 4 inches (10 cm). When sewing, fold in a 2 inch (5 cm)

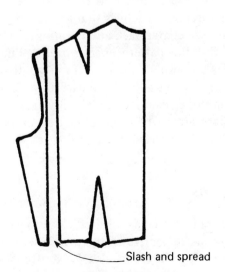

Figure 20.2

Figure 20.3

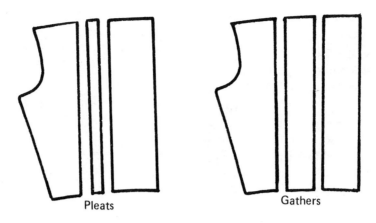

Figure 20.4

pleat that is turned toward the armscye. On the wrong side of the fabric, stitch along the top 2 inches (5 cm) of the fold line and the bottom 3 inches (7.5 cm), closing the top and the bottom of the pleat. Topstitching may be added along the fold line for decorative purposes and reinforcement. For men, follow the instructions for adding back pleats to the shirt draft (Chapter 16). Spread the pattern approximately 4 inches (10 cm) creating a wider pleat than is found in the basic draft.

Back Shoulder Fullness

Additional width can be added below a back yoke and controlled with gathers or a series of pleats. Design a back yoke as instructed in Chapters 14 or 16. Draw lines parallel to the center back that are positioned where each pleat is desired. If you plan to gather the fullness, draw two or three vertical lines that are evenly spaced between the center back and the armscye (Figure 20.4). Cut the pattern apart on each line, and spread the desired amount. Tape to tissue. If pleats are to be used, fold in each pleat, and correct the yoke seamline and the lower seamlines. If gathers are to be used, draw a smooth curve along the yoke seamline, and correct the lower seamline.

Shoulder Pleats

Shoulder pleats that are located close to the front armscye are attractive on the person with a large bustline, but they can also be drafted on the back bodice to give additional back fullness. Draw a line on the bodice front parallel to the shoulder dart, but extending from the shoulder-armscye corner. Move the shoulder dart to this location. On the back pattern, draw a line slanted like the one in front, but extend it to the bustline and to the side-waistline corner (Figure 20.5). Cut on this line from the shoulder to the waistline. Spread the back shoulder the same amount as the front pleat. If back and front pleats are both added to the design, first sew the shoulder seam. Then fold in the pleat, which is turned toward the armscye, and stitch along the fold from approximately 3 inches (7.5 cm) below the shoulder seamline in back to the same distance in front.

Wrap Skirt

Use the skirt draft (Chapter 17) to design an A-line skirt. Decide whether a front or back wrap will be the most functional. The following instructions are given for a front-wrap skirt; therefore, if a back-wrap skirt is desired, substitute the word *back* for *front* in the directions.

Create a full front pattern by tracing the skirt front sloper, flipping the sloper over at the center front, and tracing so that you have a full skirt front. Mark the center front line. On the waistline, establish a point midway between the center front and the left side seam. Draw a line parallel with the center front from this point to the hemline (Figure 20.6). For a more attractive and slightly flared opening, establish a point 3 inches (7.5 cm) beyond this line on the hemline toward

ADAPTING CLOTHING DESIGNS FOR THE HANDICAPPED • 215

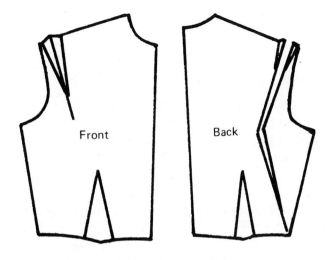

Figure 20.5

the side seam. Connect this point and the waistline point with a straight line. Cut the pattern apart on this line, and discard the smaller front section. When cutting the garment, cut left and right front pieces. Measure the waistline seam of the skirt back and both front patterns. Cut a waistband using this measurement. If ties are used to fasten the skirt, they are added to each end of the waistband. They may be cut narrower than or the same width as the waistband.

Skirt with Double Opening

Use the six-gore skirt variation of the basic skirt draft in Chapter 17. Indicate that the seams on both sides of center front are to be opened for zipper installations. The length of the openings is determined by the zipper length—9-inch zippers will be adequate for most persons. The construction technique for installing the zipper is the lapped method, but the lap must be on the left side of the left zipper and on the right side of the right zipper. The waistband must be redesigned with a double opening (see Figure 20.7).

Adapting Pants for Sitting

As clothing is designed for the standing figure, persons who sit continuously need different shaping for their clothes. Pants and straight skirts are too long between the front hip and the waistline and too short in back for this handicap. Shorten the front by drawing a line across the pattern at the hipline. Cut along this line from the center front to the side seam (Figure 20.8). Lap the cut at the center front, removing 3 to 4 inches (7.5 to 10 cm) at the center front. Correct the front and side seamlines. You may desire to move the waistline darts toward the side seams to create a more pleasing appearance.

The back pattern needs to be lengthened approximately the same amount that was re-

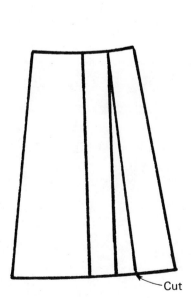

Figure 20.6

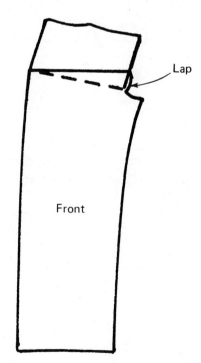

Figure 20.7   **Figure 20.8**

216 • COMPARATIVE ANALYSIS OF PATTERN TECHNIQUES

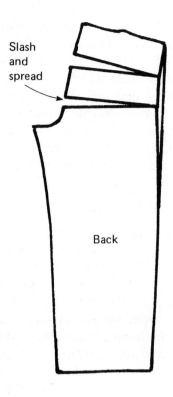

Figure 20.9

moved from the front pattern. Draw a line across the pattern at the hipline and a second line halfway between the hipline and the waistline. Cut along both lines from the center back to the side seamline. Spread each cut approximately 1 1/2 to 2 inches (3.8 to 5 cm) at the center back (Figure 20.9). Correct the center back and side seamlines to create smooth curves.

Pants with Leg Openings

A major problem of handicapped persons is getting pants legs over shoes or braces. Opening placed both in the inseams and in the side seams of pants facilitate dressing. Closures appropriate for such openings include zippers, snap tape, and Velcro. For a young child, the opening may extend the entire inseam, from the hemline through the crotch to the opposite hemline. Zippers that zip in both directions may be used in the side seams. Reaching zippers in the legs of pants may be difficult when bending or limited use of the hands is a problem. Adding a fabric tie, ring, or chain to the zipper tab may be helpful.

These suggestions are intended to stimulate your interest in designing or altering patterns for the handicapped. You will become more proficient and confident in meeting the clothing needs of the handicapped as you study and gain experience in this area. We encourage you to seek additional information from references, agencies, and persons working with the handicapped. Personal involvement is most important to an understanding of the clothing needs and preferences of the handicapped.

21
Fit of the Future

As we look to the future, there are three areas of emphasis to consider: changes in lifestyle, people with special needs, and advances in technology. Factors within each area accelerate or decelerate at their own pace, and they are interrelated. Thus, for the sake of clarity, we will discuss the factors independently, while recognizing that each factor influences other factors, creating the proverbial chicken-and-egg question as one tries to determine which came first or was the most influential.

LIFESTYLE CHANGES

Women's working outside the home has influenced today's clothing and will continue to do so in the future. Women have learned that clothing and appearance play an important role in their securing and advancing in a job. The current tight job market will continue to make women, as well as men, keenly aware of this factor. Pattern companies, fabric stores, and the ready-to-wear industry have all catered to the working woman with a variety of offerings, from fashion clinics on professional dressing to management seminars. One of the most recent developments is Saks Fifth Avenue's opening of The 5th Avenue Club. This executive shopping service is available to working women for a membership of $50, plus an annual renewal fee of $35 (*RetailWeek,* December 15, 1980).

The status symbol in fashion is rapidly changing from the socialite to the female executive. Even women who do not work outside the home find a need for executive-type clothing for volunteer and community activities. If the "electronic cottage" (Toffler, 1980) comes into being and more people are working in a home office or studio, another category of clothing will be needed. Men and women will need clothes for working at home as well as the business attire that will still be needed for business trips and away-from-home meetings. This category might well include the refined casual clothes of today. After all, one will want to be comfortable and still look professional over the videocommunications link.

Affluence is another factor affecting the clothing of today and tomorrow. During the Depression, when many families lived at a subsistence level, fashion changed little and clothing was replaced only when worn out. Today some of our affluence comes from real growth in the economy, but a lot of it comes from the number of families with two or more incomes. This affluence offers consumers the possiblity of purchasing quality that is above that of the masses, to purchase one-of-a-kind apparel, and to purchase special-use clothing (such as racketball outfits). If affluence continues, and we believe it will continue for a large segment of our society, we should see a growth in personalized or designed-to-order patterns and in custom tailoring and dressmaking.

Inflation is considered the number one problem affecting the economy, and it has renewed interest in wardrobe management and clothing as an investment. More people are evaluating their lifestyle and their current wardrobe before making new clothing purchases. This attitude has revived interest in separates and coordinated garments, especially for women who are entering the work force and who suddenly need several outfits to wear on the job. Investment clothing includes garments that can be worn for several activities and for several years. These garments must be well sewn of durable fabric and in a lasting or classic style. The color, fabric, and print must look good for the anticipated wear life (several years) of the garment. Fit is more crucial in investment garments because the consumer must find the outfit comfortable and good-looking for a longer period of time.

Another effect of inflation is that consumers shop for the lowest price in staples, yet pay a huge amount for other items. Department stores are discovering that they cannot be all things to all people: they must emphasize either discount goods or high-priced speciality items (*Forbes*, 1981). This philosophy of spending is seen over and over again as one watches teenagers pay high prices for designer jeans and professional women purchase an imported silk blouse. At the other end of the spectrum, one observes the career woman shopping at the discount or department store for the polyester blouse that looks like 100 percent silk and buying the least expensive brand of panty hose. Large pattern companies are catering to this phenomenon as they promote the less-expensive multistyle wardrobe patterns as well as the specially styled designer patterns. We expect this trend to increase the pattern offerings for special-use and custom-sewn garments.

One of the major items affecting the lifestyles of many consumers is the high cost of energy. Thus, until synthetic fuels or other methods for heating and cooling space are economically feasible and widely accepted, the need for clothing that contributes to thermal comfort will increase in importance. Several textile companies are producing fibers with moisture transport or wicking properties, and the natural fibers have become more important for garments that must absorb perspiration and keep the body comfortable (*American Fabrics and Fashions*, 1980). Quilting has been used for centuries to create warm garments, and today we have a new generation of fibers and improved processing techniques for older fibers that are used as batts or filling materials. These materials present new design possibilities as the lifestyle change resulting from the high cost of energy creates a need and acceptance of insulated garments.

The current emphasis on "self" is expected to continue with an even greater tolerance of personal differences. Thus people will increasingly desire to be recognized as individuals with a unique set of needs, qualities, and capabilities. They will be less willing to be manipulated by mass marketing and advertising. In clothing, they will seek garments that portray their individuality, and they will be less interested in fashion trends from New York or Paris. They will choose styles, fabrics, and colors that they personally enjoy and that fit their lifestyle, disregarding what is currently "in" or popular. This need for individuality is already evident in the growth of small pattern companies that offer patterns for one segment of the market, whether it be historic and folk costumes or Western attire. Even the large companies are emphasizing lifestyle patterns through their advertising and the sections within their pattern catalogs. In the future, this need could result in the marketing of patterns that are individually drafted according to one's personal measurements and figure characteristics, as well as the growth of companies that offer one-of-a-kind garments.

The desire for creativity and self-reliance is evident in every segment of our society as we observe the back-to-nature and do-it-yourself movements. In clothing, it is evident in the growth of quilting and needlework. Thus we can expect to see more patterns designed for quilting (*Sew Business*, 1980) and embellishment with needlework. This desire for personal creativity will not only advance the home sewing industry, but it may produce home designers and a new industry that produces or custom-sews these exclusive designs.

SPECIAL NEEDS

Clothing for people with special needs will increase in importance. Current legislation, sometimes known as *mainstreaming* and *disability laws,* protects the rights of handicapped individuals. Thus there are more jobs available and more opportunities for the education and training necessary for these jobs. Other laws have helped to provide transportation and easier access to buildings so that handicapped persons can work at jobs that were formerly inaccessible. Medical science and technology have helped handicapped persons become more physically and mentally able to function within the job market by providing better medical care and equipment (braces, mechanical lifts, prostheses, and so on). Therefore more handicapped persons are mobile and can function within society. Social attitude is changing so that handicapped persons are no longer shut away but are accepted as individuals and contributing members of society. Clothing for the handicapped has mainly emphasized functional garments. However, as handicapped persons work in more professional and executive positions, they will need fashionable clothing like that of their co-workers and of similar or better quality. As the demand for these garments grows, small companies will expand to produce a greater variety of clothing at various price levels.

Clothing for specific occupational groups will increase in importance as more fabrics that are engineered for specific end uses (flame resistance, thermal comfort, liquid impermeability, power stretch, and so on) become available. Clothing educators are beginning to study the needs of occupational groups, especially in the area of space and protective clothing. These studies will probably expand to other occupations and their clothing needs. Some segments of the textile and garment industries should grow as these companies expand to produce fabrics and garments for occupational groups.

These lifestyle changes—more working women, affluence, inflation, emphasis on self, and a desire for creativity and self-reliance—plus the considerations for people with special needs indicate that society wants changes in the clothing industry. These desired changes plus the following technology changes can create opportunities that may now be only dreams.

TECHNOLOGICAL ADVANCES

Technology changes and advances will create new tools and products for the pattern drafter and the apparel designer. He or she will need to become more intricately involved with fabric producers, marketing procedures, retail operations, and consumers. Communications links and accurate information will become more crucial. We, the authors, hope that the following technological advances will spark your thinking and dreams about the future.

Recent textile advances have created quality yarns and fabrics designed for specific end-uses. Currently yarns and fabrics are available that give a high level of performance and durability, plus new properties such as controlled stretch and recovery, more varied colorations, flame retardance without loss of comfort or static resistance, softness, drapability, surface interest, inherent thermal characteristics, and engineered stretch-and-shrink properties. Thus pattern designers and drafters will have more fabrics at their disposal and a wider range of design possibilities. The pattern maker and designer of the future will need to consider the fabric and its properties as well as the end use of the garment. Communication links with the fabric supplier and garment maker, as well as with the consumer, will become more critical. Designer Betsy Johnson believes that in the future, designers will be collaborators with technicians, chemists, and astronauts instead of working as they do today (*American Fabrics and Fashions,* 1980).

Computers are beginning to change the whole pattern-making industry, and they have opened the way for many future changes. At least one major pattern company is using computers to grade patterns and to create the most economical layout. Computers programmed for word processing can currently create pattern instruction guides more efficiently than methods involving typing, retyping, and printing.

Currently computer hardware is available that can draft a pattern to one's specific measurements and desired design. This possibility has begun to spawn some computer-programming efforts in this area, and small companies will grow as the project becomes economically feasible. Eventually most pattern companies may use the method, and such patterns may become obtainable through your favorite fabric store. Once your figure has been measured and analyzed for figure characteristics (e.g., sloping shoulders,), you will be able to use these figures for designing a garment over the telephone or other communications link. For example, you might choose pants with a fitted waistband of 1 inch (2.5 cm) width, two front darts, one back dart, a single-welt back pockets, and straight legs that are 14 inches (35.5 cm) wide. The store or company would enter this style into their computer along with your size and figure characteristic numbers. Very soon, perhaps via your home computer, you would receive your personalized pants pattern. Another option would be to scan the commercial pattern catalog via your home videophone and to order a computerized pattern. Both options would eliminate the pattern inventory necessary in most fabric stores. Instead the store would have a computer that would draft the pattern. You might even receive your pattern through your integrated home-computer terminal instead of by mail (*RetailWeek,* December 1, 1980).

Laser technology is another factor that is changing the garment industry. The electric cutting knife that cuts multilayers of fabric is being replaced by a laser machine that can be computerized to cut a single layer faster and more cheaply than the current method (Toffler, 1980). Thus cutting, which is often a task disliked by home sewers, could be offered by the local fabric shop. Or custom tailors and dressmakers could purchase a service that combines computerized pattern-making and laser-cutting.

The accurate measuring and analysis of one's figure characteristics is still a big problem in the drafting or altering of personalized patterns. Perhaps, in the future, we will have an electronic measuring device combined with a hologram. Thus you would stand in front of a screen that contains a special grid and have your figure analyzed and accurately measured in three dimensions.

Videodiscs and videocasettes could revolutionize the teaching of pattern drafting and altering as more people purchase videocassette players. It would make learning at home easier and more enjoyable than current correspondence courses, even those that combine printed materials with audio cassettes. Universities and the Cooperative Extension Service could both use this technique for either individual use or neighborhood groups. It would be more compact and easier to use than current closed-circuit television. As more homes have a videocommunications link, a "talk-back" capability for students could be combined with the videocassette.

How soon will these changes occur? Most of the technology is already available and waiting for some entrepreneur or company to make them happen. This technology, plus the changes in lifestyle that we see occurring daily, will make each change occur whenever it becomes economically feasible.

CAREER OPTIONS

Careers are and will continue to be available for the person who is versatile and open to new ideas and influences. Career opportunities are available for pattern designers in the fashion industry, in museums and tourist attractions, in education, and in private business.

In the fashion industry, we can expect to see a greater need for costume designers. Diversification of the industry should open job opportunities as more companies produce specialized garments. Pattern designers will probably need to be more versatile and knowledgeable about the whole industry. They will need to be very efficient in interpreting the needs and wants of a small segment of the market. Thus they will need the ability to sketch and design as well as the technical skills for drafting. Because they must understand the needs and the buying trends of their customers, they will need a working knowledge of marketing and the psychological and sociological aspects of dress.

Museums and historical restorations are stressing more "hands-on" exhibits and are using more costumed docents. Thus more people are needed for costume design and construction. The arts and recreation industries will continually need costume designers for dance and theater groups and for amusement park employees. Doll and toy manufacturers will also continue to need costume designers, especially if the desire for individuality expands the market. This desire could stimulate the market for ethnic dolls and those dressed in native and historical costumes.

Job possibilities look especially bright for persons who have the skills and the personality to establish their own business. Thus we expect to see an increased need for professional dressmakers, tailors, fitting consultants (those who draft or alter patterns for personalized fit), and wardrobe consultant/dressmakers (those who plan, design, and sew garments according to a wardrobe plan). These businesses need little capital investment, and one could begin on a part-time basis; however, success will depend on one's technical and marketing skills, sense of timing, awareness of fashion and consumer needs, and willingness to work.

As the need for costume designers, pattern drafters, and skilled dressmakers grows, there will be an increased need for teachers at all postsecondary levels: university, college, junior college, technical–vocational schools, and adult education. Therefore we predict growth for those schools or departments that offer quality training in the fitting, designing, and construction of clothing along with a general background in the social sciences, marketing, and computer technology.

Appendix

MEASUREMENT WORKSHEET*

Name _____ Date _____

	Your Measurement	Ease Needed	Total Amount Needed	Pattern Measurement	Alteration Needed (+ or −)
Height: against wall without shoes	_____			_____	
Bust or chest; around fullest part; keep tape parallel to floor	_____	+ 2″ (5 cm) =	_____	_____	_____
High bust (women only) under arms, straight across back, and above breast in front	_____	+ 1/4″ (6 mm) =	_____	_____	_____
Neck (men and boys only): around neck at Adam's apple	_____	+ 1/2″ (1.3 cm) =	_____	_____	_____
Back waist length: down center of back, first neck bone to waist	_____	+ 1/2″ (1.3 cm) =	_____	_____	_____
Front waist length: from shoulder at side of neck to line even with bust point	_____	+ 1/2″ (1.3 cm) =	_____	_____	_____
Shoulder to bust (women only): from shoulder at side of neck to line even with bust point	_____	+ 0 =	_____	_____	_____
Shoulder length: from side of neck to end of shoulder bone	_____	+ 0 =	_____	_____	_____
Back width: across shoulder blades	_____	+ 1/2″ (1.3 cm) =	_____	_____	_____
Arm length: from end of shoulder to wrist bone over slightly bent elbow	_____	+ 0 =	_____	_____	_____

*When using this work sheet for drafting, use the first column only.

MEASUREMENT WORKSHEET* (Continued)

Name _____ Date _____

	Your Measurement	Ease Needed	Total Amount Needed	Pattern Measurement	Alteration Needed (+ or –)
Shoulder to elbow (women and girls only): from shoulder point to center of bent elbow	_____	+ 0 =	_____	_____	_____
Shirt-sleeve size (men and boys only): from first neck bone, along shoulder and down arm, over bent elbow, to wrist	_____	+ 0 =	_____	_____	_____
Upper arm: around fullest part of upper arm	_____	+ 2″ (5 cm) =	_____	_____	_____
Waistline: around natural waist, over elastic or string	_____	+ 1/2″ (1.3 cm) =	_____	_____	_____
Hips: around fullest part	_____	+ 2″ (5 cm) =	_____	_____	_____
Thigh (for pants): around fullest part of upper leg _____ distance from waist	_____	+ 1/2″ (1.3 cm) =	_____	_____	_____
Thigh (for skirts): around fullest part of thigh area; _____ distance from waist	_____	+ 2″ (5 cm) =	_____	_____	_____
Crotch depth: from waist to table when seated	_____	+ 1/4″–1″ (6 mm–2.5 cm) =	_____	_____	_____
Crotch length (women and girls only): from waistline, between legs, to waistline	_____	+ up to 1 1/2″ (3.8 cm)	_____	_____	_____
Pants side length: from waist to hem, along side seam	_____	+ 0 =	_____	_____	_____
Inseam length (men only): from crotch to hem, along inseam	_____	+ 0 =	_____	_____	_____
Back skirt length: from waist to hem, along center back	_____	+ 0 =	_____	_____	_____

TABLE OF METRIC EQUIVALENTS*
CONVERTING INCHES INTO MILLIMETERS AND CENTIMETERS

(Slightly Rounded for Your Convenience)

inches	mm		cm	inches	cm	inches	cm
1/8	3 mm			7	18	29	73.5
1/4	6 mm			8	20.5	30	76
3/8	10 mm	or	1 cm	9	23	31	78.5
1/2	13 mm	or	1.3 cm	10	25.5	32	81.5
5/8	15 mm	or	1.5 cm	11	28	33	84
3/4	20 mm	or	2 cm	12	30.5	34	86.5
7/8	22 mm	or	2.2 cm	13	33	35	89
1	25 mm	or	2.5 cm	14	35.5	36	91.5
1 1/4	32 mm	or	3.2 cm	15	38	37	94
1 1/2	38 mm	or	3.8 cm	16	40.5	38	96.5
1 3/4	45 mm	or	4.5 cm	17	43	39	99
2	50 mm	or	5 cm	18	46	40	102
2 1/2	65 mm	or	6.3 cm	19	48.5	41	104
3	75 mm	or	7.5 cm	20	51	42	107
3 1/2	90 mm	or	9 cm	21	53.5	43	109
4	100 mm	or	10 cm	22	56	44	112
4 1/2	115 mm	or	11.5 cm	23	58.5	45	115
5	125 mm	or	12.5 cm	24	61	46	117
5 1/2	140 mm	or	14 cm	25	63.5	47	120
6	150 mm	or	15 cm	26	66	48	122
				27	68.5	49	125
				28	71	50	127

*This chart gives the standard equivalents as approved by the pattern fashion industry.

DECIMAL EQUIVALENTS OF PARTS OF AN INCH

$\frac{1}{64}$	.01563	$\frac{21}{64}$	.32813	$\frac{45}{64}$	.70313
$\frac{1}{32}$	.03125	$\frac{11}{32}$	.34375	$\frac{23}{32}$	.71875
$\frac{3}{64}$	.04688	$\frac{23}{64}$	.35938	$\frac{47}{64}$	.73438
1-16	.06250	3-8	.37500	3-4	.75000
$\frac{5}{64}$	.07813	$\frac{25}{64}$	.39063	$\frac{49}{64}$	.76563
$\frac{3}{32}$	.09375	$\frac{13}{32}$	.40625	$\frac{25}{32}$	.78125
$\frac{7}{64}$	.10938	$\frac{27}{64}$	.42188	$\frac{51}{64}$	.79688
1-8	.12500	7-16	.43750	13-16	.81250
$\frac{9}{64}$	.14063	$\frac{29}{64}$	.45313	$\frac{53}{64}$	.82813
$\frac{5}{32}$	.15625	$\frac{15}{32}$	.46875	$\frac{27}{32}$	.84375
$\frac{11}{64}$	.17188	$\frac{31}{64}$	.48438	$\frac{55}{64}$	.85938
3-16	.18750	1-2	.50000	7-8	.87500
$\frac{13}{64}$	.20313	$\frac{33}{64}$	.51563	$\frac{57}{64}$	.89063
$\frac{7}{32}$	.21875	$\frac{17}{32}$	.53125	$\frac{29}{32}$	.90625
$\frac{15}{64}$	.23438	$\frac{35}{64}$	.54688	$\frac{59}{64}$	.92188
1-4	.25000	9-16	.56250	15-16	.93750
$\frac{17}{64}$	.26563	$\frac{37}{64}$	.57813	$\frac{61}{64}$	.95313
$\frac{9}{32}$	.28125	$\frac{19}{32}$	.59375	$\frac{31}{32}$	.96875
$\frac{19}{64}$	.29688	$\frac{39}{64}$	.60938	$\frac{63}{64}$	.98438
5-16	.31250	5-8	.62500	1	1.00000
		$\frac{41}{64}$	.64063		
		$\frac{21}{32}$	.65625		
		$\frac{43}{64}$	.67188		
		11-16	.68750		

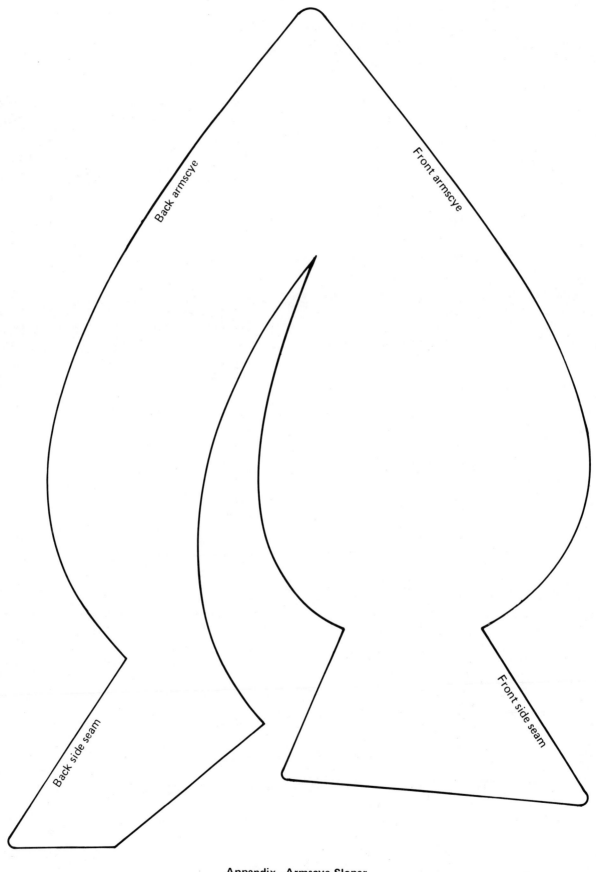

Appendix—Armscye Sloper
(this figure is 80% of original size)

Bibliography

American Fabrics and Fashions. "Report on U.S. Fiber Companies," No. 119, Spring 1980, pages 4-6 and 83-87. Doric Publishing, New York.

———. "Fashion Futures Stretch into the 80's, " No. 120, Fall 1980. Doric Publishing, New York. p. 17-26

———. "Stretch for All Seasons," Fall 1980, p. 27-37. Doric Publishing, New York.

Baker, Marjorie Y., 1980. *Clothing for the Handicapped.* Cooperative Extension Service, Oklahoma State University, Stillwater.

Bame, Louise, 1978. *Pants Fit for Your Figure.* Vista Publications, Santa Monica, Calif.

Bane, Allyne, 1972. *Flat Pattern Design.* McGraw-Hill, New York.

Blackwell, Roger D., 1979. "The Future of Fashion: The Influence of Lifestyles on Textiles and Clothing." Combined Proceedings of Eastern, Central, & Western Regional Meetings. Association of College Professors of Textiles and Clothing, Inc.

Brockman, Helen L., 1965. *The Theory of Fashion Design.* Wiley, New York.

Brumbaugh, Judy, and Jean Mowat, 1977. *His and Hers Tailoring: A Self-instructional Guide.* Anna Publishing, Inc., Winter Park, Fla.

Chapman, J.R., and Margaret Gates, 1977. *Women into Wives: The Legal and Economic Impact of Marriage.* Sage Publications, Beverly Hills, Calif.

DuBane, Janet, Editor, 1978. *Fuss-Free Fit.* Simplicity Pattern Co., New York.

Ekern, Doris, 1977. *Slacks, Cut-to-Fit Your Figure.* Sew/Fit Co., LaGrange, Ill.

Erwin, Mabel D., 1940. *Practical Dress Design: Principles of Fitting and Pattern Making.* Macmillan, New York.

Fabricnews. "Simplicity's 1980 Survey," Vol. 1, No. 9, June-July 1980. Arthur J. Imparato Associates, Beverly Hills, Calif. p. 18-19

Folk, Lois M., 1964. *Clothing for the Pre-Schooler.* Cooperative Extension Service, HE 367, Purdue University, West Lafayette, Ind.

Forbes. "General Retailers," Vol. 127, No. 1, Jan. 5, 1981, page 246-247. Forbes, Inc., New York.

———. "Apparel," Vol. 127, No. 1, Jan. 5, 1981. Forbes, Inc., New York.

Gilbert, Jeanne G., 1952. *Understanding Old Age.* Ronald Press, New York.

Goering, Lois, 1980. *Design Your Own Clothes: Flat Pattern Method.* Extension Bulletin 443, North Central Regional Extension Publication 88.

Goodrick, Jean, and Cheryl Ann Meadors, 1977. *Designs on Older Women.* Cooperative Extension Service, H.E. 454, Purdue University, West Lafayette, Ind.

Gotwals, Lois M., 1970. *Pattern Alterations.* Cooperative Extension Service, Purdue University, Lafayette, Ind.

Gurel, Lois M., and Marianne S. Beeson, 1979. *Dimensions of Dress and Adornment: A Book of Readings,* 3rd edition. Kendall/Hunt, Dubuque, Iowa.

Hackler, Nadine, 1974. *Personalized Patterns.* Cooperative Extension Service, EHA 178, University of Florida, Gainesville.

Hall, Vondalyn J., 1978. *Appearance Makes a Difference in Later Years.* Cooperative Extension Service, HE 143, Auburn University, Auburn, Ala.

Harris, Charles, Research Coordinator, 1978. *Fact Book About Aging: A Profile of America's Older Population.* The National Council on the Aging, Washington, D.C.

Hillhouse, M.S., and Evelyn A. Mansfield, 1948. *Dress Design: Draping and Flat Pattern Making.* Houghton Mifflin, New York.

Hoffman, Adeline M., 1979. *Clothing for the Handicapped, the Aged, and Other People with Special Needs.* Charles C. Thomas, Springfield, Ill.

Hollen, Norma, 1981. *Pattern Making by the Flat Pattern Method,* 5th edition. Burgess Publishing, Minneapolis.

Hollen, Norma, Jane Saddler, and Anna L. Langford, 1979. *Textiles,* 5th edition. Macmillan, New York.

Horn, Marilyn, 1968. *The Second Skin: An Interdisciplinary Study of Clothing.* Houghton Mifflin, Boston.

Joseph, Marjory L., 1981. *Introductory Textile Science,* 4th edition. Holt, Rinehart and Winston, New York.

Kaplan, Charles, and Esther Kaplan, 1940. *Principles and Problems of Pattern Making as Applied to Women's Apparel.* Streimin Studio, New York.

Kefgen, Mary, and Phyllis Touchie-Specht, 1976. *Individuality in Clothing Selection and Personal Appearance,* 2nd edition. Macmillan, New York.

Kernaleguen, Anne, 1978. *Clothing Designs for the Handicapped.* University of Alberta Press, Edmonton.

Kopp, Ernestine, Vittorina Rolfo, and Beatrice Zelin, 1975. *How to Draft Basic Patterns.* Fairchild Publications, New York.

———, 1971. *Designing Apparel Through the Flat Pattern.* Fairchild, New York.

Korda, Michael, 1977. *Success.* Ballantine Books Division, Random House, New York.

Lewis, Diehl, and May Loh, 1971. *Make It Yourself from a Picture: Patternless Fashions.* Acropolis Book, Washington, D.C.

Margolis, Adele P., 1971. *Design Your Own Dress Patterns: A Primer in Pattern Making for Women Who Like to Sew.* Doubleday, Garden City, N.Y.

May, E.E., N. Waggoner, and E.B. Hotte, 1974. *Independent Living for the Handicapped and the Elderly.* Houghton Mifflin, Boston.

McJimsey, Harriet T., 1973. *Art and Fashion in Clothing Selection.* Iowa State University Press, Ames.

McMurtry, Rosemary, Editor, 1973. *The How-to-Fit Book.* McCall Pattern Co., New York.

Mead, Marjorie, 1980. *Clothing for People with Physical Handicaps.* Cooperative Extension Service, North Central Regional Extension Publication 101, University of Illinois, Urbana.

Minott, Jan, 1978. *Fitting Commercial Patterns.* Burgess Publishing, Minneapolis.

———, 1974. *Pants and Skirts: Fit for Your Shape,* 2nd edition. Burgess Publishing, Minneapolis.

Moore, Dorothy, 1971. *Pattern Drafting and Dressmaking.* Western Publishing, New York.

Musheno, Elizabeth J., 1981. *The Vogue Sewing Book.* Butterick Publishing, New York.

Oakley, Ann, 1972. *Sex, Gender and Society.* Harper & Row, New York.

Oblander, R., D. Ekern, and N.L. Zieman, 1978. *The Sew/Fit Manual.* Sew/Fit Co., LaGrange, Ill.

Olson, Nancy, 1973. *Patterngrams: How to Copy Designs at Home.* Fairchild Publications, New York.

Ondovicsik, Maryann. "Retail Buyers: What They Want for the 80's," *American Fabrics and Fashions,* No. 119, Spring 1980, pages 32-34. Doric Publishing, New York.

Pepin, Harriet, 1942. *Modern Pattern Design.* Funk & Wagnalls, New York.

Perry, Patricia, 1977. *Fabulous Fit.* Butterick Fashion Marketing, New York.

Reich, Naomi, Patricia Otten, and Marie Negri Carver, 1979. *Clothing for Handicapped People: An Annotated Bibliography and Resource List.* President's Committee on Employment of the Handicapped, Washington, D.C.

RetailWeek. "High Technology Via Direct Mail," Vol. 15, No. 18, Dec. 1, 1980, pp. 56-59. Prads, Inc., New York.

———. "Executive Service," Vol. 15, No. 19, Dec. 15, 1980, pp. 13-14. Prads, Inc., New York.

Riley, Matilda White, and Anne Foner, 1968. *Aging and Society,* Volume 1: *An Inventory of Research Findings.* Russell Sage Foundation, New York.

Roach, Mary Ellen, and Joanne B. Eicher, 1973. *The Visible Self: Perspectives on Dress.* Prentice-Hall, Englewood Cliffs, N.J.

Rohr, M., 1968. *Pattern Drafting and Grading.* Rohr Publishing, Waterford, Conn.

Rosencranz, Mary Lou, 1972. *Clothing Concepts: A Social-Psychological Approach.* Macmillan, New York.

Ryan, Mary S., 1966. *Clothing: A Study in Human Behavior.* Holt, Rinehart and Winston, New York.

Sew Business. "Quilted Clothing: Art on Your Back," Vol. 119, No. 12, 1980. Sylvan Publishing, New York.

Sherman, William, 1975. *A Guide to Patternmaking.* Fairgate Rule Co., Cold Spring, N.Y.

Simplicity Pattern Co., Inc., 1973. *Sewing for Men and Boys.* New York.

Sproles, George B., 1979. *Fashion: Consumer Behavior Toward Dress.* Burgess, Minneapolis.

Tanous, Helen Nicol, 1951. *Designing Your Own Dress Patterns.* Chas. A. Bennett, Peoria, Ill.

Tate, Mildred T. and Oris Glisson, 1961. *Family Clothing.* Wiley, New York.

Toffler, Alvin, 1980. *The Third Wave.* William Morrow, New York.

Tuit, Ann, 1974. *Introducing Pattern Cutting.* Heinemann, London.

Tyroler, Else, 1963. *Sewing Pants for Women: A Guide to Perfect Fit.* Hearthside Press, New York.

U.S. News & World Report. "Youth on the Move: Special Section," Vol. 89, No. 26, Dec. 29, 1980/Jan. 5, 1981, pp. 72-82.

Veblen, Thorstein, 1899. *The Theory of the Leisure Class: An Economic Study of Institutions.* Macmillan, New York.

Vogue Sewing Book, 1980 Butterick Publishing, New York.

Walum, Laurel Richardson, 1977. *The Dynamics of Sex and Gender: A Sociological Perspective.* Rand McNally, Chicago.

Williams, Helen W., 1973 *Basic Pattern the Magic Tool.* Iowa State University Press, Ames.

Yep, Jacquelyn, 1974. *Clothes to Fit Your Needs.* Iowa State University Extension Service, Ames.

NOTES

NOTES

NOTES

NOTES

NOTES

NOTES

NOTES

NOTES

NOTES

NOTES

NOTES

NOTES

NOTES

NOTES

NOTES

NOTES

NOTES